TKL/VN
IC

The Art of Successful Communication

NORMAN G. SHIDLE

The Art of
Successful Communication

BUSINESS AND PERSONAL ACHIEVEMENT
THROUGH WRITTEN COMMUNICATION

McGRAW-HILL BOOK COMPANY

New York *San Francisco* *Toronto* *London* *Sydney*

THE ART OF SUCCESSFUL COMMUNICATION

Contents

Introduction

FEW MINDS lie open, awaiting your communications. Those not closed are almost certainly other-interested. Those other interests are barriers to communication.

Yet the most successful communication doesn't result from use of psychological gimmicks or even from mechanical application of clear writing techniques. Rather, it grows out of writing which is creative as well as clear, understanding as well as smartly tailored. Successful "communications writing" is creative writing at its best.

Barriers outside of the writer stand in the way of ideas he wants others to have. Like traps circling a hogback green, they threaten disaster to all except the shot that is perfect in terms of both pitch and distance. Barriers blocking entrance to a reader's mind are as high and deep as those impeding exit from a writer's.

Almost any reader, when he faces memoranda, reports, minutes, or his morning mail, lets into his mind little that he doesn't expect to be helpful. He lets in less that fails to interest him and nothing that isn't clear to him. Yet most of us persist—when we write—in thinking more about what we want to say than about how to make saying it worthwhile. We fail to practice the art of successful communication.

When we do practice this art regularly, we recognize and overcome psychological barriers. We achieve purposeful communication with individuals and with groups—through letters, reports, articles, speeches, minutes, and memoranda. We get approval of plans, break good news and bad news effectively, and get information—and perhaps a job. We find daily chances to use good writing techniques fruitfully.

A mind on the march grasps quickly the potential of written communications in achievement of personal and business ends. It recognizes that the writer's own thinking is what gives power to his communications. It learns how to encompass environmental difficulties. It translates imagination, initiative, and hard work into achievement of personal goals.

This book shows you how to write communications that get the results you want. It aims to set your mind to marching. It teaches you how to practice successfully the art of communicating in writing.

1

Personal Success through Creative Communication

ABILITY TO WRITE purposefully and creatively, more than any other single talent, brings personal satisfaction and success in modern endeavor.

Managements recognize this ability as a potent and widely needed efficiency tool. "There is a great similarity in the communication-related problems that are expressed or demonstrated by managers and executives at all levels and from remarkably different backgrounds," researchers in executive problems find.[1]

Educators see writing purposefully and creatively as a life force in the educational process. Professional men find that it unlocks doors otherwise closed to them and improves relationships with clients and associates.

The reason for these trends is simple. Qualities and talents that make for business and professional success are equally needed to produce result-getting communications. Communicating in writing forces you to exercise and develop abilities you need for success in other career areas.

[1] Charles Goetzinger and Milton Valentine, "Problems of Executive Communication," *Personnel Administration*, March–April, 1964.

1

The same mental gear-shifting required for decision making, for example, precedes the actual writing of a good communication. The best decisions result when you analyze the problem, integrate the exposed ideas or data, and bring them to focus in terms of actions or results desired.

One of the shortest editorials we recall summarized the whole process like this:

Getting things done involves three simple steps:

Incision: Cut into the problem; analyze it.

Decision: Make up your mind what to do about it.

Action: Do it.

. . . . that is all.

Your everyday decisions, minor and major, involve the same steps that are involved in writing an effective communication.

Most decisions are minor. ("Shall I answer mail this morning or shall I try to finish that report that isn't due until next week?" "Shall I follow up on that information Joe promised, or shall I hold off a few more days?")

But some decisions—and communications about them—are obviously important. ("Shall we delay production of our new designs —and lose fall sales—to permit a thorough value analysis prior to public announcement?")

In every case, situations rest on the same elements that must precede writing a purposeful communication.

Consider the three things that contribute most to sales success, as stated by *Printer's Ink* publisher Fred Decker:

1. Make sure you know as much as possible about the prospect's business, so everything you say is pitched directly at his interests.
2. Never forget that a sales call's purpose is to make a sale, and anything extraneous is a waste of valuable time.
3. Always keep control of the interview. If you lose control, you almost always lose the sale.

Each of these basic sales tenets is also applicable to communications writing. Pitching directly to a reader's interests, staying with a predetermined purpose, and keeping control of the ideas being communicated "contribute most" to communicating, as well as sales, success. Exercise these abilities in everything you write, and you will have developed them for use in any business activity.

Eliminating Blind Spots

Ability to write purposefully and creatively also helps you to free yourself from blind spots. It lets you see yourself as others see you. Few people automatically view themselves objectively, and even the most objective have blind spots. These hinder their exercise of leadership and weaken the communicable content of what they write.

Inability to take criticism is a common blind spot. Closely allied is a tendency to be competitive in thinking about statements or actions of associates.

Before writing a letter, report, memorandum, or article, you have a chance to look your thinking over and to make certain that neither self-justification nor self-will might be reflected in your words.

No effective communication will emphasize what somebody other than the writer "ought" to have done or should do. A feeling that potential improvement for a situation lies chiefly outside yourself is a hot tip to look inside. When you find yourself saying: "If only everybody would, . . ." "If only somebody would, . . ." or "If people only wouldn't, . . ." look for a blind spot in yourself.

You'll go furthest both in career and communications writing if you are aggressive enough to attack your problems but wise enough to see the other fellow's point of view; if you are ambitious enough to see around your immediate job but humble enough to meet its immediate challenges. You'll be happy tomorrow with what you do today if habitually you examine before you react, consider before you decide, and stay with it once you've started.

On the positive side, initiative, sincerity, carefulness, and interest in others' problems have to be developed broadly by the effective communications writer. And these, too, are helpful to anybody who wants to further his business or personal career. They also help the person who wants to be understood by the people around him.

In summary, learning to communicate successfully in writing is a practical way to equip yourself with what it takes to go where you want to go and do what you want to do.

Communications: Lifeline of Business

One of this century's great industrialists, Clarence B. Randall, points up these implications when he says: "Most management problems require, not knowledge of the nature of matter, but a clear mind, the power of logical analysis, wisdom born of experience, and *a talent for communication.*" [2]

On the brink of retirement a few years ago, Randall reviewed his philosophy about qualities he sought in young men to be employed by his company. He wound up with:

> Finally, I always wanted to know what talent the applicant had for self-expression. It cannot be repeated too often that the capacity to speak and write the English language clearly is indispensable today for advancement in business. Each individual in the industrial hierarchy must be able to communicate ideas, if management is to function.
>
> Within the organization, as he creates his own techniques of supervision, he must be able to pass on reliably the instruction which he receives from his superiors. He also shares at times the responsibility for interpreting to the general public the purposes and achievements of the organization that he serves.

Almost universally, experienced supervisors echo these sentiments.

"What skills or knowledge acquired in college have you used recently?" 133 executives were asked by a researching Michigan State University professor.[3] More (109) said "use it very often" of courses in business-letter writing than of any other course. "Human relations in business" was a close second (102), which recalls what the vice-president of the production and exploration division of a large oil company told an interviewing University of Chicago researcher: "Every written message is a human relations incident."

[2] Clarence B. Randall, "The High Adventure," *Harvard Today,* Spring, 1957.

[3] Rollin H. Simonds, "College Courses Executives Say They Can Use," *Michigan Business Review,* July, 1961.

And English composition (99 mentions) was third out of the sixty-odd different courses mentioned.

Other Examples

Once I asked top engineering executives of eight automobile and parts companies to list six qualities most needed in their organizations. There was little overlapping in the lists. Some forty-seven different qualities were mentioned. Only one appeared on every one of the lists—"ability to express himself effectively in writing."

Unsigned responses from 125 salesmen in a sales seminar brought twenty-four different ideas in answer to the question: "In what way could your sales manager be more helpful to you?" Six of the ideas (25 per cent) bore directly on sales managers' ability to communicate.

Each of the six ideas was directly concerned with improving communication in one way or another: (1) by communicating more promptly, (2) by being more precise and less vague, (3) by more clearly defining the salesman's job, (4) by keeping salesmen more fully informed about new product development, (5) by more clearly defining company objectives, and (6) by communicating more about general company policies. Besides, several of the remaining eighteen suggestions were indirectly concerned with better sales-manager ability to communicate.

Talking to a convocation of business school students at Northwestern University, a Chicago businessman (a graduate of Northwestern's School of Business) listed the following courses in the order of their importance:

English
Report writing and business-letter writing
Accounting
Courses that require decision making
Logic
Specialized finance courses

What was he saying to these students? "I think," says Northwestern professor Richard C. Gerfen, "he was saying that the kind of educational experience he found most useful was (1) that which developed his ability and skill in communicating and thinking, and (2) that which provided him with institutional knowledge and with facts and analytical techniques in his business capacity." [4]

The link between good written communication and thinking is as close as that between thinking and successful action. In both cases, the thinking comes first. It is no coincidence that the man who writes well nearly always can think better than those about him. To write well, he *has* to think well. Good thinking is a prerequisite to good writing. McGraw-Hill Book Company's board chairman, Curtis G. Benjamin, summarizes this succinctly: "The man who writes well nearly always can think much better than the next man." [5]

Vice-president and executive director W. Homer Turner, of U.S. Steel Foundation, Inc., reveals the full scope of the importance of written communication when he says: "Make no mistake. Your inner life, career, and family affairs, religion—your very freedom—are bound up in good communication. . . . When you enter public service, the church, business leadership of a labor union or some other group, you will find this to be true: Communication has now become a matter that embraces *every* form of conduct. . . ." [6]

Similar convictions come from hundreds of others experienced in getting things done. It is clear to almost every mature executive or supervisor that writing is a vital tool in any business success kit —*because few jobs are accomplished anymore by one man.*

Steps to Getting Results

Almost every job in industry requires getting scope and objective clear to start with. That may come in a communication of some kind from the boss—if he's good at that sort of thing—or it might go *from* you to your boss to ensure a common understanding at the outset. But written or not, communication has to take place during the course of most projects. Some things should be written down, whether or not they *must* be.

[4] Richard C. Gerfen, "The Changing World of the Teacher," *The Journal of Business Communication,* p. 12, October, 1963.

[5] Quoted in a Famous Writers School promotion booklet.

[6] Commencement address, Denison University, June 13, 1960.

And when a project is finished, a variety of communications is likely to be in order. Certainly the boss wants to know the answers, and maybe his boss does too, and his boss's boss. There may be phases to communicate to one department or one person or to many others.

In modern industry, in fact, intercommunication between people in different departments or groups is the lifeblood of effective operation. Wherever related groups must function in a coordinated manner, much of many individuals' time will be devoted to communication. Large groups could not function at all were it not for the success of their "communicators."

"There was a time," a top engineering executive comments, "when devoting time and people to communicating was thought a waste. Then came an era in which the boss was expected to do most of the necessary communicating. Now, however, communication is recognized as another form of specialization—like accounting, production, or engineering."

A reorganization of one of the country's largest engineering departments illustrates this concept. The organization is divided by function and subdivided many times. Some engineering functions are in the producing divisions of this mammoth corporation; some are staff functions at the corporate level. And each function hangs down from a different major branch of the basic organizational chart. Also, each of the producing divisions has activities such as purchasing, manufacturing, and sales—each linked to equivalent central staffs.

This engineering department produces a number of complex products and operates on a tight schedule. Obviously, such a mass couldn't perform successfully without exhaustive communication across the branches of the organizational chart—as well as up and down.

To provide essential cross communication, two men in each subgroup are assigned to do nothing but communicate, often in writing. The sole responsibility of the transmission-group communicators, for example, is to see that this group understands by the hour information, movements, or procedures of other groups which may affect their work. Also, of course, these two men export similar information from the transmission group to other groups. Communications is recognized as a necessary, specialized function.

Even in small companies today, the boss can no longer be expected to bear the major responsibility for communicating. Cross communication between subordinates is always necessary. And communicating "up" is at least as essential to efficiency as communicating "down."

Writing Skills Are Needed Everywhere

In short, it's pretty hard to find remunerative headwork anymore where written communication skills are not needed. Everywhere there is opportunity for the man who is able daily to finish projects and to connect many minds by written communication. This need exists at all levels. Neither straw boss, junior executive, nor executive vice-president completes many projects in an ivory tower. Each needs to communicate effectively with others, and writing is a most important way.

The ultimate usefulness of a completed project, in fact, is often proportionate to the number of people who understand it and are interested in it. For laboratories, proving grounds, and service organizations of various kinds, reports are often the only visible evidence of accomplishment. They produce no tangible product, so the quality of their outer-directed communications often determines the size and quality of their final achievement. Writing can be the most powerful agent in spreading understanding and creating interest.

Skills Must Be Sought

These success-producing communications skills are a do-it-yourself project for most people. Business and professional leaders increasingly criticize and view with alarm the writing abilities produced by our current educational system. But few definitely require formal training in communications writing as a condition of employment. A majority, however, actively agree with John Fischer, editor of *Harper's*, when he writes:

> Every business man knows it is a rare day when he can hire either a woman or a man capable of writing reasonably competent

English. It is easier, one executive tells me, to find people trained to write the mathematical binary language of computers. Such complaints are becoming frequent enough to suggest that the almost-vanished art of writing has become an expensive proposition for American business.[7]

Training is available in many companies, but usually in large corporations and for limited groups. Several prominent law schools have started intensive programs in writing. ("The graduates of our colleges, including the best ones, cannot write the English language," says the dean of the University of Pittsburgh's Law School.) Several engineering colleges hold periodic "refresher-course" seminars in technical writing. (One of them, Rensselaer Polytechnic Institute, has a regular course leading to a master's degree in technical writing.) Washington University in St. Louis once fathered a $135,000 project to translate the jargon of social scientists into language nonprofessionals could understand. The U.S. State Department gave a course in elementary composition to its officers to improve the understandability of their memoranda.

But the small number of such projects means that training is available for only an infinitesimal percentage of those who could profit from radical upgrading. So, as in the past, the individual must rely chiefly on his own initiative to upgrade his communication abilities.

Recognition of the need is his first step in upgrading, but more than recognition is needed. Further initiative is required (1) to do some orderly trial-and-error rewriting of one's own material on an everyday basis and/or (2) to seek guidance to study and practice from library sources or available company or outside-company evening courses.

Many who are "too busy to read" are also too busy to take the steps necessary to acquire success-producing skills in written communicating. All too typical is the next-to-top-echelon executive who asked a communications-skilled associate to rewrite an important letter for him. The letter had been returned by this executive's superior (to whom it had gone for approval before mailing)

---

[7] John Fischer, "Why Nobody Writes Good," *Harper's,* February, 1964.

with this notation: "Suggest you rewrite this to about half its length and make it clearer."

Accepting the opportunity to help, the associate said: "Sure, I'll be glad to take a crack at this for you. But you've just said you aren't any good at writing. You've just said you are too verbose, want to put in too many details. . . . Now I'll be glad to redo this particular letter for you. But doesn't this incident make you want to look into this writing thing, maybe improve your abilities along these lines?"

"Oh, no," was the response. "I'm too busy with a million things to take time out for writing. It's a knack you have that I don't have. I'm too busy to spend more time trying to write better. This sort of rejection only happens once in a while. The rest of the time, I'm doing all right."

Thousands who have achieved reasonable success think and act just this way. They fail to see that success in written communication is closely allied with openings to continued progress. When they bury the main idea of a communication in the middle or near the end, they don't realize that they are trumpeting to all a warped sense of values. They fail to see that they are publicizing their inability to put first things first, to see their problems in perspective. They are unaware of their inability to bring ideas or information into focus, to see the significance behind the facts.

Nowhere is the biblical "Seek and ye shall find" so applicable as in the development of the ability to communicate successfully in writing.

Written communication is the lever which is prying thousands of successful men out of ruts every year.

2

Writing to Get
Readers to Reach

EACH COMMUNICATION has to carry some built-in attraction to stimulate a reader to reach for what it contains.

Reaching out by a reader is essential if ideas and information are to become a part of his consciousness. He has to reach, however feebly, to make them his own, or communication isn't completed.

Few receivers, however, have firm grabbing equipment. In some folks it is so rudimentary that it scarcely can be said to exist. In others, it has become atrophied. Few minds regularly reach out and carefully con the pages thrust before them.

Each communication, therefore, has to carry some built-in attraction to stimulate the reaching process. It takes creative writing to do this, not only to open a reader's mind, but also to stir it to grab for messages.

Foremost among its creations is a bridge from your mind as a writer to the mind of a reader, a bridge which makes it easy for the reader to reach out to receive. To complete the creative process, you must send across this bridge emotions which will mix with those of your reader—ideas which will stir him to thought or action—or you must give information that he can use for his own purposes.

Creative Writing Helps Everybody

The ability to write creatively—to stir readers to clutch the ideas offered—is necessary in varying degrees for different individuals. It is essential to even satisfactory performance for the person paid to do business or technical writing. It is desirable for the scientist who must report his findings. (He can get by without such ability, but he makes much better progress if he has it.)

Between the extremes lies the daily work of most literate Americans. Particularly to be pitied is the business executive incapable of creative writing, unable to build bridges to the minds of others. He lives alone in a goldfish bowl. As he swims about in full view of associates, his mouth opens and shuts at regular intervals. But no one can "hear" what he says or profit from what he writes. He can't bring into being in the minds of his associates or customers something that wasn't there before.

There is no end to the list of arts and sciences whose practitioners benefit vastly from the ability to write creatively. There is *almost* no end to the list of endeavors in which only creative writing ability can spark maximum achievement.

How to Get Readers to Reach

No set of psychological gimmicks or even perfect mechanical application of clear-writing techniques can equip a communication to stir readers to reach. This essential grasping for knowledge is stimulated only by writing which is creative as well as clear, understanding as well as smartly tailored. Reaching can no more be stimulated by dull, lazy, or careless minds than *The Forsyte Saga* could have been written by Mortimer Snerd.

A communication's quality is mainly the result of the attitude of mind with which the communicator writes. Completed, successful communication grows more naturally from giving what you've got than from trying to get what you want. It accrues from seeking the best rather than the most.

To get readers to reach:

- Appeal to self-motivation. (Include some thought-starters.)
- Shun multipurpose communications. (Keep your reader's mind on a single track.)

- Aim at your reader's needs as well as his wants. (Help him to want what he needs.)
- Aim for appropriate timing.

Thought-starters Motivate Readers

Self-motivation will unleash the potential in every student, says educator Dr. Richard P. Reath. Its importance is emphasized by the fact that understanding is a quality of the receiver of a communication. Understanding can't be *given* by a writer. But you can start a thought in your reader's mind, and once his mind has taken off on its own *in relation to something you have written,* you have his attention. Your foot in the door becomes a step into the house.

To start a thought in a reader's mind, you can:

- Open his mind to an opportunity.
- Remind him of a duty.
- Challenge him to agree or disagree.
- Voice a strong opinion of your own.
- Inject a judicious question.

Opportunity, of course, is particularly characteristic of this "you" approach. You suggest how your reader may get something he wants, do something he will enjoy, or be recognized for his merits. Opportunity suggestion is the best thought-starter . . . when it really is an opportunity for the reader. "Opportunities" to buy something are rarely true "you" approaches.

Call-to-duty thought-starters have minimum power. Never expect a reader to read—or to do anything—because he "ought to." ("Your country needs you!") Look for an angle or a point of view for which he might have some enthusiasm. ("Join the Navy and see the world.") The chances are ten to one that this will be an angle or viewpoint for which *you* can generate some eagerness.

Challenging statements are sometimes good thought-starters. ("The results show little, if anything, to be gained from addition of tetraethyl lead." "Far from weakening the party's appeal, Mr. Conservative's nomination might strengthen it.")

A *judgment* or *interpretation* by the writer will spark a reaction in almost everybody it reaches. Agreement or disagreement is almost certain to cross the reader's mind. But you must know your particular reader well to gain the benefits and avoid the dangers of the challenge as a thought-starter. A challenge almost certainly will get a reader to reach out and pull the idea into his mind, but it can backfire worse than a damp muffler on a frosty morning.

A judicious question, casually injected, also may serve to stimulate a reader to reach. ("The trip could also include a one-day visit to Yellowstone Park. Have you been there? Or it could, instead, go through a tier of Southern states.")

Advantages of One Idea at a Time

Whatever your thought-starting gambit, you will find it best to settle for one idea at a time. When your reader starts going somewhere with ideas you have stimulated, additional thought-starters may do you a disservice. This is true because (1) the thought he starts away with will not be exactly the thought you tried to give and (2) most people are easily diverted from one thought to another.

You can be pretty sure that you reader isn't "seeing" anything *exactly* as you are. Each of us keeps changing things into thoughts every day of his life. This constant unconscious conjuring is a major barrier to communication by anybody with anybody else. To see why, pick an object in the room where you sit. Write down what it looks like, what it means to you, and what it is made of. Get someone else in the room to do the same thing. Then compare what has been written. Almost certainly, each of you will have changed the object by slightly or wholly different thoughts.

We start changing things and ideas we hear long before we have "seen" them—even with our mind's eye. That's why there is a multiple danger in putting too many thought-starters into a single communication. You know that the thought you start will be modified when your reader makes it his own. So you would like him to follow it as carefully as possible, not to knock it slightly askew and drop it for another.

This tendency to start down one line of thought and be easily diverted to different ones is common. Many people are diverted easily to totally unrelated subjects. Almost everybody is lured by tangential bypaths. So your communication has to bring about whatever focus is to exist in your reader's mind. When you start several thoughts, any one of them may lead your reader far afield. Then he is unlikely ever to return to the main point of your concern.

The single-purpose communication has a better chance also with the reader who reacts to each sentence as he reads it. Many do just this. They form judgments or react emotionally long before they "see" the communication as a whole.

Such a reader's emotions are always a little ahead of his reasoning. He reacts immediately, but later he lets the facts sort themselves out and influence him before he takes action. Multipurpose communications make him uncomfortable. His mind is always having to change itself as he reads. It is being stressed and strained instead of moved steadily, as it would be by a single-purpose communication.

Such a reader starts to fashion a reply as soon as he has read one sentence—whether it is in a letter which he must answer, a report he must evaluate, or an article he will never finish reading. The communication which tries to accomplish too many things adds fuel to his fire. It stimulates him to diversional thinking. It encourages his normal tendency to be subjective, to get off *your* track and gambol about happily on his own. Faced with a multiplicity of ideas, he becomes enmeshed in a snarl of crisscrossing thoughts. Result: He never gets back to what you really want in focus.

So try to stand up under the strain of keeping ten things on your chest while getting one off. Keep in mind that your objective is not to *state* but to *convey* a maximum of ideas or information. Never use a writing chore as a kind of emotional therapy. As you write, let your mind's eye face a listener's querulous, incredulous, angry, or placid mien. Don't sound off as you may feel—happily and aimlessly, resentfully and logically, or indifferently and carelessly.

Stick to single-purpose communications whenever you can. They will pay off in better results—partly because you will have had to bring your thoughts into good focus to write them.

Help Your Reader to Want What He Needs

Your reader doesn't always want what he needs. But appealing wholly to his desires smacks of expediency rather than clear purpose. Encouraging him to want what he needs can bring permanently more satisfying results.

To do this, the big difference between wants and needs must be recognized. We aren't always the most productive when we are happiest. We do better work for a boss whose objectives, when made clear, we respect than for one we like personally but upon whose abilities we look down.

These differences are reflected in actions and reactions by the reader of a written communication. Often he will reach for the contents of a communication which speaks to a previously unrecognized need. And sometimes he will pass up one directed to an often expressed desire. Menninger Foundation psychologist Dr. Harold J. Mendl illustrates the difference between wants and needs with a true story: [1]

A hospital night crew petitioned for the hospital cafeteria to stay open all night. Then when it was kept open, almost none of the night crew ate there. They "wanted" the open cafeteria, but they "needed" some recognition from the management that they were alive. ("Management, after all, went home at five o'clock.")

Time Can Be Critical

Good timing is a major help in getting a reader to reach out for what you have written. *When* you ask him to decide something has much to do with whether his decision will be favorable or unfavorable. The timing may even determine whether or not he considers your problem at all. What else is on his mind at the moment he gets an announcement will affect the pleasure, sorrow, or indifference with which he receives it. (Fund solicitors send out few appeals in April.)

You can't control the events or circumstances which give your communication good or bad timing. But you can consider them before you dispatch your message. Besides, you can be constantly aware of the total setting into which you are communicating.

Like all living things, communications must be capable of adapting to their environments.

[1] E. T. Moore, "Are You a Father Figure?" *Think*, April, 1962.

3

Are You Writing to Yourself?

SELF-CENTEREDNESS, the greatest single barrier to written communication, almost always results in writing to yourself.

Most of us are self-centered to some degree, especially as we write. Desire or necessity to tell somebody something usually generates the energy to write. So, when you start to express yourself, thoughts already have subjective momentum.

To be less self-centered in your writing:

• Write in terms of your reader's interests, needs, and desires.

• Write so your reader can pass your ideas along without change—to serve his own purposes.

• Listen; learn what people think and think about before you write to them or for them.

• Avoid confrontations. ("I'm right; you're wrong!")

• Warm your heart before you pound your typewriter. (Every communication has texture as well as content.)

• Use only words you are sure your reader understands.

Unless you think consciously of your reader, you will find yourself writing in terms of your own interests, objectives, and background. To the extent that you do, you will be writing to yourself.

Failure to know or sense your reader's attitudes and problems will bar complete communication almost every time. Other-

17

mindedness on your part—concern with what your reader needs —will open his mind and stir him to reach for your ideas.

Make It Easy for Your Reader to Act

If you want your reader to act, for example, write so that he can readily make your ideas his own. Write words and sentences he can pass along to others. (He may have to influence several people in order to do as you wish and suggest.)

When recommending a changed accounting procedure, for example, an auditing firm recognized that the comptroller would need his general manager's approval. So the firm wrote a letter which the comptroller could use with the general manager. (At the same time, of course, it was a convincing presentation to the comptroller himself.)

What the auditor wrote is shown in Exhibit 1.

EXHIBIT 1   *From auditor to comptroller, this letter can be used almost "as is" by the comptroller in presenting the suggestion to his general manager for approval*

Mr. Arthur Barter
Comptroller
Wharf & Warehouse Association

Dear Mr. Barter:

I'd suggest WWA set up each year in a deferred income account the unexpended portion of annual income received for research. Then your regular financial statements will show specifically the amount reserved for such future research.

Thus, I believe, WWA statements would reflect more clearly to your association's membership the execution of your director's policy—that all money collected for research shall be devoted solely to that purpose.

From an accounting standpoint, there's nothing wrong with your current procedures. But the deferred income handling, I think, would be more readily understood by your membership as a whole.

Let me know if this suggestion interests you. I'll be glad, of course, to help you work out necessary procedure revisions, though I doubt that you'll need any such help.

Sincerely,

Eugene Q. Hawker
Partner, Darnley & Hawker

Had the auditor been self-centered, he might have been totally unaware of the comptroller's problems. Or, though he was aware of the need for general-manager acquiescence, he might have left it up to the comptroller to plan the best way out. He might have completed the comptroller's communication without ensuring the total communication necessary to action. He might, in other words, have settled for something like the letter shown in Exhibit 2.

EXHIBIT 2   *From auditor to comptroller, this letter is not suitable for presentation by the comptroller to his general manager when the latter's approval is sought. The comptroller will have to make up his own presentation*

Mr. Arthur Barter
Comptroller
Wharf & Warehouse Association

Dear Mr. Barter:
   I'd suggest WWA set up as a deferred income account the unexpended income received each year for use in research. Then your financial statements would show this setting aside specifically—which they don't do as a result of current procedures.
   To do this, you should show income from this source at the same level as direct and indirect expenses. Conversely, in a year when expenses exceeded income, you would charge the deferred income account for the difference—to reduce expenses to the actual income.
   (At present, of course, you are taking into the current year's income the full revenue for research—without earmarking the unexpended portion for future use.)
   This suggestion merely changes the way WWA statements will reflect execution of WWA director's policy—that money collected for research shall be expended solely for that purpose.

Sincerely,

Eugene Q. Hawker
Partner, Darnley & Hawker

The writing which best communicates does work for the reader as well as the writer. Self-centeredness speaks with authority only to itself. It tends to limit thinking to immediate rather than ultimate objectives. It spawns writing with small impact.
   Communications which speak to the reader reveal the writer's

aims and interests in terms of the reader's. To leap the barrier of self-centeredness, tell your story or state your case within the reader's frame of reference. Don't try to write until you have at least tried to guess the environment into which your communication is going.

Handling a Reporting Assignment

Suppose your boss asks you to report a session on business opportunities in Spain at an American Management Association meeting he had hoped to attend. Inexperienced in reporting, you may begin to wonder—even as you say "Yes, sir"—how you'll go about the assignment. You may ask yourself what to report, how long the report should be, what the boss wants, and whether you'll be able to make notes fast enough.

These aren't the important questions. Rather, you should be asking yourself: "If I had my boss's job, what would I look for; what *kind* of ideas or information would be take-home pay?"

Probably he hasn't told you why he had planned to go himself, which you need to know to help answer your important question. (He probably *has* told you why he can't go, which helps you not at all.) So ask him. Also ask whether he would be willing to get the report as late as a week following the meeting. You would like to study written copies of the talks to supplement your own notes. (Then deliver the report within three days following the sessions!)

In other words, bring into some handy focus the purpose of your report. If you don't, you are all too likely to settle for a typical tyro's handling, for something like this:

> The sessions on new business opportunities in Spain were attended by about five hundred people. Seven speakers treated various phases of the general topic and brought out many interesting points and considerable specific information.
>
> First, Antonio Garrigues Walker, senior partner of a Madrid law firm, talked on regulations affecting foreign investments in Spain. He brought out that regulations differ depending on whether the foreign investor sets up a wholly controlled company, or whether he sets up a partnership.
>
> Next, Joaquin Gutierrez Cano, executive director of the Inter-

national Bank for Reconstruction & Development, Washington, D.C., explained changes in the Spanish banking and financial system. He told something of the system before its complete re-organization in 1962 and then detailed the functions of the four kinds of banks now existing.

Discussing foreign investment from a banker's viewpoint, Jaime Gomez Acedbo, chairman of the Banco Español de Crédito, Madrid, showed the difference between investment banks and the new industrial banks created by the reorganization of the Spanish banking system in 1962.

George H. Bunge, tax manager for Arthur Anderson & Co., Paris, then reviewed the probable future of the Spanish tax law, in process of revision since 1957. He detailed the different kinds of taxes, both corporate and individual, now in force and defined at some length the new "global" tax system, through which it is hoped to collect a greater percentage of the levied taxes.

Industrial sites in Spain was the topic of John Popeck, market-ing consultant, Wayne, New Jersey. He advised foreign companies desiring to buy sites in Spain to engage a consultant who knows the country.

Resources available to new industry were discussed by Felix Aranguren, industrial attaché, Spanish Embassy, Washington, D.C. He said that the work force in Spain by 1970 will be about thirteen million—out of a total population of 32.7 million. Today the work force is about eleven million. Water power is Spain's most important source of energy, he said, and he predicted that Spain would have to change its mining legislation and consider mines as natural sources for exploitation either by groups of firms or in some other way.

John D. Hendricks, project manager of Pegasus International Corp., wound up the sessions with "The Spanish Economy: An American Businessman's Appraisal." He talked about the labor supply, how Spain maintains her economy, and the fact that Spain needs giant doses of know-how from outsiders.

Without prior-to-attending focus of purpose, in other words, you may do little but rewrite in many more words the tabulated program. You may have added a few—very few—specific state-ments of what the speakers said, drawn from the notes you made when a phrase or an idea struck your fancy.

You may well have forgotten that your assignment was to write a report *for your boss,* that just *a* report wouldn't fill the bill. The chore of writing may have obscured the interesting chance to look at a complex of ideas through your boss's eyes. The chance for such business adventures on company time doesn't come every day.

You might have gotten greater satisfactions had you pretended you were the boss and approached the sessions from that point of view.

Suppose you had. Suppose you had said to yourself: "This automotive parts company my boss has been with for fifteen years has never set up European manufacturing facilities. There has been some talk of it, though, for the past five years. Since the boss suggested I take in this Spain session, maybe somebody is thinking about Spain as a possibility. . . . Well, whether they are or not, I think I'll approach these sessions as though we might be." Starting from such a base, you might have come up with something like the report reproduced in Exhibit 3.

EXHIBIT 3   *A report of a meeting which communicates to the writer's boss ideas and information the boss can use*

FOREIGN INVESTMENT CHANCES IMPROVING IN SPAIN; MANY PROBLEMS STILL REMAIN

New business opportunities in Spain look better for American investors in general—and perhaps for Our Own Co. in particular—than at any past time, according to a consensus of seven speakers at the recent American Management Association sessions. Some one hundred representatives from thirty-eight companies were there.

THE GOOD SIDE

Regulations affecting foreign investments in Spain have been importantly modified in the last five years. The process of liberalization is still going on. A recent special act reorganizing the basis of credit and banking control involves improved opportunities for private banks to promote industrial or agricultural enterprises by providing medium- and long-term financing. Spanish tax laws—notoriously lax as regards collections—are in the process of being completely reformed. Work on the revisions was started six years ago. Foreign companies investing in

Spain from now on can take profits out of Spain back to their home country freely. (There's still some question about profits on investments made prior to July 28, 1959.) Power development in Spain is going forward steadily. One American businessman, John D. Hendricks, project manager of Pegasus International Corp., says:

"Although Spain is certainly not without its problems, many of these problems are opportunities for the American investor. Spain represents the largest untapped European market. It merits attention as a potential area of activity for those American companies which feel they have something to offer in the international field."

THE OTHER SIDE OF THE COIN

But, analysis of the seven talks indicates, an American company's problems in setting up new enterprises in Spain can still be great.

Not a few problems arise because practices in Spain are so different from those to which we Americans are accustomed. In the United States, for example, we have tax evaders. Many get caught—and when caught are punished. Those who pay their taxes are an overwhelming majority of the total. But not so in Spain. It is standard practice to keep two sets of books. "Most Spanish companies do practice fiscal evasion," according to Madrid attorney Antonio Garrigues Walker. There are several reasons for this, Walker says:

"In Spain it is as difficult to be honest with regard to taxation as it is to be dishonest in the United States. . . . Tax dishonesty does not entail any risk in a practical sense; on the contrary, honesty used to be a source of trouble and complications." Neither a rigorous inspection system nor any system of relatively serious penalties exists in Spain to deter tax dodgers.

The two-sets-of-books practice results in different-from-American approaches to some common business transactions. Suppose Our Own Co. wanted to buy a tract of land for a factory outside Madrid. Then, to quote Walker: "The owner of the property is tickled to death to sell. But he will insist on establishing both an official and a private price. This type of problem will be found in many other commercial relations maintained by a Spanish company."

Other things we would find different in Spain were we to invest there include:

1. There are governmental restrictions on the dismissal of workers. Workers are entitled to appoint a representative to the board of directors for every three directors appointed by the owners of a Spanish company (which would include those where an American

company holds a "balanced position in the ownership of the company with local groups").

2. If the American company opens a branch, the branch will be "subject to a special taxation system which is not a model of clearness and accuracy."

If Our Own Co., however, or any other foreign investor, were to set up a wholly owned Spanish company of the *sociedad anónima* type (much like an American corporation), in which it owned 51 per cent or more of the stock, it would not have to get authorization from the Spanish Council of Ministers because our company is in one of a wide range of industries in which authorization isn't required. (The range includes iron and steel, nonferrous metals, machine tools, automobile tires, printing, hotels, and many others.) Even where required, authorizations have been granted in most instances (99 per cent in 1960; 86.1 per cent in 1961; 99.88 per cent in 1963).

Foreign investments in Spain may be made in (1) convertible pesetas, (2) transferable pesetas, (3) capital goods, or (4) patents, manufacturing licenses, and technical assistance.

If capital goods constitute the investment, the equipment should be new. Otherwise certain difficulties arise. With (4), authorization has to be obtained from the Ministry of Industry.

Royalties paid by a Spanish affiliate to its parent company are considered to be not deductible expenses but profit earned by the Spanish affiliate. (But, Walker says, this provision is sure to be eliminated in a revision of Spanish fiscal system scheduled for approval.)

Now a foreign investor freely can take profits from his Spanish investment back to his own country—for sure on any investments made since July 28, 1959. "Spanish laws regarding investment now are among the most liberal and generous in Europe," Walker says.

The final form of the tax-reform legislation now being drafted will be of major concern to foreign investors. George H. Bunge, tax manager for Arthur Anderson & Co., Paris, having studied in detail a sixty-page memorandum of proposed revisions circulated by the Spanish government, reports: "A very basic potential modification is the possibility of an increased direct tax rate. In part the hope is that the new legislation will raise collections. One large untapped source is personal income."

It is in raising collections that a so-called "global" method of determining tax liability is expected to help. If a taxpayer wishes to report separately, he must file notice of this intention in the first month of the taxable year. Otherwise he is automatically on the global system—which works like this:

Taxpayers are broken down into groups performing similar industrial, commercial, or professional functions and are subdivided by geographical areas. Thus all the lawyers in Madrid or all the textile mills in Barcelona may constitute a global unit. A committee for a particular global unit consists of members from the Ministry of Finance and representatives of the particular global group. Upon governmental recommendations, the committee determines the amount of net taxable income the group as a whole should have earned and allocates this total among its members. Results of the method, according to Bunge, are:

1. It has picked up a number of taxpayers who had never before reported, because their colleagues were better able than the government to gather such delinquents into the net.

2. The industry committee representatives, knowing the business and having a feeling for who is doing what, mete out a sort of rough tax justice.

Copies are attached of all seven of the papers read at these sessions dealing with new business opportunities in Spain. Of most interest to Our Own Co., I'd guess, are those by Walker, Bunge, and Hendricks.

This kind of report communicates to your boss. The self-centered, informationless report communicates to no one; it does not even refresh your own memories at a later date.

Awareness Needed

Self-centeredness precludes also the high degree of "awareness" that successful communication requires, awareness of what others think, feel, and need. A course in written communication, Prof. Arno F. Knapper of the University of Kansas says, is quite appropriately called an "awareness course." It focuses attention on the awareness vis-à-vis problems, needs, and attitudes of all with whom the writer would communicate.

Self-centeredness Widens Breaches

Self-centeredness does its crippling worst in communications involving differences of opinion.

Skill in disputing and skill in communicating rarely illumine the same piece of writing. Skill in disputing, fully exercised, usually dims communicating power. Set on winning a point, a communication may lose a customer. Bent on proving a reader wrong, a communicator may find himself without a reader.

True, it takes two to make an argument. But it takes only a single written communication to start one. Two are needed only in the sense that an argument can't go on when one party goes away —mentally or physically—and stops participating. But the argument starts when one person writes a statement which generates feeling rather than thought on the part of the other.

The argument-starting statement is almost always subjective and emanates from self-centeredness. Making such a statement, a writer is thinking first of himself and last, if at all, of his audience. The argument-starting statement rarely has crystal-clear definition of purpose. Were its aim really to convince another person or group, it probably never would have been made. At least it wouldn't have been written exactly as it was. For differences of opinion, like pieces of cloth, have texture as well as pattern. The texture, as much as the pattern, marks the quality of the discussion. In everyday work—where differences constantly have to be resolved between associates—texture becomes even more important than the pattern.

Pattern reflects the character of the differences; texture reflects the character of the written communication about them. Pattern is what everybody sees; it is the "what" of differences. Texture is the "why"—springing, as often as not, from emotional wells deep within the writer.

When you are suspicious or antagonistic, the texture of your writing tends to make differences remain differences. The same differences, stated in terms of your reader's best interests, tend to melt steadily away.

Communications Texture Illustrated

The responses of two engineers to a suggestion of conflict in technical papers point up these tendencies.

One paper was by engineer Nosreph; the other was by engineer Semaj. Both had been published in the same technical journal. A reader wrote to the editor concluding: "It looks like there is a conflict of authorities."

Nosreph, in his paper, the reader pointed out, showed the *advantages* of a full-flow filter over a partial-flow filter. In contrast to the Nosreph paper, the Semaj paper gives data and illustrations in favor of the bypass filter as opposed to the full-flow filter," the reader noted.

The editor sent the reader's letter to the two authors seen as being in conflict, suggesting that the two replies "might make good material to publish—just in case other readers aren't clear on the matter."

Nosreph responded as shown in Exhibit 4—subjectively. Everything he wrote stemmed from a self-centered approach.

EXHIBIT 4   *A self-centered letter from the author of one of two recently published articles, in response to a magazine reader's comment*

Editor
World Technical Magazine
Chicago, Illinois

Dear Mr. Editor:
Reference is made to your letter of January 19, 1965, regarding the supposed disagreement between myself and Semaj on the subject of oil filtration.

The reasons which I gave in my article for using the full-flow filter and the comparison of the full-flow and the partial-flow filter were based on very extended and thorough tests performed by the engineering staff of my organization.

I definitely have no desire to engage in a typewritten debate on the subject. My article was intended generally to give our thinking on all the features incorporated in the engine discussed, and that is all it is supposed to do. It was not intended as an article to settle the controversial questions involved in the matter of oil filtration.

I think it would be too much to expect that somebody else's findings would correspond entirely to our own, and it is also, I think, too much to expect to have complete agreement between any group of engineers from different organizations.

Very sincerely yours,

Barton G. Nosreph
Engineering Vice-president

Semaj's response (Exhibit 5) was clearly an attempt to help the reader to understand. It offers specific information bearing on the question brought up. The inquiring reader is the authority for the conclusion that the Semaj letter not only offered but also conveyed to him a maximum of information and understanding and that the Nosreph response conveyed nothing of interest or value.

EXHIBIT 5   *An author's objective response to the same reader's comment which drew the subjective response (Exhibit 4) from the other author*

Editor
World Technical Magazine
Chicago, Illinois

Dear Mr. Editor:

The apparent discrepancies between Mr. Nosreph's article and mine can be resolved very easily.

There are full-flow filters which are very effective in removal of small abrasive particles. But there are other full-flow filters which are not very effective in removal of these particles. The difference between these two filter types is often in the pressure differences available for filtration. When the pressure difference required for filtration is low, less satisfactory contaminant removal is achieved. Most so-called by-pass filters operate with a pressure difference of between 30 and 40 pounds per square inch. This pressure difference permits a very effective removal of small particles. So, if the flow through the bypass cartridge is ample, it is possible to remove the contaminants entering the engine as fast as they either are formed or work their way in.

Another factor, often overlooked, is that the so-called full-flow filter does handle the full flow of oil from the oil pump but not the flow of oil which is not pumped but circulated by throw-off from the crankshaft and splash from the main bearings leakage—and drainage from the cylinder walls back on the crank.

If the part-flow filter is effective, it can reduce wear on the core and rings more effectively than wear on the bearings. The full-flow filter, however, may reduce wear on the bearings. But unless it is very effective, it may not reduce wear on the splash-lubricated parts of the engine—bores, rings, and pistons.

So, I do not believe there is any real conflict between Mr. Nosreph's statements and mine. It is a matter of more detailed understanding of the mechanism of lubrication and wear in engines.

I hope this explanation will help to clear up any apparent discrepancies between us.

Very truly yours,

Anton Semaj
Engineering Vice-president

Professor Richard Saxon, of Fordham University, illustrates but oversimplifies with his story of the two Catholic priests who were inveterate smokers. One of them wrote to his supervising bishop asking: "Would it be permissible, Father, for me to smoke during prayers?" He received an explosive "No!" along with a stern lecture on attitudes becoming the cloth.

The other priest wrote the same supervisor asking: "Would you approve, Father, of my praying while I smoke?" He was rewarded with a prompt and pleasant "Yes."

Helpfulness Douses Self-centeredness

The simplest way to avoid self-centeredness is to try to be helpful. Nothing attracts a reader so quickly or holds him so firmly as writing which recognizes *his* self-centeredness.

But the recognition must be logical, sound from the writer's standpoint, and above all sincere. When the appeal to the reader's self-interest is little but a restatement of the writer's self-interest, it is self-liquidating. Not even the least sophisticated are much impressed by the sales message which promises great benefits if one buys the product, takes the travel tour, or invests in the securities. Only when confidence in the source is established does such assistance from sellers "reach" us in depth.

And confidence is established only by repeated experiences. That's why you should take pains with *every* communication. Each letter, report, or memorandum you write plays its part in building or destroying confidence in your sincerity, accuracy, and objectivity. Only by experiences do others buy your honest interest in their affairs and open their minds automatically to your communications.

Professional Slang

Use of special words, professional slang, or trade lingo is a major manifestation of the self-centeredness that so surely bars complete communication. Vocabularies that have a special meaning to special people say nothing to those not in the know. Every business and profession has its constantly growing quota of special words. Sometimes writers use this esoteric language to impress "outsiders" with the fact that they are "insiders." Sometimes they use it in always unsuccessful attempts to dazzle others of their own profession. As teen-agers ride new slang to death in every generation, so their parents joy in dotting their writing (and conversation) with the newest business, engineering, or scientific jargon.

Whether you are writing to outsiders or to insiders, you should choose the words and phraseology which will make it easy and pleasant for your readers. Professional slang is a sort of shorthand that speeds up communication among those in the know—when adapted to that purpose. But even insiders appreciate clarity, brevity, and simplicity. A tendency to use special language when it isn't needed goes hand in hand with verbosity and dullness. Phraseology common to a profession can become trite within the profession, even though it is understandable.

The engineer who wrote:

> The ease with which inspection, servicing, and maintenance operations can be performed is an important factor in operational safety as well as in minimizing operating cost and attaining high airplane availability.   (31 words)

might better have written:

> Ease of inspecting, servicing, and maintaining an airplane importantly affects its safety in flight, its operating cost, and its readiness to fly regularly.   (23 words)

When he wrote:

> It has been proved that installations and components which are not readily accessible are often neglected or poorly serviced, especially when the airplane utilization is high.   (26 words)

he might better have written:

> Inaccessible parts of an airplane are often poorly serviced, especially on planes kept in the air much of the time.   (20 words)

The profound is not always differentiated from the verbose.

Too wide use of your special language or professional phraseology is sure to result in your writing to yourself. So, too, will reckless use of such language when writing to others who are *supposed* to understand. Even to sophisticates, its only virtue is to convey meaning quicker than would be possible with words understandable to everybody.

Never should professional, special language be used to *exclude* readers or to impress a reader with your sophistication. It should never be used to make understanding harder for the reader even though he is capable of understanding your jargon. It should always be used to give him a message faster and more easily.

Too often the master of a specialized terminology lacks the ability to use it effectively. Sometimes he is so self-centered that he seems to dare his reader to understand what he writes. He equates quality of writing with complexity of sentence structure and sophistication of phraseology.

Special terminology should be shunned when it narrows an audience to those familiar with it and when more familiar language will permit others to benefit from the same piece.

Special terminology or professional slang always limits—never expands—an audience. At best it serves a limited audience better than more generally understood terminology would. It's dynamite. Used in the right places, it helps build bridges to readers' minds faster. Used indiscriminately, it blasts barriers into being which weren't there before.

Worse-than-meaningless Words

Some special terminology can be worse than meaningless; it can actually mean the wrong thing to the unsophisticated. When professional slang gives uncommon meanings to common words, it will mislead positively when written to professionally unsophisticated readers.

The language of statistics offers some good examples. "Population," "sample," "normal distribution," "percentile," "mean," "average," "standard deviation," "variance," "confidence interval," and "confidence coefficient" are just a few commonly used words that mean one thing in a statistical discussion and something entirely different elsewhere. Used as statistical terms, for example:

Population means: All possible data on a subject; rarely available; treated mathematically as an infinite number of data points.

Sample means: Data actually available; used to estimate the underlying population.

Normal distribution means: A frequency polygon for the population, scaled so that its area equals one; mathematically calculated as a normal probability density function.

Percentile means: Probability of population being less than a particular value.

Mean means: Most typical value of a symmetrical population, or the center-of-gravity value of a skewed population distribution curve.

Average means: Average of sample values used to approximate the population curve.

Only to a sophisticated statistical theorist will "population" mean "all possible data on a subject; rarely available; treated mathematically as an infinite number of data points." And so with the other terms listed. Use of common words to mean something uncommon is the ultimate of writing to yourself.

Scientists Are Self-centered Too

The scientific explosion of the 1960s focused attention on the self-centeredness of scientists. The need for the explosion to be understood by nonscientists has become great. Leading scientists, unable to get through to financiers, administrators, and politicians, themselves criticize severely the overuse of professional slang and obscure writing in general. They frown upon a scientist's writing any longer to himself. The director of Oak Ridge National Laboratory, for example, sees "the unclear way in which our scientists and engineers usually express themselves" as "the single greatest block to effective use of their written material." Then, exhibiting some of the faults he seeks to correct, he adds: "Much of the discussion of language by documentalists today is concerned with how the language looks to the neural network within a computing machine. Much more important is the analysis of the syntactical structure of a language with an eye to how the language looks to the neural network within the human brain." [1]

Clear, Interesting, and Helpful

To overcome the self-centeredness which finds so many ways to mar written communication, try to put three things into *every* communication you write:

- Clarity—to the people who will read
- Interest—to the people who will read
- Helpfulness—to the people who will read

In short, get your mind on your reader—and off yourself—as you prepare to organize your thinking before you start to write.

[1] Alvin M. Weinberg, "The Technical Writing Crisis," *The Rensselaer Review.*

4

Barriers to Communication: In the Writer

MANY BARRIERS IMPEDE exit from your mind of thoughts and data you want a reader to reach for. Self-centeredness is the most common, but it is not always the hardest to remove.

Even greater psychological barriers bar entrance to your reader's mind and impede his intake from your writing.

Barriers to Exit

These barriers to exit of ideas as you write combine to constitute your attitude. Your attitude, in turn, determines the texture as well as the pattern of your communication.

Pride, envy, laziness, anger—all are common, though often unrecognized, barriers to writing effectively. Fear, impatience, suspiciousness, cunningness, or anxiety often fashions the texture of a communication. Sometimes they joggle clear thinking so sharply as to affect the pattern as well.

To recognize this tedious train of unhelpful impulses is the major step toward eliminating them from writing attitudes. Few people are consciously prideful or envious, fearful or cunning, or impatient or lazy. We spot these qualities in letters we receive more quickly than we spot them in ones we write ourselves.

A normal tendency to rationalize prevents us from seeing our own attitudes as others see them. How often do we look on our own vacillation as prudence, our doubting as calculation, our hesitancy as forethought? Are some of our long, careful analyses of what to write really fear of a decision's consequences? You are unusual if you sometimes haven't hidden behind the old Haitian maxim or its equivalent: "Never insult an alligator till after you have crossed the river" . . . when you were just plain scared of drowning.

One deep-seated barrier in most of us is self-interest—the acute form of chronic self-centeredness. What to write comes most easily when we aim to benefit our reader as a person, not just as a reader. When we truly are telling him for his own good, we have little worry about how he will take it. We worry most when we are still trying to convince ourselves of the soundness or rightness of our viewpoint. Good reason exists for the general unwillingness to be suspicious of the motives of a person who speaks plainly.

Disputing Is Not Communicating

A not uncommon tendency to be competitive in our thinking is another inside-the-writer barrier to written communication. Skill in disputing is the opposite of skill in communication.

Winning an argument or defending a position may weave a communication clear in pattern but coarse in texture. Argument turns a reader's mind from what a communication is saying to what he plans to say in rebuttal. Friction from a communication whose texture is woven of argument and debate cuts its power to penetrate. Compulsive arguers are rarely adept in the art of successful communication.

Readers are mirrors. When our writing seems to attack them, they read defensively. When we write to prove a reader wrong, what do we communicate? Chiefly, our low opinion of his thoughts or actions and only incidentally the rightness of our impeccable logic.

More effective is injection of "our side" in contexts already at least partially acceptable to the reader. Blasting his concepts to nothingness and offering ours as replacements is simply the hard way. Self-satisfaction accruing from "winning" a written exchange rarely compensates for failure to achieve sound communication.

To Say "No," Kiss 'Em, Kick 'Em, Kiss 'Em.

Saying "no," for example, is among the more discomforting of communication tasks. Deciding that "no" must be said may have involved you emotionally, at least to a small degree. Usually you want to leave your reader "feeling good," as good as possible, at any rate. Yet the surrounding circumstances may make your chances small.

However difficult the situation, a kiss-'em–kick-'em–kiss-'em communication will make the best of it. I have seen it used successfully over more than three decades. It has said "no" harmoniously to everything from an irate advertiser's demand for positions opposite editorial text to a magazine owner's desire for publicity for his friends; from a potential advertiser's request for 1,000 free copies to a student's request for excessive thesis help. To kiss-'em–kick-'em–kiss-'em:

First: Find a way to thank, congratulate, or compliment your reader, if there is any possible reasonable basis for doing so and if you can make any statement that will not sound contrived. ("We appreciate your having thought of us as a possible source for information about pollywogs.")

Second: Tell him *"no"* clearly. Being as gracious as you can, explain why the answer is "no." Explain very specifically and very briefly. ("We don't, however, have the sort of pollywog data you seem to be looking for. Our concerns are almost exclusively with deep-sea game fish.")

Third: Close with the best practical, specific suggestion you can think of to point him to a source where he might get what he needs . . . and/or with a courteous, meaningful sign-off—as personalized as seems appropriate. ("I have an idea the Pollywog Protective League might supply the information you need. Here's hoping we can do better next time you call on us.")

The kick-'em part of such a communication should be as long or as short as need be. The kiss-'em parts should always be short, crisp, and gracious.

The KKK technique is well applied in the following letter:

Mr. George Tanken
Development Manager
Salzer Realty Co.
Whatown, Iowa

Dear Mr. Tanken:

Thank you for the opportunity to bid on installation of oil burners and hot-air heating systems for twenty homes in your Shady Acres housing development.

Other immediate commitments make it impossible for us to meet the time requirement of your specifications, so it isn't feasible for us to compete this time.

We are particularly sorry to be unable to respond to this first chance we have had to bid on a Salzer Realty job. We have long hoped we might be able to serve one of your projects. We hope you will keep us on the list for the next time around.

Best wishes for your satisfactory completion of the Shady Acres development in time for occupancy next spring.

Allen Bester
Manager, Heating Systems, Inc.

Both the texture and pattern of this letter, incidentally, reflect a writer alert to an opportunity to communicate positive values where only routine response is required. By imaginative handling of kiss-'em paragraphs, he kept the door open for later business.

This KKK technique is effective in any communication—memorandum, report, or letter—where the answer has to be "no." Having to say "no" to a request for contribution of prizes to a trade-association golf outing is a particularly unenviable duty. A general manager had to tell his sales manager to refuse such a request. He had to give him an excuse the sales manager could use to refuse the association's request. (The association's committee chairman, of course, was an important customer of the company being solicited.)

Unable to grant permission because of parent-company policies, the general manager made the best of a tough job by writing as shown in Exhibit 6.

EXHIBIT 6   *Saying "no" is never easy. Here's how a general manager tried to make a refusal easier for his sales manager to take*

TO Mark Hopkins
  Sales Manager

Dear Mark:

I think this is a good time to congratulate you on having consistently sold to the tractor industry on the basis of product, not personality. It should stand you in good stead when you have to say, "Sorry, no" to Carl Candor and his TMA Outing Committee.

I'm not naïve enough to think Carl will relate the two ideas and be happy about our not contributing to his prize fund. But I doubt that he'll be unhappy enough about the prize matter to affect our tractor sales volume in any way.

You had best just tell him the truth about why we have to say "no." I wouldn't be defensive. That could only get us into unfruitful discussions. My thought would be to write him something like this:

> Carl Candor
> Chairman, Outing Committee
> Tractor Manufacturers Association
>
> Dear Carl:
>
> When we became a division of Bigtime Industries last January, we gained some real improvement in production speed and manufacturing costs. But, along with the gains, we got some minor policies to administer that reduce our promotion flexibility in some areas. "No contributions or donations to social or athletic events sponsored outside the division" is one of these inherited policies.
>
> So, we aren't going to be able to participate in the prize pool for the TMA outing this year.
>
> I'm looking forward to seeing you at the outing. And I hereby promise not to win any prizes or, if I do, to pass them along to some more deserving charity!

Good luck, Mark. I know you'll do your best.

Sincerely,
Pendle Hill
General Manager

Sincerity, clarity, and specific statements, of course, are necessary to achieve success with the kiss-'em–kick-'em–kiss-'em communication. Lacking any one of these ingredients, it is more likely to infuriate a reader than to make him feel good.

Bad News Is Hard to Tell

Conveying bad news is a communications problem which usually involves the writer's emotions. A boss having to criticize an employee, for instance, usually has emotional barriers to overcome before he's ready to write (or talk).

Fear of personal discomfort from possible adverse recipient reactions, in fact, obsesses some executives. In writing, they seek distractedly for ways to say "You're doing a poor job" without saying it. They tell themselves they don't want to hurt the employee's feelings; they can't decide what to write because they are so strongly concerned with his interests.

Often their concern is more for the employee's reactions than for his interests. In such cases, emotional turmoil blocks rather than stimulates objective consideration of the reader's (employee's) future.

Barriers Overcome: A Case Study

To salvage a department head's future for his company's benefit, a vice-president started with analysis. The department manager had a brilliant mind, but he couldn't seem to focus it in terms of everyday business needs. His contributions to essential group projects were especially gauche. They were rarely out of order. Yet they were almost never entirely appropriate.

The vice-president's problem: To communicate management's dissatisfactions in a way which would stimulate self-correction in the department head. To do this, the vice-president had to overcome several barriers to exit of sound ideas from his own mind. Among them were:

Fear that an angry, defensive reaction by the department head might result in slowdown sulking or in his quitting the company entirely; that a personally unpleasant, emotionally uncomfortable confrontation might ensue; and that a positive attack for improvement might backfire and make matters worse.

Impatience at the failure of so brilliant a man to recognize what was perfectly obvious to all his associates as well as to management.

Resentment because the department head had failed to respond spontaneously to many "suggestions" for changing his ways and because working on this problem kept the vice-president from more attractive tasks.

Then he had a special worry. Person-to-person communication might end up far afield, as did so many other conversations with this department head, whatever the subject.

To reduce this worry barrier within himself, this vice-president decided to start with a written communication and follow it with a conversation. He reversed the order usual in such cases. His aim was to have the written communication serve as a focus—a sort of informal agenda—for the personal discussion.

He recognized the need for objectivity in his own thinking to avoid other barriers to exit of sound ideas. He decided to write strictly in terms of the objective he had set down: "To communicate management's dissatisfactions in a way which would stimulate self-correction in the department head."

He couldn't avoid discussion of the department head's personal characteristics. To correct them was the sole reason for communicating. But he could, he decided, talk of those characteristics impersonally, as he would if they were possessed by anybody charged with the same company responsibilities.

The very process of thinking thus before starting to write muted incipient impatient thoughts. Diverted also was the resentment which had fleetingly entered his consciousness. Finally, knowledge that his stated objective was truly to help both department head and company did much to shunt fears from the doorsill of his mind. In short, concentration on a mutually beneficial purpose cleared the way to getting major obstacles out of his own mind.

When he got to shaping the communication itself, he saw the perfect opportunity to apply the KKK technique. The resulting communication—which did pave the way for a well-focused, fruitful personal discussion—was the "Dear Harold" memorandum which is shown in Exhibit 7.

Dear Harold:

You've got an anniversary coming up. Soon you will have been supervising our canning operations for five years. In those years, you have held costs almost level, while other department costs were rising. You've done a more accurate job of budgeting than your predecessor. And you have developed and implemented important mechanical and operational improvements.

In short, your management has been characterized by initiative, imagination, and hard work. It has resulted in no small measure of practical development.

So, you must have been asking yourself: "Why doesn't management see me as a logical man for further promotions? I don't think they do. I sense lack of confidence every time I'm involved in a project with our manufacturing vice-president. But why? For heaven's sake, why?"

You are entitled to more than an answer to those questions, Harold. You should have an answer designed to help you gain management's confidence, so that we could use your talents more widely. So here goes.

– – – – – –

Five personal characteristics currently make you unavailable for broader services—unless radical changes occur.

First, you like to play a lone hand. Given a project, you keep everybody in the dark until it is completed. This is your idea of taking responsibility. It is fatal to accomplishment where others of equal or higher rank should be participants. They can't follow your leadership because you rarely let them know where you are.

Second, you can't seem to concentrate on what to do about a specific problem at a specific time. (You wouldn't answer "yes" or "no" to "Should we let employees off at noon the day before Christmas?" Instead, you would philosophize. After thirty minutes you might be saying: "So, you see, fifteen other elements of our personnel policy equally need revision. We should review the whole area and. . . .")

Third, you are insensitive to your audience's reactions—in conversations of all kinds at all levels. Result: You constantly arrive at slightly incorrect or *non sequitur* conclusions about the thoughts of others.

Fourth, you say: "I come out all right when I prepare myself ahead of time and plan what I'm going to say, even at informal conferences or in informal conversations." But you rarely do prepare.

Fifth, you're a great starter but a poor finisher. You are easily diverted from a project that needs finishing to totally irrelevant ideas for projects which intrigue your ever-active, keen mind.

In summary, you are far too subjective in thought and action to achieve maximum success as a member or a leader of a group.

You are capable, in my opinion, of hurdling all these barriers to maximum accomplishment—*if:*

(a) you recognize them as barriers

(b) you decide they are worth jumping

Blessed are the meek, for they shall inherit the earth.

Let's talk further at your earliest convenience.

Sincerely,

(Jackson Crosby)
General Manager

Two Separate Attacks Often Help

Often barriers to exit of ideas from your mind can be lowered, as in the case study cited, by making two separate attacks on a problem, one in personal conversation and the other in writing.

Most executives, faced with the need to discharge an employee, know they should do the job in person. No written communication, from the pink slip to the gobbledegook of bureaucracy, is ever quite satisfactory. But once personal contact has made the separation as harmonious as possible, a written communication can be a great help to the former employee's future. Wherever he goes, the first question he'll be asked is: "Why did you leave your last job?" A personal letter at the time of separation, written by the man who discharged him, can be of real help.

A general sales manager in California effectively overcame some strong emotional barriers to write such a letter to a salesman, coincident with discharging him.

This salesman was being fired because (1) his sales had declined steadily over a period of three years—while sales in other territories had increased—and (2) he had become increasingly critical of the product and the management policies behind its development. Having completed the separation process in a series of personal conferences, the sales manager wrote this letter. Every statement in it was true; every sentiment was sincere.

> Dear Arthur:
>
> I wouldn't want you to leave Canyon Products without knowing about my high personal regard for you as a man and as a skilled and effective sales representative.
>
> Within a year or so after your arrival, our product sales increased appreciably—in your territory as well as in Denver, where you trained a newcomer. You brought to us and maintained a graciousness of personality which made you friends throughout the organization.
>
> And, working under what I know you felt to be product-quality handicaps, you contributed measurably to improving the Canyon Products image in our industry, where you have so many friends and clients.
>
> If we can assist your future plans in any way, be sure to let us know. We'd welcome an opportunity to help.
>
> > Sincerely,
> >
> > General Sales Manager
> > Canyon Products Corporation

Never Write in Anger

Anger in any of its aspects is a major barrier to generating the kind of thinking that results in a successful communication. The ill effects of writing in anger or pique are so obvious that it is surprising to find many communications so written.

None of the excuses for speaking in anger have validity for the communications *writer*. It's far easier to think before you write than before you speak. When writing, *you* can dictate the length of a cooling-off period. A temper strong enough to overcome the natural tendency to procrastinate about writing pays its owner no dividends.

A wholesaler, writing to one of his fifteen manufacturer-suppliers, for example, had second thoughts before writing the following letter. But that wasn't enough. Had he lengthened his cooling-off period, this wholesaler probably would never have written as he did:

Darling Imports
New York, New York

Dear Mr. Darling:

I wrote a letter to you this morning in lieu of sending a collect wire and just tore it up because my associates think I was a bit too angry to send a letter that I had written in that frame of mind. I'm sure they are right. So I'll start all over again.

To begin with, we have told you how disappointed we are in the deliveries this season—or rather the lack of deliveries. Attached are three typical examples—pardon, only two. (The third is one I'm about to mention in this letter.)

One of these letters (The Crossroads Store) is one we wrote you about on November 11. We haven't even had an answer, and they have written us a second time. The third I mention is the order for Nargog Imports (our order No. 740), which we took on September 13. They haven't received a thing and have called us twice on it. The Cat and Bottle order was written September 6 for $134.12 . . . nothing shipped.

In checking our records the other evening, I became aware of how darn little reorder business we are writing for Darling. When I checked further, it was easier to understand why. Many of our accounts never received their first orders. (They usually place a first order to test it for sales appeal.) So, naturally, they haven't reordered.

Will you please tell us what is happening, what we can tell our customers, and when you expect deliveries to be made more promptly?

At this point, we are pretty well discouraged. We had never had these types of complaints about the Darling line, and now we find that we are writing more business than ever and yet also have more complaints than we ever had about lack of delivery.

Sincerely,

Product Distribution, Inc.

The faults of this letter are typical of any communication written in anger or pique. Its texture is calculated to arouse equal anger barriers to reception in Mr. Darling. Its pattern is confused, and the movements of its thought are frequently tangential.

As received in Mr. Darling's mind, the letter said something like this:

(Paragraph 1) I'm madder than hell with you.

(Paragraph 2) I've told you before that your deliveries are bad.

(Paragraph 3) Now here are two or three new examples.

(Paragraph 4) What's more, people aren't reordering your line, because you don't deliver the first order promptly.

(Paragraph 5) What do you suggest we tell our customers? . . . to get them off our backs.

(Paragraph 6) Having gotten this much off my chest, I'm not quite as mad as I was, but I'm even more fed up with your poor delivery performance, and the lack of reorders isn't *our* fault. We're writing more business all the time.

At no point, incidentally, does this wholesaler ask the only business question worth writing about: "What can be done to radically improve deliveries of Darling articles to our customers?"

Thought Turns Outward

Once you recognize unhelpful emotions for what they are— major barriers to effective writing (and living)—half their power to warp your thinking is destroyed. The other half will fade as you turn your thoughts outward to consider barriers to ingress into your reader's mind.

5

Barriers to Communication:
In the Reader

THE UNSEEN BARRIERS impeding entrance to a reader's mind also are related to the self-centeredness common to most humans. To communicate, accept self-centered readers as normal, even while exorcising self-centeredness from your writing.

These barriers are numerous and chameleonlike. They differ from reader to reader and within the same reader at different times. So you had best concentrate on a few that are common to most readers, most of the time. Among these are:

- Built-in opinions
- Impatience
- Tangential thinking
- An easily diverted mind
- Touchiness and competitive comparing

There are others. But if you can regularly get past these five hindrances, you will complete your communication more often than not. (A good way to identify these blocks is to check your own reactions to communications you receive.)

Danger Signals: Built-in Opinions

The known generalities about people's behavior are danger signals rather than positive helps. Few of us, for example, are very pliable. Faced with an unsolicited communication we are likely first to scan it mentally for reinforcement of views or information we already have. (Editorials and other opinion-molding devices usually do very little molding, editorial consultant Edgar A. Grunwald says the behaviorists report. Editorials make the fellow who agrees with them feel rosy. Those who don't agree quickly turn their backs.)

Whatever the subject, some previous knowledge or misconception is in a reader's mind. There is a way he *wants* to read what you are trying to say. His built-in opinions may be due to ignorance. They may arise from a general fearfulness about life in general or from special fears related to the subject. They may come from doubts about your accuracy, reliability, or objectivity. Your communication credit rating—his collective impression of your past communications—may be low or high.

Many of these *built-in opinion barriers can be avoided* rather than scaled. *They can be avoided by sticking to the point throughout the whole communication.* When your purpose is communication, you need face only those prejudices that are clearly germane to the problems and purposes of the particular communication. As Grunwald suggests, direct attack is unlikely to change the opinions; it *is* likely to sidetrack your whole communication.

Whatever the subject, you should have a purpose—stated specifically before you start to write. That purpose should involve benefit to your reader. Sticking to that kind of a point, you will run head on into a minimum of built-in prejudices. Such prejudices are born of self-centered, subjective thinking. Your objectively purposed communication will be running on a different track, between different terminals.

Impatience

Impatience sparks hasty reading, inaccurate reception, and limited comprehension, so it's best to visualize your communication as being an interruption to a man intent on his own concerns. He doesn't have to be busy to be impatient with your interruption. He can be just as impatient if his daydreams are broken. And saying: "Pardon me, do you mind if I interrupt for a moment?" only makes matters worse. ("And this program will continue after a word from our sponsor.")

To keep impatience to a minimum, relate your communication to your reader's concerns as quickly as possible. "The first thing to learn in intercourse with others is non-interference with their own peculiar ways of being happy," said philosopher-psychologist William James. Answer as promptly as you can the questions impatience is likely to stir in your reader's mind.

> "What's the point of this communication?"
>
> "What—if anything—am I expected to do about it?" ("Is it just 'for information'?" "Is it for my approval? Am I expected to take some action if I approve? Or can I approve without letting myself in for more work?")
>
> "Is it something I *have* to do something about?" ("Is it from my boss, from somebody to whom I'm under obligation, or from some group to which I have committed myself?")
>
> "Or do I have a choice?" (Remember the bridegroom at the shotgun wedding who responded to the preacher's "Do you take this woman for your lawfully wedded wife?" with "Do I have a choice?")
>
> "Or is it just a sales solicitation of some kind—where I'm in the driver's seat and I can take it or leave it without having any reasons?"

Such unsorted questions tumble through a normally self-centered reader's mind (often subconsciously) almost every time he picks up a communication.

Your most potent counter to impatience is to *state your main point first.* Then answer your reader's other questions *by the way you write* what you have to say. Couch your statements in terms that will provide the answers incidentally.

For example, here are two versions of an interoffice memorandum. Version 1 simply emits the information in the order in which it entered the consciousness of the writer. The recipient must read clear through to get answers to: "What's the point of this communication?" and "What—if anything—am I expected to do about it?"

Version 2 was written *from* Asche (the writer) *to* Hessar (the recipient). Version 1 was just written. Version 2 is designed to allay any natural impatience in Hessar. Version 1 was written without thought of possible Hessar reaction—impatient or otherwise.

TO   C. Hessar, Office Manager
FROM   J. Asche, Receiving Department

Version 1

A shipment of 12 dozen ball-point pens and 16 dozen lead pencils arrived here yesterday. The invoice shows they were ordered by your department three weeks ago, on August 3. There is, however, no indication as to whether or not they are to be delivered directly to your department or whether they should go to the stock room.

Please let me know which you would like to have done.

Version 2

Shall we deliver to you or send to stock the 12 dozen ball-point pens and the 16 dozen lead pencils delivered yesterday, which you ordered August 3, Order No. S9487?

In simple situations such as described in Versions 1 and 2 writing to allay impatience is *desirable,* but with more complex problems writing (at more length, of course) is *essential* to completing communication.

Above all, to allay impatience *don't apologize*—especially at the start of a communication. Nothing makes a reader so impatient as apologetic windups before he finds out just what the writer has in mind. No communication profits from an "I-probably-shouldn't-say-this" introduction or from "You-probably-know-this-but-I'm going-to-tell-you-anyhow," "You-probably-won't-agree-with-this-but," and all the train of apologies they drag behind them. (If apologies are really needed for what you are writing, then write it differently.)

Don't apologize for what you are about to say, even when your communication itself is an apology.

Tangential Rambling

The tendency to think tangentially, common to most readers (and writers), was noted in Chapter 2, "Writing to Get Readers to Reach." A tendency to ramble tangentially is an even greater barrier to the entrance of ideas. It emasculates them on their way in.

You may write: "The flat drive, characteristic of modern tennis, takes the ball more quickly to its destination than the topped drive of yesteryear." Without continuing to your subsequent comparisons and discussion, my mind may leave your communication to wool-gather thus:

"Yes, but the margin of error is smaller . . . Tilden used a slight top spin on his drive . . . and Tilden was the greatest player of all time . . . I don't care what anybody says. And I've seen 'em all from Norris Williams on up to now . . . I'll never forget the first time I saw Williams . . . in Pittsburgh . . . right after he had been among those saved in the Titanic disaster . . . that was a terrible thing . . . I remember there was a movie about it, . . . Clive Brook, the suave English actor, was the lead in it . . . Wonder what's happened to him? . . . I haven't heard of him, etc., etc., etc."

Directly, you can't do anything to prevent this common sort of reader rambling. But by recognizing the likelihood of its presence, you can *keep your communication tightly knit*. You can hold it to a single subject and write only in terms of that subject. You can make sure that when your reader does return to your second sentence, he is back on *your* track.

An Easily Diverted Mind

The easily-diverted mind barrier is closely allied to the tangential-rambling hurdle. It is just another form of the same human characteristic. It's harder for the average mind to stay on one subject than to move aimlessly. You can't prevent your reader from listening to errant thoughts or intruding people while he is trying to read your communication. You can't be sure his tangential rambling won't come to focus on a subject alien to that of your communication.

But here again, you can make sure your communication itself doesn't divert him. A department manager's report to his company's operating committee illustrates the positive dangers of diversion-prone statements. He wrote:

"We are about to change both design and production operations to use the metric system. The advantages of such a change are familiar to this committee. They involve. . . .

"The disadvantages—which seem to us to be more than offset by the advantages—are. . . .

"Now if this committee approves this change at once (as I hope), I am sure we can encompass the change within the next twelve months. I've set up all the details of doing it. The cost will be about $50,000—which I have included in our department's next year's budget. (The $15,000 of this total, which, I figure, we will spend in the current fiscal year in getting the changeover started, I'm planning to handle as a deferred expense.)

"So, we are all ready to go if this final consideration is approved by this committee."

At the committee meeting held to discuss and approve the changeover to metric, the comptroller *immediately* objected to handling as a deferred expense the $15,000 to be spent in the current fiscal year. "Regardless of how it's handled on the books," he protested, "we have to take the actual dollars from someplace this year. To do that, we must ask the finance committee to approve an extra budgetary expenditure this year."

This led to a decision to do as the comptroller demanded— following lengthy discussion, which included protests about the delay necessarily involved in following that procedure.

Discussion of the changeover to metric—for which the committee had convened and for which the report had been written— was never mentioned until the tangential accounting-procedure item had been completed. The department manager had recognized the tangential character of the item and had put it in parentheses. But he failed completely to recognize its diversionary potentials. By including this item, he delayed by several weeks the start of his new program. He also gave himself some extra communications to write—to explain the problem and make the request to the finance committee. (It could have been handled later, outside the official committee framework.)

In writing, you can at least *avoid inclusion of potentially diverting concepts or information.*

Touchiness and Competitive Comparisons

A good many people are "touchy"; a few are extremely so; some take as implied criticism any statement that remotely can be so interpreted.

Most readers of individual communications are touchier than they admit. Also, most tend to compare themselves and their performance to figures, statements, or opinions in communications directed to them. ("The average income of bachelor of arts graduates five years after graduation is $8,000 a year" brings every B.A. reader the thought: "Let's see, mine was so-and-so.")

As a writer, you should recognize the existence of such mental habits.

Check your communication over before it starts for its destination. Have you opened the way for any particularly "unfortunate" comparisons or touched any obviously tender nerves?

Barriers Are Low to Requested Communications

When your communication responds to a request or demand, the reader has reached for it before it is written. When it arrives, he will lower his own mental barriers. He is almost sure to read it —perhaps with eagerness and certainly without initial irritation.

The easiest report to write, for example, is one your boss asks for. You know your audience; you know or can readily learn the use to be made of the report. Your opening, main-idea sentences can be determined by analysis of this knowledge.

So it is with letters, memoranda, and other written communications. When they respond to a request, they will be received and read. The asker-receiver is reaching for the ideas or information— probably with his best reaching equipment.

Responding to requests, therefore, is a special opportunity to communicate effectively. Relatively, the barriers are down. A creative report, letter, or memorandum has a good chance to stir enthusiasm, get action, or convey a maximum of information. Only the naïve and the lazy will see the request as a chance to get by with a mediocre response. Others will recognize it as their best chance to communicate fully, comfortably and fruitfully.

Only a little more difficult is responding to a request you yourself stimulate. The bars aren't down as far as they are when the request is spontaneous. *But they are further down than they are when a communication is received that has not been asked for at all.* Even if you stimulate by "Yes, I wish you would get me that information," your response is pretty sure to be read. You have opened a channel into a future reader's mind. The communication won't have to do its own bulldozing.

So seek, don't avoid, requests which require that you write a communication. The requested communication has maximum potentials for achieving its purpose. The reader automatically lowers major barriers to entrance of its contents into his mind.

How to Scale Reader Barriers

To scale the barriers which impede entrance to a reader's mind, in short:

- Avoid built-in opinion barriers.
- Have a purpose for every written piece.
- Relate your communication to your reader's concerns as quickly as possible.
- State your main point first.
- Don't apologize.
- Keep your communication tightly knit. Hold it to a single subject, and write only in terms of that subject.
- Avoid inclusion of potentially diverting concepts or information.
- Check your communication over before it starts for its destination.
- Seek, don't avoid, requests which require that you write a communication.

6

Writing:
A Tool to
Penetrate Realities

FIT YOUR COMMUNICATIONS purpose to the realities of each individual situation. Sharpen the outline of that purpose to penetrate the realities of the problem. Then make the purpose positive, and your writing will achieve the ends you envision.

A statement of purpose as well as objective appropriate to the special instance will sharpen your writing's definition. You *do* want to have an objective—an aim or end to your action of writing, a point to be hit or reached. But purpose is even more important—an end which you set yourself as an object to be attained. Statement of objective clarifies where you are going; statement of purpose clarifies what you hope to do when you get there.

Suppose you want a job as assistant to the office manager of a particular company. The objective of your letter of application is to reach the office manager with information about your qualifications. Its realistic purpose is to get him to hire you.

This conscious definition of purpose should always precede thought about what to write and how to write it. The writing should be tailored to effective achievement of that purpose. The purpose shouldn't be modified or bent to make expression easier. Never emulate the rookie cop who dragged a dead horse a block from Kosciusko Street to Smith Street because he had to turn in a written report and couldn't spell "Kosciusko."

Suppose you'd like your yearly progress report to stimulate additional appropriations for the coming year. Don't start writing, and, finding it hard to express so forthright a purpose, end up with a straight, factual report because it's easier to write. To avoid this all too familiar sequence, clarify your purpose mentally before you begin to write. Then write to that purpose.

Assume you decide—hours or weeks before you write—that your progress report should help to ensure new, needed appropriations. Then you can organize your material to point up this purpose. Each sentence will begin to flow naturally in the same direction. The result will be totally different from what it would have been if you had proposed winning the company's annual award for "greatest departmental progress last year." Data and material would be the same in either case, but the presentation would be different.

Aiming at additional appropriations, your report might unfold along these lines:

> With a minimum of overtime work, Department XYZ has completed two-thirds of the test program designed to learn the behavior of oil-water mixtures in separators.
>
> At this point we are sure that so-and-so occurs. But until two further tests are run, we can only speculate that so-and-so is always a characteristic of the reactions.
>
> Other results of the tests to date include:
>
> .
> .
> .... etc.

> ### Conclusion
>
> To achieve this progress to date has cost about 90 per cent of the $100,000 budgeted this year. We have, in other words, gone two-thirds of the way on about $90,000.
>
> To go the final third will not involve another $45,000. The final tests have already been programmed, personnel are at work, and equipment is already in operation. These tests should be

completed and reported on for less than $35,000—of which $10,000 is left over from the current budget.

Based on the same data and material, a report aimed at winning the company's annual award for "greatest departmental progress last year" might unfold more like this:

In the last twelve months, Department XYZ has run 843 tests in a program designed to learn the behavior of oil-water mixtures in separators. This seventy-per-month record exceeds by 16⅔ per cent the sixty-per-month estimated in the original programming.

Economies effected in purchase of budgeted equipment, plus personnel training which kept overtime to a minimum, resulted in operating expenses of $90,123—almost 10 per cent under the budgeted $100,000.

From these 843 tests, a number of technical conclusions are already feasible, though 280 additional tests are contemplated to complete the scheduled program.

At this point, for example, we are sure that so-and-so occurs. Other conclusions already feasible to date include:

.
.
... etc.

Conclusion

The chief progress by Department XYZ in this calendar year is in the improved personnel training program and in reorganization of selection-of-new-equipment processes. These two improvements are chiefly responsible for the better-than-estimated production of tests and the better-than-budgeted cost records. (A detailed rundown of how these two improvements were achieved is attached.)

Clarification Produces Success

Now this clarification of purpose is the most potent single step in producing a successful communication. It is more than thinking before writing. It is thinking through your problems—big and little. It is thinking so you can act on your problems, not just to react to them. It is essential to creative communications writing. But it helps in every phase of living.

In getting your own mind clear about the purpose of a contemplated communication, you face the realities of the particular situation. As soon as you say to yourself: "I'd like Harry Heptane to send me a bibliography on tax aspects of cost accounting," inevitably you wonder what chance there is of his doing so. Harry works in the headquarters staff of the Cost Accountant's Institute, of which you are a member.

You muse: "He'll feel under some obligation to help. But his work is in the membership department. He knows little about accounting himself; almost certainly he is unfamiliar with the literature. He won't have any such list at hand. To dig it out personally would be a very big job. . . . But maybe he could tell somebody else to ask. I can't think of anyone else myself. . . ."

So, the purpose of your letter to Harry becomes finding out where you can get the information. There is some chance of Harry's supplying a source but almost none of his supplying the information. Ask him for a source, and you probably will get it. Ask him for the information, and you'll probably get nothing—though Harry may package the nothing in gracious and deft words.

Such definition of purpose helps even when communicating about simple, minor matters like the bibliography. But it can make or break success when writing toward solution of complex, important business or professional problems. Here, a definition appropriate to the specific situation can eliminate most major barriers to entrance to your reader's mind. An inappropriate definition can raise insurmountable ones. The handling of similar presentations by two company industrial publications will illustrate.

Two Case Histories

Industrial publication editors in two similarly organized concerns each had become aware of growing criticism of their publications. Neither publication had been subjected to major editorial or format changes for nearly ten years. Both were achieving a high reader satisfaction, according to reliable reader-research studies.

In both cases, the overall publication policies were directed by a company publication committee, of which the general sales manager (the editor's boss) was chairman. Both editors realized they must act to reduce or eliminate the criticisms. Each decided on a presentation to his company publication committee.

Editor Ardmore went right ahead with his written presentation. He didn't pause to think through to a precise purpose. He marshaled his data, pointed up his rebuttals, and logically justified his position that the magazine was doing a good job. As a brief in a court of law, his presentation could not have failed to win a verdict.

But to a committee responsible for development of the best possible company publication, it appeared defensive, unimaginative, and slightly stubborn. Those committee members who had voiced criticism felt "put in their place" rather than convinced of their error. They were slightly resentful rather than better educated.

Editor Bonsell, on the other hand, decided to act, not react. He stopped to clarify in his own mind exactly what he hoped his presentation would accomplish. He sought not only a specific definition of purpose but also a definition appropriate to this particular situation. His thoughts ran something like this:

"When you get right down to it, I'm after the same thing the committee is: the most effective company publication we can get out.

"Some changes probably *are* indicated. But not those my critics have been suggesting! They haven't the slightest idea practically what to do to eliminate their dissatisfactions. Let their ideas edit the magazine for a year, and they'd wreck it.

"So, I'd better get out ahead of the committee and suggest changes that should and could be made. Better to get committee approval of a program *I* know can be executed than to have to try to carry out a program dreamed up by the committee's non-professionals."

Such thinking led editor Bonsell to aim his presentation at getting committee approval to develop and execute an editorial improvement program. He knew that a plan already in motion is easier to approve than one in mind. So he wrote:

> THE ACME STAR has in process editorial changes which when completed will reflect a radical improvement in today's satisfactory publication.

Next January will mark completion of the operationally involved process of changeover to the improved publication. Changeover completion will be signaled by the entirely new typographical format and layout which will debut in January.

Your editorial staff was motivated to go forward with plans for this new *Acme Star* by several things:

• Study of long-range reader-research implications makes clear that a basically new editorial approach is needed to face up to some chronic dissatisfactions on the part of a limited number of important readers. In a nutshell, readers like and read the *Acme Star* and react most favorably in an overwhelming percentage of cases. But they disagree violently among themselves about the *subjects* they want treated most emphatically.

• Spontaneous in-person comments from some of the foreign readers in recent months confirm the need for radical change in handling domestic-as-related-to-foreign news material.

• Several experienced company "elder statesmen"—including three members of the committee—have expressed need-for-change thoughts in terms which can be translated into action in a practical way.

THE ADVANCE, INSIDE STORY of this new *Acme Star* is told in some detail in the attached editorial staff report.

The staff report which editor Bonsell attached contained generalized statements of specific changes contemplated. It was specific enough to be meaningful to the committee of nonprofessionals. But it was general enough not to invite picking-the-grunts-out-of-pig-iron discussion by the committee.

The committee approved going forward along the lines of the suggested program, asked for progress reports as the program moved ahead, and OK'd the substantial budget increase necessary.

What the committee really approved, of course, was the initiative and imagination revealed by the presentation. These qualities gave promise of effective action in a direction the committee members *felt* was desirable. The specific program had to accompany the presentation to prevent suspicion that it didn't exist. But the committee didn't "expert" on the program itself. It did "expert" on the character of the thinking which had produced the written presentation of the program.

Editor Bonsell's presentation brought him an opportunity and a challenge of the kind most editors long for.

Face Realities

Usually, the work of writing is less when you are clear about your purpose before taking pen in hand or putting fingers to typewriter. In the cases cited, the thought-out-in-advance communication was more effective because it was tailored to existing circumstances—and it was just as easy to write as well.

So try to fit your communication purpose to the realities of each individual situation. Communicate to a particular person or group with consciousness of their limitations as well their self-interests, of their capacities as well as their prejudices.

A realistic definition of purpose appropriate to your specific situation will lower the barriers to a reader's mind better than by any other single method.

7

Focus: Keystone of Successful Writing

FOCUSING IS GETTING to the point, by means of a written sentence. It is a written statement inspired by your predetermined purpose. Usually it will spark the first sentence (or sentences) of the communication itself.

Similarly, the opening lines of each subdivision of your communication should be a written focus of the main idea or ideas of the subdivision. Each paragraph should be focused in its opening sentence, and each sentence in its opening words. Actually, each word should be selected to fulfill the pointed purpose of the sentence.

To bring ideas to a point in writing involves disciplining, but not limiting, your thoughts. It requires crystal clarity about the smallest and largest projects. It involves awareness of an almost infinite spectrum of directly and remotely related concepts. It makes that total awareness concrete *in terms of* the specific purpose already defined.

Focusing would be easy if it meant merely selecting data and discarding what isn't pertinent. But it means more even than letting in fresh thoughts and new information. It requires letting the fresh and the new unfold in relation to what is already in your

61

mind to start with. It means relating the partly known to the fully known, the future to the past.

And finally, it means condensing the partially related to a pinpoint of direct relationship. Focus, in other words, is the practical end of relaxed thinking, the meeting place of variegated visitors to your mind.

Defining purpose integrates your own thoughts. Those thoughts, put into words which open a communication, bring your reader's mind to focus on what you have to say. The written words are proof that your purpose is clear. Former Life Saver president Sidney Edlund writes: "No idea is clear, no goal is clear until you put it into words."

This written focus acts as piers for the bridge a creative communication seeks to build from your mind to a reader's. Your definition of purpose is the survey which precedes the bridge building; the focus in writing sets the piers exactly along the surveyed lines.

If you can't translate your definition of purpose into written focus, the trouble is with your definition, not with your writing ability. Don't permit yourself to rationalize: "I know exactly what I want to say, but I can't seem to put it in words." Clear thinking will almost inevitably produce clear writing. Ability to express your main idea in a sentence tests whether or not you are ready to write. Until you can do it, don't write.

"But," you may say to yourself, "I'd never get my writing chores done if I followed this advice. I wouldn't have time to do anything but answer my mail. I'd never get to the reports expected of me, write the minutes of that last meeting before the next one occurs, and get out those instructions to suppliers. This focusing idea is for the birds. It isn't practical, especially on short, minor-problem communications—which make up most of what faces me."

And you're right—if you think defining purpose means making a major production of every communication you write. But it is the *only* practical way to communicate complex ideas successfully —day in and day out, year after year. And if you look on minor writing obligations merely as chores, you'll never form the communications habits necessary for attacking the big jobs.

There's no need to stay awake nights defining the purpose of a letter responding to an invitation to become a member of a committee or a request for your estimate of next year's sales.

The purpose of your response in the first case is to accept or reject—graciously and clearly. In the second, it is to give the estimate—with or without supporting data. The process of defining purpose can be a matter of seconds. But defining in routine instances fashions the habit which ensures defining when to fail to define is fatal.

Bringing your communication to focus gets your reader thinking at once about what you want him to think about. It gets attention *for the ideas or facts you have to convey.* It turns a reader's mind in the direction your communication is going to take.

Defining purpose solves the attention-getting problem—always satisfactorily and usually in the best possible way. (Contrived attention-getters too often get attention for something foreign to the writer's purpose. They actually lead the reader's mind astray and interest him in something foreign to the communication's message. The nude adorning a calendar advertising an axle gets the truckdriver's attention, but not for the axle.)

Immediate pointing up of the main ideas to be communicated serves your reader by informing him. Also it makes it easy for him to decide whether or not he is interested. This serves you as a writer, too. If you can't interest the reader in what you *really* have to say, you are going to have to try some other-than-writing approach anyhow. In the meantime, you have left a favorable impression. You have saved your reader the annoying work of "discovering" that what you are really getting at isn't to his taste or need.

Focus also ensures clarity for your communication because it puts in writing exactly the purpose your prethinking has defined. It ensures unity for your communication because it guides and limits what you shall put in and what you shall leave out. It ensures proper emphasis because it illuminates the main idea or fact you want your reader to take in. In ensures coherence because each subsequent paragraph or sentence becomes a proof, an explanation, or an amplification of that main idea.

Successful focus involves both analysis and synthesis of *all* involved factors. Too many writers analyze the problems they are writing about but stop there. They sort out the elements of the problem; they see and face the facts. But the hard, careful work of recombining the elements to achieve the defined purpose is so rarely done as to make outstanding the communications of those who do. Even rarer is encompassment of *all* problem elements in terms of both the purpose and the reader.

Naming inability to communicate the "most prevalent source of weakness in executives," Roy Pearson concludes in "Where Do We Go from Here?": "He doesn't get to the heart of what he wants to say [when he writes]. He has a dozen ideas, but no point. He has all the parts of the puzzle, but hasn't taken time to put them together. So he lands hard on the inconsequentials, and slides over the significant issues with no awareness of their meaning." [1]

Three Approaches

Ability to focus a communication is influenced greatly, of course, by the mental habits of the writer and the problem approach characteristic of him. These influence particularly the focusing in terms of predetermined purpose.

Three men whose communicating I have known intimately for years well illustrate this point.

Jack tends to take each problem at its face value. If it seems to be a troublemaker, he tries to find an immediate and direct way out of the particular trouble threatened or existing. Then he faces the next problem when it arises.

Sam tends to look so far past the immediate problem to the ultimate possible solution of all similar problems that he loses his reader, who usually has a Jack attitude. Frequently, Sam proceeds remorselessly with every last detail but omits any clear explanation of the main point.

George does a little of both. He tends to look for a way to solve the immediate problem, as Jack does. Thus he establishes and maintains mental liaison with his Jackish audience. But he tries also to settle only for an immediate solution applicable in princi-

[1] Roy Pearson, "Where Do We Go from Here?" *Think*, July–August, 1964.

ple to all other similar future problems. (But his communications say little if anything about the future. He doesn't insist his reader be interested in anything except solution of the immediate problem. However, he doesn't permit himself a final focus until, in his own mind, he can see how it will fit the future.)

George's approach satisfies the Jackish readers, who *must* be satisfied or the immediate problem remains. But it doesn't run counter to Samish readers. Either they interpolate for themselves or write back and ask questions about the future.

It's easy to see how these three approaches might bring a different focus in writing, even if defined purposes were identical.

Suppose $20,000 had to be eliminated from a $2,000,000 preliminary budget before submission to the board of directors. Jack's focusing sentence might be:

> To bring the budget within desired limits, I recommend we delay for a year construction of the proposed new $30,000 storage facility. I am sure we can make do with present facilities for a while longer and that this would be the least harmful elimination we might make at this time. Actually, we might redistribute the extra $10,000 to strengthen some other elements of our program. . . .

Sam's focus probably would arrive thirty minutes before the final deadline for recommendations because he kept thinking of so many different ways the cut might be made and the possible ultimate effects of each. It might run like this:

> The desired $20,000 budget reduction might be effected in any one of several ways. We might eliminate the proposed $30,000 storage facility, stretch out our schedule of salary increases, reduce the size of our promotional budget, cut our advertising budget, or do any one of several other things without seriously harming the year's program. Or we might accomplish the same purpose by developing plans to ensure greater income.
>
> Development of more income seems to me the best method because it would ensure a maximum effort on the positive side of our long-term development. A restudy of our pricing policies alone might give us the key to the right way to move. . . .

George's focus probably would be much more like Jack's. It might read something like this:

> To bring the budget within desired limits, I suggest that each of our eight department managers cut 1 per cent (wherever he sees fit) from his department budget. This would get the necessary $20,000 total and yet require no noticeable modification of any currently planned program. (Few figures now in the budget have a plus-or-minus 1 per cent accuracy.)
>
> Were the problem to cut $200,000, an across-the-board reduction of this kind would make no sense. But to get the $20,000, this method seems best. It can be executed quickly and easily and yet will require almost no program readjustment.

Jack's focus, in other words, grew largely from expediency thinking, but it was clear and easy to execute. George's was equally clear and easy to execute. But it was better fitted to the future and just as well fitted to the present. Sam's *thinking* was probably the soundest of all. But his focus was fuzzy and probably frustrated the budget balancers who read it.

Focus is fundamental. With it, a communication is almost bound to be clear, however phrased. Without it, the communication can't be clear, however crisp and polished the words, phrases, and sentences.

So when pressed for time in preparing a communication, don't skimp on the thinking before writing.

How to Focus in Writing

First, decide what ideas or facts are most likely to achieve the purpose you want your communication to achieve. Then write them down in a single positive statement, a one-sentence statement if possible.

Suppose you are an accountant newly employed in a small manufacturing company. You have found that the company has no integrated system of receiving merchandise and equipment. When an invoice accompanies incoming merchandise, it is copied on a receiving sheet in duplicate by whoever happens to be around at the time. One copy is sent to the accounting department; one is held by the department to which the merchandise is delivered.

You feel that all merchandise should come in through a special person or department. You decide to write a memorandum to the general manager. Defined purpose: To get established and properly functioning a company receiving facility.

So you begin playing with words for a sentence which will focus in the general manager's mind the main point you want him to get. He agrees that an integrated receiving department is what is needed, so you focus directly on how to establish the needed receiving facility—needed because of the losses and inefficiencies inherent in the existing loosely coordinated methods.

So you *do not* write:

> It seems to me that our company's present method of receiving incoming merchandise might be considerably improved by having all merchandise come in through a special receiving facility, established for that single purpose.

Nor do you write:

> A special receiving facility, through which all merchandise passes before distribution to using departments, might save us money and time through better checking of shipments before acceptance and by the insurance of prompt handling.

But you *do write:*

> I suggest establishment of a special receiving department responsible for (1) inspecting all merchandise on its way in to our plant, (2) checking incoming invoices against purchase orders, (3) recording all incoming material on proper receiving forms, and (4) promptly delivering incoming shipments to using departments. Such a facility—set up under the supervision of the production, administrative or accounting department manager's supervision— could, I believe, save time and money and reduce errors.

The seemingly slight difference in order and emphasis of ideas in these three written focuses can make the difference between day and night in practical results achieved. The *do write* statement *immediately* starts the general manager thinking about establishing the new department, not wondering what ought to be done to correct a loosely handled company operation or agreeing that a new department would be a good thing. His thought is pointed immediately toward action—not agreement or approval. And he gets some immediate help in thinking about the action. He gets reasons favorable to the action, potential benefits from the action, and suggested ways to implement the action. (As the *do write* memorandum went on, of course, it would amplify, explain, and support with facts these same points.) The help is in the form of suggestions, clearly showing the writer's recognition of the general manager's decision-making responsibilities and authority.

Maintaining the Focus

To maintain focus throughout your communication:

• Keep the reader's mind moving in the direction of, and toward the end indicated in, your opening statements.

• Bring out the unfavorable points your reader might think of as well as the favorable ones you hope he will accept.

You keep your reader's mind moving by follow-through on your opening focus sentences. Let them guide and limit everything else you write into that particular communication. Let nothing divert his thought. Keep out extraneous material. Keep your communication moving on that straight line which is the shortest distance between two points.

You can best achieve this guided motion by:

1. Presenting your ideas in the order which your opening focus sentences have led your reader to expect

2. Writing everything "in terms of" the opening focus

3. Keeping out tangential material—especially at the beginning and end of your communication

Suppose your opening focus sentences were those of the *do write* example on page 67. Your second paragraph would begin to discuss the effects of a receiving department on quality control of incoming merchandise. Next, you would go on to what such a department could achieve through coordination of incoming invoices with purchase orders. Then you would discuss what a receiving department might achieve in improving inventory control and, finally, in achieving prompt deliveries.

You would treat these subjects in this order because that is the "expected" order—the order of the particular *do write* opening sentences. And, by maintaining a "receiving department" as the subject of each subsidiary discussion, you would be discussing everything in terms of your original focus sentence. In these two positive ways, you can best keep your reader's mind on your subject and avoid giving it the slightest encouragement to wander.

You encourage a reader's mind to wander when you discuss, say, inspection of merchandise on its way to the plant as a new or separate subject. You prevent wandering when you discuss it in terms of (or as a subsidiary to) the main idea: *establishment* of a receiving department.

Inserting tangential material—as so many communicators do —is going out of your way to lead your reader's mind astray. If your main purpose is to get a receiving department established, where's the sense in starting off with a discussion of the inefficiencies of the existing system? Such a beginning may lead your reader's (general manager's) mind in any one of several directions. He may start wondering about the efficiency of his personnel or begin working out ways to improve details of his existing processes. He may even have thoughts of guilt about his own inadequacies, which permit so bad a situation to exist. He might start thinking in a hundred other directions, but only by chance would his mind *wander* to establishment of a receiving department.

So don't encourage—at all—the natural tendency of his mind to wander. Don't defeat your own purpose. Encourage your reader to stay on the subject of your choice.

Tell the Whole Story

Telling the *whole* story also helps to keep your reader focused on the subject of your communication. When he spots the omission of a germane point or fact, almost inevitably his thought will digress. He'll start asking himself: "Why did he omit it? Is he trying to cover up something? Or does he think I'm too stupid to catch him?" Your omission will have diverted his mind. But also you will have raised doubts in it, doubts which will color his thinking about everything you have to say.

If the receiving department is likely to cost an additional $5,000 a year, for example, be sure to mention it. You may be able to make him see it as "only $5,000 a year." If he "discovers" it, it's almost sure to be "$5,000 a year!!" When he has any such reaction, his mind is diverted—slightly or violently—from the communication's main line of thought.

Fulfilling a Reader's Expectancy

So straight-line writing—in which one idea leads to the next idea the reader expects—is necessary to maintain focus. Whether you mean it to or not, every statement he reads gives a certain momentum to his mind. Recognize this fact, and use it to your advantage. Otherwise you may be leading your reader further and further from your communication's purpose.

When your idea sequences fail to preserve an "expected" relationship, your reader's mind will constantly be overrunning in a given direction. The impetus given by a previous statement will impel him tangentially—not directly—to the next one.

The opening and closing paragraphs of a technical paper about power takeoffs, read before an engineering society, provide an excellent example:

> PTO problems have been with us for many years, and the situation has not improved. If anything, it has deteriorated. However, in the hope that repetition might someday lead to improvement, this paper is being written.
>
> In the field of dump bodies and packer bodies, there are three major areas of concern with PTO applications: the variety of PTOs required, clearance for mounting, and power output available. All the remarks in this paper will be confined to highway type of equipment, since we feel that the three problem areas have been largely overcome in the case of off-highway dump equipment.
>
> The truck equipment division of the Yakamon Co. is almost 100 per cent hydraulically actuated, using a side-mounted PTO on the chassis transmission as the power source. The optimum PTO output speed for this equipment is about 1,000 rpm, which requires PTO-to-engine ratios of about 50 to 80 per cent. Confining ourselves roughly to these ratios and to single-shaft, single-speed PTOs, at last count we listed almost two hundred in our price list.

Admittedly, this number is swelled due to the listing of medium, heavy-duty, and lever- and wire-control PTOs. Still this is a fantastic number of PTOs with which to deal.

Installations over the years have become increasingly difficult and expensive. . . .

This author's first paragraph indicates that his communication will focus on chances of PTO problems getting worse before they get better. The second paragraph begins the tangential movement. It moves from the better-or-worse idea to the statement of three main problems of dump- and packer-bodied trucks. Then it moves tangentially again to note that the communication really is only about highway units.

Further tangential movement takes place with the beginning of the third paragraph. Here starts a description of Yakamon PTO equipment. By the end of the third paragraph, it gradually becomes evident that the Yakamon equipment is mentioned simply as an example of the first of the three main PTO application problems: the variety of PTOs required. The writer doesn't relate it until the last sentence in the paragraph: "Still this is a fantastic number of PTOs with which to deal."

Nowhere in these opening paragraphs is there more than a hint of the writer's real purpose: to recommend three actions by truck manufacturers that would alleviate the three major problems of applying power takeoffs to highway dump trucks.

The writer's real purpose was focused by the opening paragraphs of a brief article by a technical editor. The editor's article started with:

> Three actions by truck manufacturers would alleviate the three major problems involved in applying power takeoffs to highway dump trucks. The problems. . . .

and finished with:

> The three alleviating actions highway dump truck manufacturers might consider are. . . .

Focus Is Fundamental

Focus is fundamental. With it, a communication is almost certain to be clear, however badly written. Without it, the communication can't be clear, however crisp and polished the words, the phrases, and the sentences.

To ensure focus for your communication:

1. Condense partially related ideas or information to a pinpoint of direct relationship to the writing's purpose.

2. Analyze all factors of problems to be dealt with or elements of discussions or descriptions.

3. Synthesize all involved factors by translating your definition of purpose into a written focus, a single sentence expressing the main idea you want to give your reader.

4. Keep the reader's mind moving throughout the communication toward the end indicated by your written focus, on which the communication's first sentence should be based.

5. Present ideas in the order your opening sentences lead the reader to expect.

6. Exclude all material that can't be expressed in terms of relationship to the opening focus.

7. Tell the whole story to prevent the reader from digressing when he spots the omission of a germane point or fact, and when pressed for time in preparing a communication, don't skimp on the thinking before writing.

8 | Using Words to Move Ideas

SKILL IN HANDLING words goes far toward completing the communication process. It helps greatly to get ideas from a written page into a reader's mind. Sentences that march from subject to object make clear the purpose you have defined and the focus you have achieved. Words that live add zest to the clarity effected by thinking through a communication before writing it.

Sentence structure sets the pace, the thrust given ideas or data by your communication. Sentences should be neither staccato nor long with literary flourish. It is best to aim to have them march along steadily, briskly, smoothly, and naturally. Then use "live" words to beat time for these sentences that march. Say what you have to say, or wish to say, in simple, direct, and exact words.

The term "march" connotes steady, brisk movement in a pre-determined direction. It suggests pace without hurry—a happy medium between long, meandering statements and telegraphic rat-a-tat-tat. It implies what engineers call "dynamic balance," balance while in motion. (When an automobile crankshaft is not balanced dynamically, it will wobble endwise, thus setting up vibrations in the engine.)

"Live" applied to words means crisp, moving, trim, and active. A word is live when it does something to the reader's mind as he reads it. Size, derivation, and familiarity condition, but do not determine, its liveness. Like electricity, which has to be defined in terms of what it does, the live word—caught and harnessed— can be turned to powerful use.

How to Recognize Marchers

The best way to recognize sentences that march is to look for them in your everyday reading. Then, if you keep writing with "march" in mind, you'll gradually come to "feel" a marcher and a nonmarcher without having to debate. Your feel will be about the same as the next man's for practical purposes. You and your reader will seldom disagree.

Let's examine some sentences together to see how this works. Probably neither of us feels any marching quality in:

> It may be interesting at this point to report briefly on some aspects of the case which have been emphasized by different supervisors from various organizations when we have talked with them about it.

But we might feel a little in:

> Aspects emphasized by supervisors may be interesting at this point.

We'd feel no march in:

> It would seem as though the perpetual harping on production difficulties currently being experienced would give an unfortunate air of unreality to the problems likely to be faced in the future and thus ensure, rather than avoid, major troubles sooner or later.

Converted to a two-sentence passage, however, some feeling of marching enters:

> Perpetual harping on today's production difficulties seems likely to make future problems seem unreal, nonexistent. This approach can only ensure, not avoid, major troubles sooner or later.

There is no marching quality in:

> This is the analytical procedure which is the heart of the greater part of research work you meet on all sorts of subjects.

But this sentence marches rather well:

> This analytical procedure is the heart of most research work.

This sentence doesn't march:

> Details of new design progress in most companies are the deepest of secrets, but XYZ Company executives are proud of their design ideas and talk about them freely, within certain limits, of course.

But these do:

> Most companies guard design progress details as deep secrets. But XYZ executives are proud of their design ideas. They talk about them freely—within certain limits.

Most sentences in the following passages, we might agree, could properly be called "marchers":

> Almost invariably businessese is marked by heavy use of the passive construction. Nobody ever *does* anything. Things *happen*—and the author of the action is only barely implied.[1]

> People at work are not so different from people in other aspects of life. They are not entirely creatures of logic. They have feelings.[2]

> Who gets more value out of things? The persons who hold title to them, or the persons who put life into them and thus appreciate and use them? The latter, of course.[3]

> Defining your audience means more than naming it. It requires bringing to a mental point what you know about it.[4]

> The air cleaner often gets clogged with dust and dirt. This difficulty will restrict passages of air, just as a partly closed choke will.

> When a laser is fired, the focused light will fall on the sample in a very bright, concentrated spot. Some of the light will be reflected, and some absorbed. The absorbed light will heat the

[1] W. H. Whyte, "Language of Business," *Fortune,* November, 1950.

[2] Malcolm McNair, quotation of Fritz J. Roethlisberger, *Harvard Business Review,* April, 1957.

[3] Ralph W. Sockman, *The Higher Happiness,* Abingdon Press, Nashville, Tenn., 1950.

[4] Norman G. Shidle, *Instincts in Action,* Society of Automotive Engineers, 1963.

small area of the sample to the melting temperature. If intense enough, vaporization temperatures will be reached.

The difference between a boss and a leader is not always discernible to the naked eye. Each is distinguished by the fruits of his efforts.[5]

A man who is going somewhere is almost bound to bump into something once in a while. No bumps often indicate no movement.

Try converting into marching sentences the ideas expressed by the following nonmarchers. Make it a game rather than an exercise.

It's fun to achieve motion through the use of words.

The nonconformist today may find himself in the position unanticipated by Mill, of an eccentric who must, like a movie star, accept the roles in which he is cast, lest he disappoint the delighted expectations of his friends.[6]

After the conclusion of peace the government was chiefly occupied with the problem of feeding the country, which necessitated various measures prohibiting export and authorizing the requisitioning of home-grown foodstuffs.[7]

On the way home from the factory that afternoon, the shop steward pondered statements made at the local's meeting the previous night and asked himself how sincere he had been when he had openly supported them.

To write sentences that march into a reader's mind requires following a few simple practices. Regularly applied, these become positive insurance against really poor communications writing. Using them, you will gradually form good sentence-writing habits. You will deviate from them only consciously, for a good reason. As your skill increases, so may your conscious deviations. But experience will affirm the capacity of these practices to stimulate a

[5] Norman G. Shidle, *Getting Along with Others in Business,* B. C. Forbes & Son Publishing Co., 1947.

[6] David Riesman, *The Lonely Crowd,* Yale University Press, New Haven, Conn., 1953.

[7] "Belgium: Internal Affairs," *Encyclopaedia Britannica,* vol. 3, p. 355.

wide range of good communications writing. Their outlines can be evolved from analysis of the marching and nonmarching sentences given on previous pages.

Marching and Nonmarching Characteristics

Length. The marchers are uniformly shorter in length. Few, if any, of them run more than twenty words. None of the passages average more than twenty words per sentence. (A Famous Writers School textbook says: "Few successful authors today average more than twenty words per sentence." *Time* magazine's average sentence length used to be less than seventeen words.)

It is hard to write nonmarching sentences of less than twenty words. ("A cat is often referred to by the appellation of 'feline.'") And few everyday writers produce passages that give readers a keep-moving effect when average sentence length goes higher.

Construction. Usually marching sentences have a straight subject-predicate-object construction.

"Subject" isn't just a grammatical term in relation to sentence construction. It is the main idea of the sentence. So make a habit of starting each sentence with the word or phrase that is its subject.

Immediate mention of what the sentence is about orients the reader promptly and lets him in on its main point. Then he can readily relate to that subject what the sentence goes on to say. A sentence commenting on a subject before naming it gives the reader nothing to which to tie the comment: "Unless a company has minimum objective standards which must be met by employees before they can be placed in engineering classifications, lower engineering classifications may become populated with nonengineers." Finally having found the subject of such a sentence, the reader has to start over again. Only thus can he examine the preliminary comment intelligently.

Also, the subject-first habit usually helps a sentence to march. A subject-predicate-object construction usually speeds movement of the sentence's thought. Passive constructions slow it down. "John passed the butter to Mary" is almost always better than "The butter was passed by John to Mary." A good rule: Use the passive construction only consciously. Use it to fit a particular case or to express a particular idea, where *you decide* it will be best.

Here are comparison sentences to illustrate that, more often than not, sentences are shorter as well as clearer when the real subject is at the beginning:

> President Tennet stated that the *future of the organization* is dependent upon younger accountants.   (14 words)
>
> *The organization's future* depends on younger accountants, President Tennet said.   (10 words)
>
> The association's cardinal objective is aimed at the *improvement of skiing and the association's skiing members.*   (16 words)
>
> *To improve skiing and its skiing members* is the association's cardinal objective.   (12 words)
>
> He went on to explain that at the company's annual sales convention, *younger members had been effectively utilized in key roles.*   (21 words)
>
> *Younger members were used in key roles* at the company's annual sales convention, he then explained.   (16 words)

The first words of each of the rewritten sentences are the subject. The reader's mind is directed immediately to what the sentence is about. In the original sentences, on the contrary, he is asked to wade through somewhat weedy verbiage to discover the subject.

Ideas per Sentence. One or two ideas per sentence are characteristic of the marching-sentence examples. The flowing prose of Sir Walter Scott and the oratorical periods of William Jennings Bryan, or even the complex sentences of William Faulkner, are not for the creative communications writer. Most successful communicators in writing couldn't write like Faulkner if they would —and wouldn't if they could.

The most effective communications usually converge on a single idea for the piece as a whole and tell everything in terms of that focus. (See Chapter 7.) The sentence focused on a single idea communicates surefootedly and clearly.

More often than not, the same ideas or information can be conveyed in *less words in several sentences than in one.* The long, involved single sentence doesn't even save words. In the following nonmarcher, for example, there are fifty-three words. Rewritten, the same information is conveyed in three marching sentences totaling forty-two words, with an average of sixteen words per sentence:

Nonmarching Sentence:

> But the alternative solution presents problems, too, because the widely held concept of director or associate director as "boss" meant that Korksky and Bagnall would be taking directions from a supervisor who did not have a Ph.D. and inevitably lacked some of the important technical and theoretical knowledge the younger scientists had acquired.[8]

Marching Passage:

> But the alternative solution presents problems, too. A director or associate director is usually thought of as "boss." So Korksky and Bagnall would be taking directions from a supervisor lacking both a Ph.D. and their own degree of technical and theoretical knowledge.

The same is true of the following forty-six-word nonmarching sentence when it is rewritten into three sentences which total thirty-seven words.

Nonmarching Sentence:

> Following each subject heading will be one or more document or article entries, each comprising a document number and a Notation of Content (NOC), which may be the title or a version of the title believed to be more indicative of the contents of the article.

Marching Passage:

> Document or article entries will follow each subject heading. Each entry will comprise a document number and a Notation of Content. (This NOC will be a version of the title indicative of the contents of the article.)

[8] Ralph M. Hower and Charles D. Orth, *Managers and Scientists,* Harvard Business School, Division of Research, Cambridge, Mass., 1963.

In both these examples the number of ideas per sentence has been decreased. Result: Each of the ideas marches directly into the reader's mind. (The reduction of word totals results from using only work words and eliminating all not absolutely needed.)

The following encyclopedia definition may seem an extreme example. But it is all too characteristic of writing by experts to lay audiences. If you are a scientist, lawyer, philosopher, teacher, historian, or engineer, you may have written sentences like it. In this one-sentence definition, subsidiary statements black out information already seriously obscured by excessively long wording. (The special language of erudition completes the communication blackout.)

DEFINITION:

The necessary and sufficient condition for an object to be recognizable as a living organism, (and so to be the subject of biological investigation), is that it be a discrete mass of matter, with a definite boundary, undergoing continual interchange of material with its surroundings without manifest alteration of properties over short periods of time and, (as ascertained either by direct observation or by analogy with other objects of the same class), originating by some process of division or fractionation from one or two pre-existing objects of the same kind.[9]

Such a sentence provides very limited service to the average user of an encyclopedia. The writer has neglected to write for his main audience and has concentrated on avoiding *possible* criticism from meticulous fellow experts. More information would enter the encyclopedia reader's mind if this communication (definition) were shorter. More information would penetrate the reader's mind if it were given in fifty-one of the hard-to-grasp words rather than in ninety of them.

DEFINITION:

A living organism is a discrete mass of matter with a definite boundary, undergoing continual interchange of material with its surroundings without manifest alteration of properties over short periods of time. Also, it originates by some process of division or

[9] "Living Organisms," *Encyclopaedia Britannica,* vol. 3, p. 606.

fractionation from one or two pre-existing objects of the same kind.

True, the average reader may get nothing from either the original or the rewritten definition. Even so, the rewrite is a favor to him. He can get nothing faster from fifty-one words than he can from ninety.

Qualifying Clauses. A noticeable lack of qualifying clauses characterizes the marching sentences and passages. The writer says what he has to say and rarely seems to qualify or play safe.

A tendency to apologize, leave a way out, or insert an alibi bogs down thousands of sentences and hundreds of communications. Scientists, lawyers, engineers, diplomats, and politicians are particularly insistent on using qualifying clauses. But few people are free of this writing fault. It stems from fear and can be overcome by courage and reason.

After all, few statements can be absolutely true. No desert is absolutely dry; no liquid is absolutely wet. No floor is absolutely level; no point in the universe is absolutely fixed. The entire truth about anything is almost impossible to tell within practical limits. So give your reader a break, and qualify only to the extent that it makes any real difference to him.

Be Specific. The best of marching sentences state specific facts, unfold specific ideas, or give specific information. The worst of the nonmarchers deal with generalities. Being specific imparts a marching quality to almost any sentence and gives penetrating power to almost any communication. Specific facts are baited hooks which catch in a reader's mind. A fact-filled sentence will always march better than one of the same length devoted to generalities.

Often you may read with interest a specific fact about a subject in which you aren't interested. Perhaps you couldn't care less about art. But you may have been interested in the journey of the "Pietà" to the New York World's Fair. You may not care that:

> In the phase of incipient population decline, the conditions for advancement alter significantly.

But you might—even if you are an engineer—read on about:

When population declines, average yearly earnings of lawyers tend to [increase or decrease].

See how specifics up the pace and catching quality of these sentences:

School needs will require considerably more money next year.	Next year schools will cost $40,000 more than the $425,000 expended this year.
Yesterday I picked a lot of pinecones from my lawn.	Yesterday I picked more than fifty pinecones from my lawn.
My experience as a sales manager qualifies me, I believe, for the marketing-manager position you have open.	Seven years of increased sales during my ten years as sales manager may qualify me for the marketing-manager position you have open.
Leading professionals will be on hand to give tips and instructions.	Arnold Palmer, Sam Snead, and Tony Lema are scheduled to be on hand to give tips and instructions.

Be "Unmistakable." Be sure a sentence can mean only one thing. References to pronouns especially should be unmistakable. Your reader can't verify his guess, as a listener can in personal dialogue:

"And," he said, "if Arthur decides against Henry, send him to me."

"Henry?" I asked.

"No, for goodness sake! Arthur."

Slight carelessness can obscure meaning and make reader comprehension inaccurate. "I dropped a nickel in the slot which I found in my pocket" isn't prone to misinterpretation. But "Harry bumped into Joe and broke his teeth" is a toss-up.[10]

Unmixed Metaphors Bless. Metaphors and tropes enliven communications writing when they flow naturally from the writer's imagination. Like any embellishment, their effectiveness is destroyed by the slightest ineptness in their use. The everyday writer had better shun metaphor than risk mixing it, as a science writer

[10] For further information, see David Lambouth, *The Golden Book on Writing*, The Viking Press, Inc., New York, 1964, pp. 22–24.

did when he described laser technology as a "virgin field pregnant with possibilities," or as the newswriter telling of President John F. Kennedy's stand on disarmament did: "Kennedy is determined to keep the fire going under the cold-war thaw...."

Avoid Triteness. Trite metaphors and tropes, as well as inept ones, are also anti-effective, as all trite phrasings are.

To hope that a trite expression will give color to a sentence is like expecting Harry to be pleased when you slap him on the back with a hearty "Hello, Joe!!" A shopworn expression, like a shopworn mink coat, marks its user as trying for an effect that isn't achieved. Both expression and coat were good products in their day. But they are worn out now—the trite expression, because everybody has overused it. All written communications live better without trite phrasings.

Compare, for example:

> Proceeding via shank's mare, Walter Gaul's pace was as slow as molasses in winter. He had gotten the cart before the horse by arising after only two hours' sleep to get an early start. Joe Sougher would have hit the hay early last night. He'd probably be sharp as a razor and think as quick as lightning.
>
> "I'd better take the bull by the horns," Walter mused, "and call the meeting off. Otherwise I'll find myself buying a pig in a poke. Then tomorrow I'll get with it and turn over a new leaf. I'll be in fine fettle for the postponed meeting."

with:

> Walter Gaul walked slowly. It had been a mistake to make so early a start after only two hours' sleep—though this had been necessary to make the meeting on time. Joe Sougher would have gone to bed early last night. His head would be clear; his thinking alert and active.
>
> "I'd better postpone the meeting," Walter mused. "Otherwise I won't know exactly what I'm buying. Then tomorrow I'll rest up and be mentally alert for the postponed meeting."

Plain, straightforward wording always affects a reader more favorably than trite or shopworn phrasing.

A business executive concerned with communications writing

was honoring false gods when he said: "A shoo-in candidate for another Pulitzer Prize is any man who can write 'Indeed the dismal downpour made my intended visit to Niagara Falls seem redundant.' Wonder why I can't write like that?" A natural communications writer of high skill, this executive goes awry only when he takes pen in hand and self-consciously indites an epistle. Noted as a natural, successful storyteller when speaking, his self-conscious writing produced:

> I can even try to tell about five men in a four-man putt-putt as they cajoled their fast-swamping skiff to a doubtful landing across a deluge-crazed lake. From the diaper stage to uncertain senility, one never knows what it is like to be authentically wet, until he sits, as we did, on water, in water, surrounded by water, with driving rain from all sides. Only then does one know what it's like to be fully emulsified. In our adventure, tempestuous doses of lightning, thunder, rain, hail, and wind came howling at us as though nature were dumping her choicest exaggerations at once into our already crowded boat. It looked like the ending of a life cycle from "mostly water" back again to "mostly water." No dust this time!

This executive is not alone in mistakenly approaching writing as primarily a juggling of words. Communications writing especially is *use* of words to achieve an objective, to fulfill a purpose, and to assist a reader. Communications readers are less stirred by new words than by fresh thoughts, less by fancy words than by moving ideas. They are better informed by plain words than by contrived phrasings.

Trite Wordings Are Not Colorful

Trite words and phrases are characteristic of the unskilled communicator. Sometimes they are an awkward attempt at "fine" writing. Sometimes they are a lazy man's uncomfortable try for informality. Always they mark a writer who has chosen weak means to reach sound ends.

Working Words. Every word does some useful work in most of the marchers. Say-nothing words are exorcised. So unless a word makes a positive contribution, leave it out. When it says nothing whatever, take it out.

Frequently, you will find, words and phrases like the following detract rather than add to clarity. They are characteristic of non-marchers:

"On the other hand"

"In order (to)"

"Nevertheless, it is apparent that"

"It follows logically that"

"Therefore, it would seem that"

"Thus, it is clear that"

"Fundamentally"

"Basically"

"However"

"Of course"

. . . and others like them.

To be convinced that such words usually can be omitted, watch for them in your own reading. Stop a moment when you run across them, and mentally rewrite the sentence without them. This practice will go far to make you feel all right about leaving them out of your own writing.

Active Verbs. The best marching sentences have verbs which are active-sounding as well as of active construction. Few everyday writers will go wrong trying for "headline" verbs. More of your sentences will march with:

get	than with	*obtain*
need	than with	*require*
shows	than with	*illustrates*
named	than with	*appointed*
use	than with	*employ*
split	than with	*divide*
stress	than with	*emphasize*
aid (or *help*)	than with	*assist*
claim	than with	*allege*
cut	than with	*abridge*

Live verbs do more to make sentences march than any other single element. Dead and overweight verbs are ill fitted to function as the "part of speech expressing action."

Live Words. Words that live for your reader are words he understands—without using a dictionary or a thesaurus. Use such erudition as may be yours to choose words familiar to the particular reader. A word doesn't serve well if it doesn't mean the same thing to both writer and reader. Even when writing to fellow professionals or to highly educated readers, don't go all out in using uncommon words. To ensure communication, play it safe.

The size of your vocabulary is not half as important as the accuracy with which you use the words you know. Too many communicators belong to the Humpty-Dumpty school of word selection. (Remember, Humpty-Dumpty told Alice in Wonderland: "When I use a word it means just what I choose it to mean.") The true dimension of your vocabulary isn't how many words you can identify, but the number you can use appropriately.

Word selection does more than make understanding easy, for words are the foundation of all understanding. One human bundle of nervous processes spins out words. Another human bundle picks them up and responds in some fashion. These symbols are supposed to mean something in terms of reality. But symbols aren't the reality. At best they are links to reality. And what the reader receives—not what the writer sends—determines the closeness of the link.

Always beware of "trigger" words—words that will almost certainly trigger emotional reactions. Words like "communism," "fascism," "foreign aid," "traitor," and "capitalist," for example, have come to be what Michigan State's Prof. H. R. Jollife calls "emotive symbols that tend to cast a blanket of fog around specifics." Friction with mental prejudices often turns general words into trigger words in particular instances.

Much unclear writing results from using too many broad, general words. Such words have many possible meanings, so each person reads his own special meaning into them.

So shun the use of general words that can mean anything a Humpty-Dumpty decides they shall. When you do use them (you'll have to occasionally) somehow inject exactly what you mean them to mean. And remember: The more general the word, the fainter the picture it gives to your reader. The more specific the word, the brighter the image projected.

Get in the habit of using plain words. Then an occasional unusual or special-purpose word can be effective as a change of pace. Each time you inject a new word as synonym—perhaps to keep from repeating in the same or adjacent sentences—test it to be sure it is understandable and *alive.*

To be alive in communications writing, a word should be:

1. Understandable to the particular audience and to the total possible audience for the particular communication

2. Not worn out by overuse and not trite

3. Not overweight

The simple word—as opposed to the complex or contrived word—is comfortable both to write and to read. A word the writer never would use in conversation may lose him contact with his reader. Use unusual words in communications writing to achieve unusual effects, never to show the breadth of your vocabulary.

Stilted is: "They cogitated on the enigma and then decided to tarry." More effective is the normal: "They thought about the problem and then decided to stay." "He made a forcible ingress" communicates less than "He broke in." Only those educated beyond their intelligence would write:

> He took umbrage because he wished to be exculpated rather than calumniated.

instead of

> He got mad because he wanted to be vindicated, not maligned.

Overweight words. Overweight words cut down the ability of sentences to march. Too many words of any kind stop them from marching. When an overweight sentence is composed of overweight words, the reader stops reading.

A World War II memorandum about air-raid protection included this overweight passage:

> Such preparations shall be made as will completely obscure all Federal buildings occupied by the Federal Government during an air raid for any period of time from visibility by reason of internal or external illumination. Sure obscuration may be obtained either by blackout construction or by termination of illumination. This will, of course, require that in building areas in which production

must continue during the blackout, construction must be provided that internal illumination may be continued. Other areas may be obscured by terminating the illumination.

One recipient suggested this revision:

> In buildings where the work must go on, put something across the windows. In buildings where work can be stopped for awhile, turn out the lights.

In communications writing, a word is overweight when it has more syllables than another word that gives the same idea. A sentence is overweight when its marching quality is lost. Short words are better than long ones because they reduce lifting effort for the reader's mind. Short sentences, as opposed to long, do the same thing.

The more complex your thought, the more you should try to express it in simple, short words. *Because* profound ideas are harder to understand, they demand easy-to-understand words even more than simpler ideas do. The professional man who must use his trade lingo should keep all other words as short and plain as possible.

The idea that big words go with big thoughts was started by self-centered pundits. They wrote to *express* their thoughts, being too lazy to *communicate* them.

Complex ideas and profound thoughts can be expressed most effectively in simple, short words. Of a random 198 consecutive words from Jesus' Sermon on the Mount in the King James Version of the Bible (Matt. 5:13–19), only thirty-six, or 16 per cent, have more than one syllable. (Twenty-seven have two syllables; nine have three syllables. None has more than three.)

The following modern illustration is more pertinent. Titled "Needed: More Talk, Less Communication," it was an editorial by A. Q. Mowbray in *Materials Research and Standards*, published by the American Society for Testing and Materials.

> SCIENCE—both the pure and the not so pure—is a vast book in which man writes all that he learns of the world that he can touch, see, hear, smell, or taste. At this hour in the life of Man, when he

can hang in space to see the earth, and at the next stroke may touch the moon, those who write in this book must strive to use words that strike the minds of all men. For it may have come to this: to see is to live; to be blind is to die.

This is not to say that man will be saved by science. It is to say that each man must learn the lore of science, he must learn the thoughts of those who work in science, he must learn to put the fruits of science to their best use. But if he is to learn these things, the men of science must learn to speak to him in his own tongue.

There is no law, so far as we know, that says a man must use short words when he talks and long ones when he writes. Nor is there a rule to force us to seek out the big word when our thoughts run deep. In fact, when the urge to tell burns in us, we turn to the short word. When we swear, we slash and bruise with the sharp, curt word. When we pray, our souls soar on wings of light, brief words. When we love, the sweet, spare words pierce straight to the heart. When we urge or drive, the words are pruned and clipped, they dart to the mind in one clean stroke. The long words bounce off the shell, weight us to the ground, probe in vain for the path to the heart or to the mind.

Each man who takes his pen in hand to tell his peers what he has thought or done should make this pledge: "I swear that what I write will speak to men in words that they can seize and hold. I will shun the blunt, stiff, thick words that clot the brain and turn clear minds to sour ooze. I will cleave to the keen, terse, brisk words that bear true to the mark and shed a pure gleam in the dark. My one aim will be to see that those who scan my words can read my thoughts."

QUIZ: *Which word in this piece has more than one syllable?*—A. Q. M.

Grammar

Grammar is a basic tool for the communications writer. The grammar of a language *is* the language, the system which governs its use at every step.

But it is a "great mistake to think of grammar as compilations of 'rules'—often factitious, and sometimes unfortunately expressed when they really do contain a reliable truth," counsels Babson Institute's Louis Foley.

Foley differentiates real grammar from that which is an affair of textbooks, rules, and abstract theory. "Real grammar," he posits, "is the very life of the language. Without it, relationships of ideas could not be made clear. It is not something which anyone can use or not as he chooses. Everyone handles it easily, without taking thought, in all ordinary situations to which he is accustomed. With new or complicated ideas, he may become entangled or confused."

You can't communicate a thought that isn't clear in your own mind. And that's where what grammar you know comes into play. It enables you to plan a sentence. It prevents your writing sentences that get lost and become incoherent because they are unplanned. Each sentence you write can know just where it is going before it starts out.

If you aren't already reasonably well grounded in English grammar, you can't hope to communicate successfully in writing. There are good reasons for the most commonly accepted ways of constructing a sentence. These you should know and accept—or take time out immediately to satisfy yourself about. Breaking the rules of grammar is not fatal to good written communicating. But good communicating is impossible without the help available from a knowledge of the most common of these rules.

The best and quickest refresher course for adults is *The Golden Book on Writing*, by the late Prof. David Lambuth, of Dartmouth College. From less than sixty pages of scintillating prose, the modern communications writer can learn all he *needs* to know about grammar—though I don't recall that the word "grammar" is mentioned. (First published in 1923, this book was republished in 1964 by The Viking Press, Inc.)

Summary

In summary, if you want the words you write to move your ideas into others' minds:

1. Write sentences that march; keep them to an average of twenty words or less.

2. Make a habit of using short words. When two words mean the same thing, use the longer only when you decide consciously that it's better in that particular sentence.

3. Make every word in every sentence useful. Eliminate every one that isn't needed either to express meaning or to convey feeling.

4. Put the main idea first—even in sentences.

5. Be specific. Avoid generalities.

6. Be unmistakable. Write sentences that can mean only one thing.

7. Lean *toward* use of active verbs, and *away from* passive sentence constructions.

8. Get *The Golden Book on Writing* if you need to brush up on your grammar.

9

Good Looks Invite
Good Reading

TO BE GOOD, a communication has to look good. Good looks open a reader's mind and stimulate his idea-grabbing equipment. Attractive appearance, like sound thinking, is a product of the creativity that builds bridges from writers' to readers' minds. Good looks are the broad, inviting approaches to the bridges.

Fruitful communications writing involves three elements:

> What you say
> How you say it
> How you present it

You haven't finished your written communication until you have made it look good. Sound reasoning can be obscured by inept packaging. Doubt can be cast on the accuracy of facts by careless-looking dress. What you say and how you say it are of major importance. But how you present it mechanically is important too.

Too many everyday writers let go a communication once they have written the words. They feel the *creative* job is done. It's up to a secretary, an assistant, or a specialist to carry on from there. ("What do I know or care about presentation? That's a typist's job —certainly on letters, memoranda, and informal and semiformal reports.")

But that's like fashioning two legs of the stool with craftsmanlike skill and giving the third to Junior to whittle on. Your secretary, your assistant, or available specialists can help immeasurably to complete this phase of your communications writing. But *responsibility* for completing the communication remains yours, the writer's. You should develop skill in using available assistance. Concern for your brainchild, however, should extend to the clothes it wears into the world where it seeks acceptance.

An indifferent presentation will dull your communication's points, however sharp your writing has made them. A logical, imaginative presentation, as well as content, is needed. Such an approach can be fruitful in:

1. Avoiding negative reactions in the reader
2. Attracting the reader

To avoid negative reader reaction, presentation of any written communication should be:

- Typewritten
- Clean and reasonably neat

To attract the reader, to get his idea-grabbing equipment into action, one or a combination of several devices may help:

- Indentions
- Listings—like those on this page (or with numerals instead of dots)
- Double spacing—or single spacing with wide margins and double spacing between paragraphs
- Practical paragraphing and punctuation

Typewriting Helps Communicate

A typewritten or printed piece of writing always communicates faster and more clearly than a handwritten one. Handwriting is better only for communications for which social usage still demands it, and those cases are steadily becoming fewer. To few today does handwriting per se denote a special sincerity of sympathy or warmth of invitation.

The typewriter has become a personal tool to a vast majority of college graduates. It is used by very large numbers of recent high school graduates also and by a growing percentage of all literate Americans. About 38 per cent of United States' homes own some kind of typewriter, Royal McBee Corporation's marketing-research manager estimates. More than 30 per cent of all $5,000- to $8,000-income households own a portable and more than 30 per cent own a standard machine, according to *Newsweek* tabulations from a *Simmons Standard Magazine* report. Of the more than 5½ million homes where the head of the household is a college graduate, this report shows, nearly 3.3 million own portable typewriters; over 1.4 million own standard machines.

Personal typewriter use is now so common that inability at least to hunt and peck may come to be regarded as a form of semi-illiteracy. Learning to use a typewriter sufficiently well for personal, everyday purposes isn't nearly as hard as learning to drive an automobile.

Few of us handwrite with anything like the clarity of a typewriter; many write quite illegibly. A piece of typewritten copy—even when replete with x'd-out words—is easier to read than nine out of ten handwritten pieces.

Even when stenographic assistance is available, a personal typewriter often is a communications help. Few dictated communications measure up to those written personally. And the first draft given your typist will be closer to the last if it is composed on a typewriter. A typewritten first draft can be corrected interlinearly and edited *before* it goes to the typist. Then there's a good chance that the first copy she makes can be the last. Much time can be saved by communicating clearly with your typist!

Keep It Clean

A clean, neat presentation keeps your reader's mind on what your writing is trying to communicate. Interlinear corrections, ragged margins, and smudges stimulate the tangential thinking you are trying so hard to prevent. Besides, noticeable sloppiness is an irritant. It actually predisposes some readers to reject your message.

So it pays to keep your presentation clean and reasonably neat. How neat is reasonable depends on the particular communication and the particular recipient. You won't go far wrong if you insist on a presentation which would honestly satisfy you if you were the reader.

Good presentation habits help equally on informal communications you type yourself and on more formal ones where you have expert typing aid. In both instances, you will be using available mechanical devices to express your thoughts. Even when your copy is turned over for retyping, the typist will be influenced by your rough drafting.

Tabulation and Indentions

Often, indenting or tabulating some material will help mightily to complete communication more clearly and quickly. Your rough draft should indicate lines to be so emphasized. Don't expect your typist to make such decisions accurately.

The best way to indicate tabulation on your rough draft is to tabulate as you write. Think in terms of presentation as you write. You'll be surprised how much tabulating, in particular, will help to keep your thinking straight.

Indented tabulation of a series of facts or ideas often improves clarity and makes things easier to read. The longer the list, the more useful this device is. And the more abstract the ideas, the more it helps to keep the thinking clear for the writer as well as for the reader.

Compare, for example:

> Quality factors in marketing processed foods are color or appearance, flavor, texture or consistency, and freedom from defects.

with:

> Quality factors in marketing processed foods are:
> * Color or appearance
> * Flavor
> * Texture or consistency
> * Freedom from defects

or compare:

> French literary work of the 19th century repeated on a larger scale the work of the 16th, broke up and discarded such literary forms as had become useless or hopelessly stiff, gave strength, suppleness and variety to such as were retained, invented new ones when necessary, enriched the language by importations, inven-

tions and revivals, and brought into prominence the principle of individualism.[1]

with:

The French literary work of the 19th century:
  • Repeated on a larger scale the work of the 16th
  • Broke up and discarded such literary forms as had become useless or hopelessly stiff
  • Gave strength, suppleness, and variety to such literary forms as were retained
  • Invented new literary forms when necessary
  • Brought into prominence the principle of individualism

Double Spaced or Single Spaced?

Many single-spaced pieces of writing would communicate better had they been double spaced. Single spacing, effective and standard for one- or two-page letters, often hinders communication of ideas and information in memoranda, reports, minutes, and very long letters.

A double-spaced typewritten page is easier to read than a single-spaced one, however wide the margins and generous the spacing. Six pages of double-spaced material will attract and hold many more readers than three or four pages of single spacing. (Effective single spacing requires wider margins than double spacing and should always have double spacing between paragraphs. So material which runs six pages double spaced should run more than three pages single spaced.)

Single spacing often is used primarily to get a given message into the fewest possible pages. Many communicators measure the length of a communication by the number of typewritten sheets it occupies. But their readers, consciously or unconsciously, measure it by the time it takes to make the communication's message or data their own. (Communications writers who use single spacing to get a message into the fewest possible pages often make matters worse by skimping on white space.)

[1] "19th Century French Literature," *Encyclopaedia Britannica*, vol. 9, p. 794.

Make Editing a Routine

Whether single or double spaced in final form, the first draft of almost every communication should be double spaced. A single-spaced first draft discourages the careful editing and rewriting that almost every purposeful communication requires. The dictated communication, particularly, should come back to the dictator double spaced. He should give it detailed pencil-in-hand attention before retyping it in final form. Too many dictated communications are dictated but not read, and labeling isn't necessary to prove it.

However experienced the communications writer, his first draft will rarely be perfectly organized. Even less often will he have written throughout sentences that march with words that live.

To illustrate double spacing's greater readability requires examples covering a number of typewritten sheets. (Where relatively few lines are involved—as in the average letter—the superior appearance of properly positioned single spacing more than outweighs the greater readability of double spacing.) Why not have your next long communication set up both ways? Then deliver both copies to your reader. Later check back and get his comments.

(If you are appalled at the number of pages required for the double-spaced version, do a final editing before delivery. The chances are that 10 to 25 per cent of the words you have written are unnecessary, and perhaps 20 to 40 per cent of the words you dictated. Besides, you may have included some tangential material just because you had it and hated to throw it away.)

Paragraphing and Punctuation

Punctuation is the most important device available for helping to make things easier to read. And that's what it's for. It's for you to use.

So go ahead. Use a paragraph, a period, a colon, a semicolon, a dash, a series of dots (. . .), or any other punctuation mark. Use them to convey in writing as nearly as possible what you "feel." Use them much as you naturally use pauses and stresses in talking.

Don't worry or argue too much about academic rules and regulations.

Unless you want your reader to pause more or less than usual between two words, you will have nothing between them except white space. If you want him to stop a little longer than usual, a dash may seem natural. A hyphen will move him more quickly than usual from one word to another.

You can apply the same idea to sentences. A period means a normal pause between sentences; a semicolon or a colon means a shorter-than-usual pause. When you want a long pause between sentences, a new paragraph is indicated. (Stephen Leacock suggests: "A paragraph is not a break in the sense, but a break in the type.")

Summary

Good appearance, liberal use of white space, double spacing other-than-short communications, and free punctuating help greatly to complete written communication. Possessing these qualities, a communication attracts readers to sample its contents. It invites them to share the writer's information or thoughts.

Your wishes or orders will be followed best when your reader is attracted to understand them. All your communications should look good—including those to people who have to read them. Few of us get much out of material we read because we "ought to."

10

Writing
to Individuals

AN INDIVIDUAL RECEIVES every idea or piece of information that is communicated. What you write isn't received by directors of a corporation, members of an association, or readers of a magazine. Each individual reader "has to reach, however feebly, to make ideas and information his own—or the communication isn't completed." (Remember Chapter 3?) Individuals—not groups as such —do whatever reaching is done and grasp whatever is taken in by individual minds.

The same idea will need different wrappings when presented to different people. A new product, for instance, will interest different people for different reasons. Suppose it is a new design of electric toaster. An engineer will want to know first of all *how* and *why* it works—its design, producibility, and durability. The sales manager will want to know *what* it does, particularly what it does better than previous models. The engineer is interested in cost; the sales manager, in price.

To interest another in our ideas, we must tie them to something with which he is already concerned. We can always do this when writing to an individual. When we can identify a single person as our reader, we can tailor a communication specifically to him. Thus we multiply many times the communication's chance to achieve its purpose. When writing to one person, it is feasible to serve known needs, surmount familiar barriers, and meet predictable requirements.

Specific data usually can be obtained about any one-man or one-woman audience. Get all you can with a minimum of effort. At least let your mind focus on what you already know about the person to whom you are about to write. Think first of his probable immediate and temporary concerns. Then consider, even though fleetingly, his general mental traits and his habitual reactions.

For example, suppose you are a publisher trying to get an author to move his deadline ahead. He has just asked for postponement from October 15 to December 15. You know he is reasonable in general but allergic to orders or ultimatums. He's stubborn when pushed, responsive when led. You know a feasible deadline date depends on the author's allocation of work hours between his book and his new country home. You have to grant some delay—but December 15 is too late. Here's what one successful publishing executive wrote in just such a case:

> I'm sure your manuscript will be well worth waiting a little longer for!
>
> However, will you please try for December 1 instead of December 15? Then I can officially transmit it through our processes before the Christmas holidays. This would enable us to come out in May, which would be a very good time.
>
> Cordially yours,
>
> (Publisher)

To the particular recipient at the particular time, this letter was perfectly constructed. It elicited a "yes" response to the December 1 date. But, more important, it stimulated the effort necessary to produce the finished manuscript on December 1. Before writing the letter, the publisher gave a few moments of consideration to the characteristics and work environment of the author. That's all that was needed. Failure to give advance consideration, however, might have resulted in a self-centered letter like this one:

> We're disappointed, of course, that you can't finish your manuscript by October 15, as originally agreed. But we understand the

problems you've had and are glad to push the deadline back a month or so.

But December 15 is really too late. Can't you finish please by December 1 at the latest? If we don't get the manuscript until after that, I can't get it through our processes before the holidays —which I would very much like to do. Then we could get it out in May, which, I think you will agree, would be mutually advantageous.

Cordially yours,

(Publisher)

However routine the communication, at least cursory thought about the particular recipient is well worthwhile.

Writing on important matters, what you know or don't know about the recipient may spell complete success or dire failure for your communication. Suppose it's vital to you that a complex communication achieve its purpose. Then real prewriting research is justified. You probably need to know everything you can about the man you are writing to or for.

Finding out before Writing

Much background information about individuals can be accumulated through simple awareness of others. You will know something about 90 per cent of the people with whom you communicate.

To "know" the remaining 10 per cent is equally possible. But it isn't always worthwhile; occasionally it isn't feasible. Here, you must let the communication's importance determine how much researching is enough.

Even about comparative strangers, however, you can often accumulate a surprising amount of information without investigating much.

First, of course, you will turn to your ready-at-hand, informal sources. These include your associates, your subordinates, your superiors, your secretary, your friends, your files, and even your social acquaintances.

Next, you might consult membership lists or headquarters staff personnel of trade associations or professional societies. Check groups to which you suspect your prospect might belong. (Available in many libraries, published by the United States government, is a list of all national organizations.) These sources are likely to yield the person's correct last name and initials as a minimum. His current job title and his correct home address and business address are reasonable expectations. The organization's headquarters staff might yield something about his special interests. These would be revealed by his committee assignments or his administrative posts. It is also possible to learn from such sources of papers your "prospect" may have written or of speeches he may have made.

Then there are scores of standard directories, financial reference books, and *Who's Who*. Usually these are available in big-city public libraries and in big-corporation company libraries. They will yield data only on people who have achieved at least some slight prominence in their working environments. But the total of such listings is great. Even the most selective lists record thousands of names. Don't skip these sources thinking your prospect isn't prominent enough to be included.

Though not a usual source for communications writers, credit reports provide a variety of information about almost anybody. Where an important communication makes pertinent a reader's personal financial standing, this source can be well worth its cost.

Using the Information You Have

Whatever information you accumulate, your skill in using it rests in your ability to interpret it suitably. (Here you put to work your understanding of Chapters 4 and 5.) Synthesized, the information should help to mold the texture, pattern, and timing of your communication. It will also help you to recognize probable barriers to a particular communication. (A political liberal attempting communication with an arch conservative, even on a nonpolitical, noneconomic subject, might recognize some special barriers to exit of ideas from his own mind. Surely he would be aware of special ones in his reader's.)

What you know about your reader should guide your writing around and over recognized hurdles. It will do just this, each time you consciously use it. Too commonly is admission that "knowing your reader is essential" combined with failure to think of him before writing.

How often do you marshal for use knowledge of your reader before you address him? How often does intimate knowledge of close working associates facilitate your communication with them? Not often, if you are normal. Few put such knowledge to work to make their communications click. Few are conscious of how much using that knowledge can strengthen a communication's impact.

Writing to an individual opens the way for a personally tailored, maximum-powered written communication. To take advantage of the opportunity this offers requires only:

1. Conscious consideration of your knowledge of each reader before starting to write each communication

2. Willingness to seek and ability to synthesize what you know about a reader as a guide to communicating with him through writing

Writing to individuals gives a chance to communicate in depth and breadth unavailable to writers for publication and to speakers. Recognizing this, each can add a new dimension to his practice of the art of successful written communication.

11

Writing
to Get and Give
Information

WHETHER SEEKING FACTS or opinions, a good information-getting or information-giving communication should:
- Make it easy for the reader to respond
- Make it hard for him to misunderstand

Written requests for information produce best results only when the writer does his share of thinking and research. Specific questions always get more specific answers than general inquiries. A request receiver must know exactly what is wanted before he can possibly give a useful answer. If the writer isn't sure of what he wants, the reader can't be expected to be. And if the reader isn't sure—without expending too much mental effort—he just doesn't bother to find out.

Since techniques for both giving and getting information are largely the same, discussion first of getting information is indicated. It may be more blessed to give than to receive, but it's more usual to seek than to give.

Getting Information by Writing

Obvious self-interest is inherent in communications which ask for information or make requests. However worded, they say, "I want something of you." Any attempt to conceal that essential quality is specious at best, dishonest at worst, and unlikely to succeed in any case.

So recognize that when you ask for information, you are always under obligation to your reader. Be sure that recognition is reflected in the texture of what you write—in your communication's "tone of voice." Though a reader may be obliged to you in other relationships, *you* ask a favor of *him* when you write for information. Though you may be his largest customer, you will get more of what you want if you put him in the driver's seat. If positions are reversed (he is your best customer), your approach, of course, needs a maximum of tact and sincerity.

You will, in short, seek the approach best tailored to the particular situation. You will want to consider advantages accruing to your reader from complying with your information request.

Who is your reader in relation to you? A customer? A supplier? A fellow professional? A lodge brother? A member of the same trade association?

You will express your reason for asking in terms appropriate to the relationship—and briefly too. Briefly, because this "why I am asking" should come first in your communication, along with the statement of what you want. Combined, these should create a favorable environment for the more detailed request to follow.

So the opening paragraph of a request for information should be worked over carefully. Its effect will determine how much trouble is too much for the reader to take in responding. It should always indicate what you want of the reader. It should refer to him, to his problems and interests. Your problem should be mentioned only in relation to him.

Suppose you are writing a paper on the influence of presidents on company advertising themes. You write for information to an advertising manager, asking what the relationship is in his company.

Do not begin:

> I am writing a report on the influence of company presidents on their company's advertising themes. For use as background material in developing this paper, I would very much like to know the situation in your organization. . . .

Do begin:

> Does the company president in your organization exert direct or indirect influence on the company's advertising themes? If so, how does he manage to inject his thinking into the process of setting advertising goals?
>
> With similar information from twenty or thirty other companies, I aim to develop a paper for presentation to an industrial advertisers' association meeting early next year. . . .

When a request is for information the reader normally would resist giving, establish some yes-environment before detailing your request. The data wanted should be revealed in the opening paragraph, of course. So your try for a yes-environment has to be combined with the data-wanted statement. Often this can be achieved by reference to the exact use to be made of the information.

A company, for example, unwilling to reveal details of its salary structure might be willing to release the percentage of total salaries accounted for by officers, other supervisory personnel, office workers, and factory workers. If so, an editor's request for the percentage figures would be fruitful; for the salary figures, unfruitful.

The same company might give its salary figures to a local chamber of commerce researcher. He might have established a yes-environment by promising to hold the data confidential and provide a copy of his final report.

Asked to aid development of a student program by answering the question: "Where did you attend college?" a professional society's members responded enthusiastically. A few, tested on the same question without the "student-program" preface, responded hesitatingly, even grudgingly. The way you ask influences answers strongly. So does the context in which you ask. To play safe, think of your reader as prefacing his first glance at your request with a mental: "What the hell does this fellow want?" Tailor your approach carefully to each particular reader situation—if you really want the information.

Because information-requesting communications must be precisely tailored, examples can only suggest the kind of approach appropriate to the kind of situation posed in each example.

EXAMPLE 1

A young buyer in a West Coast buying office (for a nationwide string of department stores) was responsible for running down information about new or different products. Often leads came from local department-store advertisements. Older heads counseled a variety of indirect procedures for getting the needed background details—manufacturer's name and location, detailed product description, breadth of the line, supply capability, and so forth. The young buyer felt comparative shopping and other indirect research to be time-consuming and to be avoided if possible.

So she adopted the simple procedure of writing directly to the department-store buyer involved, asking frankly for information desired. A typical letter ran something like this:

> Dear Mr. Furniture-store Buyer:
> Would you tell me the name of the manufacturer of the attractively carved-wood table lamp pictured in your Bonton's advertisement in today's *Examiner?* It is beautiful enough to have been hand-carved, but it isn't priced at hand-carved levels.
> Our buying office serves only stores outside of Southern California. All are completely noncompetitive with Bonton. Should I be able to interest some of our stores in this item, your manufacturer, I am sure, would be appreciative of your favor in referring us to him.
> Thank you greatly for your assistance.
>
> Sincerely,

To scores of letters using this direct approach over a three-year period, this young buyer never got a turndown.

EXAMPLE 2

The head of a very large Middle Western law firm had declared himself a candidate for United States senator. A young accountant, eager to volunteer his services to the lawyer's campaign organization, used his own employer's letterhead and his own title when he wrote to the prominent lawyer as follows:

Mr. Edgar Jerrold
Jerrold, Munster, O'Reilly, and Uppenmeir
Midwest City, Iowa

Dear Sir:

Should you or your organization in the near or distant future be able to use the talents and abilities of an enthusiastic, hard-working, aggressive young man, please call me.

I would be honored to support and be a part of your organization.

Very truly yours,

(Abe Martin)
Accounting Division

A response from the law firm's accounting manager acknowledged receipt of the letter and said that they had no openings at present but that his letter would be kept on file.

To achieve its real purpose, of course, the letter should have either (1) been addressed to Jerrold at his campaign headquarters —not his law office—or (2) made it clear that it was volunteer help being offered to the political campaign organization.

EXAMPLE 3

A Vermonter, willed a small piece of California property, wrote to a California appraiser to get an idea of the property's value. He detailed the location of the 5 acres of land and noted that it included a "one-room bungalow, suitable for occupancy." He asked the appraiser to provide him with:

. . . a short-form appraisal indicating the present market value for sale and/or mortgage purposes of this land, as well as a general background including future possibilities of the area and indicating what would be the best use of the land.

Responding, the appraiser included a statement that:

The land contract range of price would be from $1,900 to $2,400, and a cash sale price might range from $1,200 to $1,600.

Earlier information had made the Vermonter feel that the property *might* be worth $5,000. Proceeding from that mental environment, the appraiser's statement was not clear to this particular recipient. He wasn't sure whether the appraiser meant "per acre" or "for the entire 5-acre parcel." (Responding to a second letter, the appraiser made it clear that his quotations were for the entire 5-acre parcel.)

Had the appraiser used the words "for the entire 5-acre parcel" in his original response, the second exchange would have been unnecessary. Also, had the Vermonter asked more exactly for what he wanted originally, the appraiser's response might have been more exact.

Make It Easy to Give

The way you ask for information has much to do with how easy it will be to get. It has everything to do with how easy the information will be to give. The easier it is to get information, the easier it is to give it. The easier it is to give, the greater the likelihood that it will be given.

To make it easy to give, state specifically what you want. State it so specifically that your statement can't possibly be misinterpreted, can't possibly be read two ways. Be sure it can mean only one thing.

To be specific, you have to bring your wants into focus. And that is necessary. Your reader won't do it for you. Not when *you* are asking *him* a favor. Pointed questions make pointed answers easy. Doing your own synthesis in question-laden communications is your big chance to make it easy for your reader. Many common requests are for information which the reader already has and which he may be expected—and sometimes is eager—to give. So doing your own synthesis is the most practical way you can compensate him for the favor of responding.

If you ask a manufacturer the price of his X128 cable, no special appeal should be needed to stimulate a response. But suppose you really need the information promptly. Then, be sure before writing that "X128 cable" identifies exactly what you want—and *only* what you want. For example, X128 might be a number applying to a line of cable made in several sizes. If so, you'll get the wanted prices faster if you specify X128 A or X128 B or if you give the specifications of the cable you want so that the manufacturer can match it with the right X128 letter.

Clarity in the request makes a prompt, accurate response possible. Also, it makes a response more likely!

So state specifically what you want—in phraseology that can't be misinterpreted.

Don't ask for "automobile prices by makes at the present time."

Do ask for "retail delivered price in New York of the highest-priced 1968 model four-door sedan in the following passenger-car lines: Ford Galaxy, Chevrolet Impala, etc."

Neither expect nor require your reader to guess or reason—even slightly. "Automobile prices," in the above example, could mean any one of a dozen things. It might be meant to include trucks, for one. More likely it might mean the price of every model of every passenger-car line—an awesome task (Chevrolet alone builds more than three hundred different "models.")

Nonspecific requests like this one

1. Set the reader's mind searching, not for the information, but for the best way to say "no" to the request.

2. Force the reader to guess or figure out what probably is meant. (Then, at best, he will give what he thinks you want; at worst, whatever he has handy without effort—whether it's close to what he thinks you want or not.)

Reader Won't Do Your Work

A reader won't do work for you which *he* thinks you might have done for yourself. "Why should I do this fellow's work for him?" is a normal reaction to the nonspecific request. "If he isn't interested enough to figure out more exactly what he wants, why should I think it through for him, then find out whether my analysis is correct, and go get the information also? Let him do his own homework!"

You've probably reasoned this way yourself when on the receiving end of fuzzy information requests. When your request is fuzzy, your reader will reason that way too.

So the chance for receiving a satisfactory response will vary directly with your success in organizing the request communication. That success, in turn, relates to the quality of your thinking before writing.

In the automobile-data case cited, for example, the requester wrote immediately as his need arose. He wrote before he was sure exactly what information he really did need. "I'll just get somebody to send me all the data he can. Then I'll figure out later what parts of it are applicable to my current problems." Thus his information request was poor—and probably fruitless. More often than not, preparation needed to ask intelligent questions is preparation applicable to solution of the problem which sparked the questions.

Students as Question Askers

College students faced with term papers or theses are among the most prolific and most self-centered information requesters. Every business and technical magazine editor—and many, many business and professional men—get college-student requests regularly. Students often write: "Please send me all the information you have about the shipping industry. I need this in connection with a thesis I am writing." The veteran editor of a shipping-industry publication responds to these perennially similar requests with almost a form letter. It runs like this:

> Dear Mr. Student:
>
> If you can give me a list of shipping-industry data needed for your thesis, I will be glad to send you whatever we have available. (I may be able to suggest other sources for data which we do not have.)
>
> Or if there are any specific questions on which you would like my thoughts, I will be glad to try to answer them.
>
> For general information about the shipping industry, I suggest you do a thorough research job in your college library. There you can select as you go along material that will fit into your thesis outline—which, I am sure, you roughed out as your first step.
>
> Your own library research, in fact, will probably stimulate just the sort of specific questions and data needs on which I might be of help. I think you can realize the impossibility of my taking time to figure out what *might* be useful to you.
>
> Sincerely,

This slightly tongue-in-cheek letter could be briefed, of course, to something like: "Listen, Bub, why don't you do your own homework?"

A student's inexperience may excuse his writing before he is prepared to ask purposeful, likely-to-be-fruitful questions. One irritated executive, however, seeing the student as a shirker, wrote with unbecoming frankness: "If you are not interested enough to figure out what you want to know, you may be sure I'm not. You're not asking for information. You're asking me to write an outline for your thesis and then fill it in." But a student's gauche approach usually is accepted as being naïve, rather than as shirking responsibility.

Lazy Question Askers

What may be judged by harsher standards are the generalized gambits from long-out-of-school information requesters. Adults stand the chance of being dubbed just plain lazy. Almost every supervisor or executive has received (and bristled at) letters written by lazy-thinking adults. Many such letters come from people who should know better. An example is one from compilers of a new encyclopedia who told a woolen-industry executive: "We will appreciate your sending us such source material concerning your field as you may deem appropriate for inclusion in a work of this type."

So the successful information getter starts by giving his communication a pleasing texture, by making it tactful and sincere. Then he makes response easy for his reader by stating exactly what he is asking for. He brings into clear focus his information need. He doesn't leave to his reader the task of organizing the request.

Let the Reader in on Information Use

The successful information getter lets his reader in on the use he plans to make of the information requested. He outlines that use, if possible, in terms of possible benefit to the reader.

Seeking figures, for example, to indicate widespread use and availability of typewriters for personal communication, we wrote the sales manager of a typewriter company as follows:

Sales Manager
Royal McBee Corporation
850 Third Avenue
New York, New York
10022

Dear Mr. Sales Manager:

Can you help me convince thousands of people (I hope) to: "Never send your writing to a reader in your own handwriting unless you can't get hold of a typewriter"?

In a new book, to be published shortly by McGraw-Hill, I'm saying:

"A typewritten or printed piece of writing always communicates faster and more clearly than a handwritten one. Handwriting is better only for communications for which social usage still demands it, and those cases are steadily becoming fewer.

Can you give me—or tell me where to find—up-to-date estimates or guesses of:

- Percentage of college graduates (total or recent years) who can operate a typewriter
- Percentage of high school graduates (total or recent years) who can operate a typewriter
- Percentage of literate United States citizens who can operate a typewriter
- Number of United States homes in which a typewriter is available, as compared with number having telephones, refrigerators, or some other common utility
- *Any specific* figures to help prove my point

Somewhere there must be better data than I had to use in 1951 in my *Clear Writing for Easy Reading*, when I used an *American Magazine* promotional survey.

I shall greatly appreciate and be glad to acknowledge any aid you may give.

                                                    Sincerely,

Appropriate suggestion of a reader's interest isn't always feasible, but it's the best way to motivate him willingly to respond. Once interested in your project, he tends to become a mover in it. In the dark about the information's use, ease or difficulty of gathering it alone may determine his response. Give him a chance to be interested.

Besides, knowledge of projected use often stimulates information in addition to that asked for. A responder often knows more than the asker about the problem or area involved. Often, he sees need for additional information, need unsuspected by the writer. Such situations are common, rather than rare. Suppose, for instance, that the request for "automobile prices by makes at the present time" (see page 110) came:

> *From* The president of the Salk Center Rotary Club
> *To* The secretary of the Automobile Manufacturers Association

Suppose, also, that the AMA secretary knew the data were destined for a member information bulletin recently inaugurated by the Salk Center Rotary. Suppose, also, that he decided to help this local group. Myriads of complications in producing any such list suitable to the bulletin's two mimeographed pages were immediately apparent to him, and yet they were unsuspected by the local merchant asking for information. So the secretary's helpful response did not aim to produce the information asked for. Rather, it aimed to suggest a specific form for the information which would be applicable to the intended purpose. He wrote:

> I suggest that you publish as your August information bulletin the Salk Center delivered price of the highest- and the lowest-priced four-door sedan in each of the following lines: Ford, Mercury, Lincoln, Chevrolet, Pontiac, Oldsmobile, Buick, Cadillac, Valiant, Plymouth, Dodge, Chrysler, Studebaker, Rambler, and Rambler American, and I suggest that you list prices obtained from dealers in or near to Salk Center.
>
> This would give you a rough, reasonable comparative list, short enough to be complete in the space of your two-page mimeographed information bulletin. Any attempt to develop a full price list of all models of all makes would be extremely difficult, if not impossible. No published list is available; we have none here at AMA. And if it were available, its publication would take many times the limited space you have available.
>
> Sincerely,
>
> P.S. Ask the dealers for the delivered prices suggested which include *only* such equipment as is included in the factory delivered price. That will ensure comparable figures.

The responder in this case didn't supply the information requested. He did a far better thing. Knowing the proposed use of the requested information, he suggested a practical solution to the writer's problem. He didn't supply the information, but he suggested specifically what to ask for and where to ask for it.

So let your reader in on the use you hope to make of what he sends you. Give him a chance to be interested. You'll be surprised how often your bread comes back buttered.

Check and Double Check

Requests involving figures, "yes" or "no" responses, or one- or two-word answers account for a good percentage of all information requests.

Such requests lend themselves to listings, tabulations, and questionnaire formats. These the respondent can fill in with minimum effort. *Carefully worked out,* such formats can both stimulate response and bring exactly the data required.

The number of direct-mail responses, for example, is usually inversely proportional to the effort required to return an order. More will make a check mark than will write in a word. More will order two items if the proposal totals the two prices than if it lists the two prices without a total.

The questionnaire format tends to force a writer to bring into focus each item on which information is requested. A rambling questionnaire, of course, gets information no better than rambling, unorganized text. But putting a request into questionnaire form ensures some thinking on the part of the writer before the communication goes on its way. It's impossible to prepare even a very poor questionnaire without bringing your thoughts into some kind of order. (It's all too easy for fluent dictation to run on at length without having been organized at all.)

This tendency to produce a better-focused request makes the questionnaire format easy for the reader. It reduces to a minimum what he has to write in response. But more importantly, it minimizes the thinking he has to do. Glancing at the questionnaire-type request, he knows whether or not he can respond without gathering further data. Also, the amount and kind of data gathering necessary probably are readily apparent. The reader needs to give little if any thought to the form of his response. The listing, tabulation, or questionnaire provides the form.

When voluminous information is requested, a tabulation or questionnaire attached to the request communication is best. Then both texture and pattern of the communication itself can be deftly fitted to the particular receiver.

A few well-stated specific items may better be made a part of the letter itself (as in the letter to the typewriter company, page 113). The decision to attach or incorporate sometimes can depend on whether the receiver will want the letter for his files. If not, he can make his responses on the letter itself and return it.

Timing Is Touchy

Timing is touchy as related to communications asking for information. Good timing is important to any written communication. But it rates special consideration when you are asking the favor of information. *When* you want the information may determine whether or not you get it. *When* can be as important as *what* you want and *how* you want it.

If need for the data is not immediate, timing is not critical. You simply ask for the information at your reader's convenience. Usually, though, you do need the material for use within some definite period of time. You would like a response *before* your final deadline. You would like to be able to process the data without haste.

A graduate student once gave inadequate consideration to the time element—and got completely unsatisfactory results. On Wednesday, July 22, he wrote to the treasurer of a large industrial corporation asking for information needed for a term paper due Monday, August 3. The letter reached the treasurer's office on Friday, July 24. When his secretary read the letter, she underlined the last sentence before she put it on his desk: *"Incidentally, the paper is due in two weeks (August 3), which leaves very little time."* Beside the underlining, she wrote: "Five working days between now and the time the response would have to be in the mail. August 3 is a Monday."

Here was the information requested:

> What is the percentage gain or loss in sales of the year to date versus the year before, and what are your estimates for the entire year in both units and dollars; how does this compare with the previous year?
>
> What is the sales mix by brands for this year, and how does it compare with previous years?
>
> What is the company's trend vis-à-vis the industry, and what is the current percentage of industry sales, i.e., the trade position, and what future position do you forecast?
>
> To what do you attribute any deviations above or below the industry trends?
>
> What efforts are being made to further foreign penetration, and what significance will this have for the overall company sales picture?
>
> With regard to research, what amount and percentage of sales are spent annually on research? In what areas is research conducted, and how productive has it been? Has it produced new products or improved methods?
>
> What is the average age of top management? Is it centralized or decentralized? What provisions are there for recruiting and training executives?
>
> Concerning earnings, have any cost savings programs been instituted? What is the trend of earnings to date versus a year ago, and can you provide a rough estimate of per-share earnings for the entire year? Have there been any nonreoccurring items?
>
> Lastly, what is management's prognosis for the future of the industry? In this regard, is continued diversification contemplated? If it is, in what areas and to what extent?

The date on which you would *like* to have a response is the place from which to start thinking. If you suggest that date, how convenient will it be for your reader? Would the response you want require serious or slight interruption of his normal routines or his regular responsibilities?

Another Example

A comptroller used good judgment about timing in asking budget data from the manager of a subsidiary company. The comptroller was committed to present a consolidated budget proposal to his finance committee on October 1. He needed thirty days in which to consolidate the collected data. He *had to have* fifteen days. To ask for returns before September 1 (thirty days) was impractical because the subsidiary manager would lack necessary data with which to work. Asking for a date prior to September 1, in other words, would provide no extra safety factor and would simply ensure lateness. But, the comptroller knew, the subsidiary manager *could* produce a response by September 1. So he asked for the information on or before that date. He knew from experience also that this particular manager was a procrastinator. He was likely to be late. So the comptroller injected into his request for budget information some sense of urgency about the September 1 date, even though he had fifteen days' leeway before facing a real crisis. He wrote:

> Dear Joe:
>
> This year we'll need your next year's budget estimates not later than September 1. You can count on our being satisfied with the best approximations you can develop in time to make that deadline.
>
> It's especially important that I get them on time this year because the finance committee has asked for alternative budget estimates depending on whether or not we go through with rebuilding of our major production facility. I'll be in a real jam if my regular consolidations can't be made September 1, as planned.
>
> Thanks for your help.

This request—from a staff to a line executive—makes clear the need and gives reasonable grounds for emphasizing promptness. It also removes a possible excuse for lateness. This request illustrates a sound approach to the establishment of a time limit. Besides, it is tailored to a particular situation. The same sequence of thinking is applicable to any information-asking communication. The writer must envision specifically and realistically his relationship to the person he's approaching. Next, he should establish both a desirable and a "must" date in his own mind. Then comes the decision on the date to be suggested, based on consideration of the reader's situation. The date suggested to the reader has to be a date which, from *his* standpoint, is possible without serious discomfort—emotional or mechanical. This reasoning applied uniformly to every information-asking communication will result in communications specially tailored to the particular instance. This means a different timing decision and a differently flavored communication in almost every case.

Asking for Ideas and Opinions

Getting ideas or opinions or recommendations is the hardest communications task. It's hardest because the respondent has first to think and then to do some work.

You are after *his* ideas, the result of *his* thinking. If *you* set up a list of choices, making it necessary for him only to check the one he prefers, you will be getting only his choice of your suggestions. This excellent easy-for-the-reader way to get relatively factual information backfires when baited for creative or spontaneous thoughts. A reader will react as students do to the multiple-choice examination paper. Instead of putting forward their own best thoughts, they simply meet the multiple-choice requirements. Thus they avoid the intellectual effort involved in marshaling their thoughts and expressing them coherently.

When getting idea-type responses, your part is to stimulate a reader's mind to creative thinking. You can pin down only the *kind* of response you want. You can make doubly clear the use to be made of the response so that the reader can think how to fit his concepts helpfully toward achievement of that end. You can go at least that far to make it easy for him.

To get a respondent to "marshal his own thoughts and express them coherently," you must interest him. You must stimulate his mental grabbing equipment to action. When you can't be sure of the right questions to ask, make it easy for your reader to jump to his own conclusions. Psychologically, this is the reverse of your approach when asking for specific, factual data.

The Thought-starter Method

Start your reader's thoughts playing about the end point of their projected use. You then have him participating with you to achieve your aims.

A technical magazine editor, faced with a special information-getting problem, used the thought-starting technique effectively. For an "about authors" page, he wanted specific, offbeat information. He was aiming for "profiles," as opposed to standardized biographies. So he sought to ask questions which would spark a reaction, a partly emotional reaction—questions the author would *want*, not just be willing, to answer. He framed his questions so that they would bring answers related to the author's article or the subject.

One such letter brought him a deluge of personalized "history" which gave him the basis for an additional short article, as well as a good profile. Written to a technically minded author, it read:

Dear Mr. Garrison:

We're just in the process of doing an article for *Technical Magazine* based on your interesting proof of the thesis that:

"A realistic program for guidance of human nature is necessary to the exercise of effective management control."

Along with the article we would like to give our readers some hint of how an engineer—whose formal biography indicates only research and design interests—got around to the penetrating management and psychological concerns so evident in your paper, "The Heart and Soul of a Development Program."

How, when, or where *did* you become so constructively aware of the importance of these areas? Did some out-of-the-ordinary professor at the University of Colorado start you speculating along these lines some years ago? Was it some extracurricular reading that set you off in this direction? Or did you just find yourself facing business and engineering problems that you couldn't solve "without a realistic program for guidance of human nature"?

Thanks greatly for whatever background you may feel like letting us in on. I'm going to be greatly interested personally—as well as "officially."

Sincerely,

(Editor)

The thought-starters in this letter happened to hit the jackpot. The author turned out to be more interested in human relations than technology. He wrote the editor an interesting summary of his philosophy of life as related to the article's subject.

Another of this editor's thought-starter attempts fell on less fertile ground. But it did start some thoughts in a technically concentrated mind. It produced a better profile than a straight biography response and request would have. This letter ran:

> Dear Mr. Mirskai:
>
> When did you first get involved in the problems of clean-room personnel—about which you write so interestingly in your forthcoming *Technical Magazine* article? Did they just come up in the natural course of your work at XYZ Corporation, or had you been involved elsewhere—and came to XYZ because of your experience?
>
> We'd like to give *Technical Magazine* readers a chance to know a little about you at the time they read your article, "Clean-room Techniques Paced by Fast-improving Techniques." They'll be interested, I think, because in that article you have drawn so clearly from your personal experiences.
>
> Thanks greatly for whatever background you feel like letting us in on.
>
> > Sincerely,
> >
> > (Editor)

The more you know about your particular reader, of course, the better aim you can take to start him thinking. (The editor's letters were based chiefly on knowledge of the man's company connection and business title. He had also such meager internal evidence as the article itself revealed.)

Thought-starting about Job Applicants

When checking a job applicant's references, you can profit from thought-starting suggestions to the executive from whom information is asked. Here, your aim presumably is to get the true and full personal opinion of the man queried. You want also information not available from a factual résumé. Thought-starting suggestions usually are necessary to prevent a mere recital of already known or easily guessed facts. Characteristic of one successful personnel officer are letters like this one:

> Dear Mr. Jones:
>
> Could you tell me something of your experience with Roscoe Kisset, whom we are considering for a place on our market-analysis staff?

Our immediate need is for a man who rates high on accuracy, reliability, and application to his work. The work load in this department is enormous right now, and we are adding personnel to get that load back to normal as quickly as possible.

Should the man we hire happen also to get along well with others and have some ability to synthesize and a touch of imagination, he might go far here. The department is sure to continue to expand, and we will have need for additional supervisory personnel—which we like to supply by promotions from within if possible.

How do you think Kisset would shape up on the immediate requirements?

Thanks greatly for such help as you may give.

Sincerely,

(Personnel Manager)

P.S. We'd appreciate also your noting any negative personal qualities or habits of Kisset's, as you see him—qualities which would tend to impair his effectiveness.

This letter starts its reader's thoughts in the direction most useful to the personnel manager. But it doesn't influence the character or quality of the thoughts generated. It aims primarily to get positive information applicable to the man's performance on the new job. It recognizes the normal reluctance of most employers to emphasize the negative traits of a former employee—even when they have fired him.

This letter is a good example of the thought-starting method properly applied. Whenever asking for information which must result from your reader's thinking, suggest the direction to be taken by the thoughts started. Then outline the use to be made of the hoped-for thoughts. This makes responding relatively easier. Your asking communication, like the above letter, should shape the form of the expected reply without influencing its substance.

Giving Information

Other things being equal, it's to your advantage to help others get the information they ask for. But in justice to your employer (even if you are self-employed), be reasonably selective about how far to go to satisfy any individual query.

Your judgment of the contemplated use is a fair basis for your selectivity. When an inquirer simply asks for facts—without indicating what he wants them for—accept his request at face value. If you have what he wants, give it to him. If you haven't, tell him courteously that you don't. Chances are you can't do everything everybody asks of you. So why not give your extra efforts to the asker who invites you into his project, whose query is interesting as well as exact?

Take every opportunity, however, to help your inquirer achieve his purpose when he does let you in on it. Often this plus service to him may mean less effort for you.

One sales manager, Charles Funckle, for example, asked Gerald Harris, a fellow member of the Sales Managers Association, for the latter's (1) dollar sales by territories for the last three years and (2) salary and expense figures by territories for the same periods. "I'm working out our sales costs," Funckle wrote, "and would like to have your figures for comparison. The comparison will be useful, I believe, even though our products are different."

Harris replied: "Here is a list showing our percentage of expense to dollar sales by territories for the last three years. 'Expense' includes the salary and commission figures in each case. The percentages vary, as you can see, from 12.5 per cent in our Pacific Coast area to 13.4 per cent in our Atlantic Coast states. Our total sales expense, including home-office salaries and expenses, has run consistently between 12.5 and 13.0 per cent through the period involved."

For Harris, simple listing of ten percentages meant far less work than assembling the several pages of detail requested. And Funckle was saved from having to make any calculations. Both product and territorial lines of the two companies were unlike, so it was evident that Funckle's desired comparison would have to be in relative terms—in percentages. (Sure, Funckle should have asked for the percentages in the first place! But he didn't.)

How much help is your response likely to be to your inquirer? The answer isn't a bad basis for deciding how to allocate your responding efforts. Whether or not you are under self-interest obligation to reply, the how-much-help criteria is applicable. Using this yardstick is likely to bring a maximum of satisfactions and a minimum of irritation and frustration.

Sometimes you can best help achieve your questioner's aims by telling him *specifically* of other sources. It doesn't help, of course, to refer him to other sources merely to get him off your back. But it can help greatly when you have good knowledge of the other sources. Then you can guide him to reasonably sure help. In every referral case, try to give the name of an individual in an organization, and the address at which he can be reached.

Never use a referral to achieve a brush-off. So used, it will breed ill will where a courteous "I'm sorry, we don't have the information you need" would have been acceptable.

Guides for Getting and Giving Information

WHEN GETTING:

1. Make it easy for the reader to respond.

2. Recognize that you are always under obligation to your reader.

3. Tailor each communication to a particular situation.

4. Establish a yes-environment before detailing requests.

5. State specifically what you want. Bring your wants into focus.

6. Make it hard for your reader to misunderstand. Be crystal-clear.

7. Don't expect a reader to do work for you which *he* thinks you might have done for yourself.

8. Use listings, tabulations, and questionnaire formats when requesting figures and statistical data.

9. When asking for idea-type responses, inject some thought-starters.

10. Give your reader what he will deem plenty of time to respond.

WHEN GIVING:

1. Do your best to help an inquirer achieve his purpose—when he lets you know what it is.

2. Respond simply and directly when only facts are asked for.

3. Decide consciously how far you should go to satisfy each individual inquiry.

4. Never use a referral to brush off an inquirer.

12

Writing to Get Approvals

GET YOUR MIND on the reader's need for what you have when you write for approvals. Then shape your communication to meet that need. Make the writing a tool that *he* can use or a power plant to move his projects and programs.

Don't be satisfied with an OK. "OK" may mean only "I see nothing wrong with it." Aim to get full understanding of your communication's potentials. Aim to have your approver see exactly what's right with it.

A communication aimed through, instead of to, the approver can transcend the indifference which generates a laconic "OK." It can hit the approver's target for him.

Here's a simple example: An office worker wants permission to add a week to his regular vacation without pay. He asks permission of his supervisor, who says: "Write me a memorandum on it, because I'll have to get an OK from the personnel manager. It's all right with me, if it is with him."

Writing to his supervisor, as requested, the office worker might normally have written:

> As I mentioned the other day, I would like to take an extra week's vacation without pay at the end of my regular vacation this

125

year. My regular vacation runs from August 1 to August 15. This extra week would take me to August 22.

I'm most appreciative of your willingness for me to take this extra time, but I realize that personnel approval also will be necessary.

Thank you for your help.

This communication is perfectly keyed to the supervisor to whom it is addressed—and who had asked for it. It would readily get reaffirmation of his already given approval. But it wouldn't help him to present the request to the personnel manager.

The supervisor might communicate effectively to the personnel manager, or he might not. Much would depend on the degree of his interest and on his communicating ability.

The office worker's memorandum was written *to*, not *through*, the supervisor. It wasn't suitable for passing along to personnel.

Writing *through* the supervisor, on the other hand, the office worker might have done the supervisor's work for him. He might have written a memorandum suitable for passing to personnel with only a penciled note from the supervisor. Thus the supervisor would be relieved of a chore, and the office worker would have controlled the way his story got to personnel. Writing *through* his supervisor—not just *to* him—the office worker might have addressed his supervisor thus:

> I'd like an extra week (without pay) on the end of my vacation this year so that I can give my wife a special treat on the occasion of our fifteenth anniversary. I've promised her a Caribbean cruise for so long that she doesn't believe anymore that we'll ever really go.
>
> And the fine cruise I've set my heart on takes an even twenty days.
>
> So this special request is for a special situation.
>
> As mentioned when we talked the other day, my work is in such shape that I should be able to catch up without difficulty within a few days after my return.
>
> Thanks for your consideration.

To write this note, of course, the office worker had to know what was routine and what was special procedure.

This note includes information the personnel manager needs to permit him to decide favorably. And, whether he actually passes the note along or not, his "presentation" to the personnel manager has been both outlined and detailed.

Getting Approval Means Getting Action

As in this simple example, getting approval usually means seeking action. Writing *through*, rather than *to* your approver multiplies many times the chance of getting desired action.

Applied to complex problems and many-patterned projects, "writing through" can be the most potent of all communications techniques. But it is also the most difficult to execute. It always requires getting complete data about the whole problem or project in advance of writing. It always requires clearheaded analysis and imaginative synthesis of those data.

But writing through is more than the best way to get approvals. It can be a channel for easy movement of complex ideas through lazy thinkers to successful action. Potent in every form of communications writing, it contributes particularly to getting action-powered approval of a report writer's recommendations. (An extensive example of writing through in a complex intracompany situation is included for study (Exhibit 11) in Chapter 13, "Writing: Reports to Be Read.")

Writing through can have indirect advantages too. Consistently practiced, it is probably the best do-it-yourself executive training technique ever devised. To apply it successfully is to have acquired skill in what makes good executives—at high and low levels. It is effective in communicating up and communicating down in an organization. It is useful in writing to strangers and to friends. It is especially potent in seeking approval to act or refrain from acting.

Practicing the Art of the Possible

Writing through is particularly helpful to those sure achievers of limited objectives who are the shock troops of business progress. It pays extra dividends to these practitioners of the art of the possible—the supervisors adept at getting the best out of existing circumstances. These men build castles—but not in the air; they accept but don't embrace the status quo. They propel progress.

And writing through is a surefooted way to get approvals for their practical proposals. It can be potent also in getting the widespread informal approvals which are usually necessary.

An example is the working out of a scrap problem by one such supervisor. This tractor-company comptroller functioned best in his existing environment, whatever it happened to be. It was company policy to consign to each new retail outlet replacement parts for three models preceding the current one. So the final production run had to cover two years' needs, including parts to stock an uncertain number of new outlets. Estimating existing outlet needs two years ahead was difficult enough. Estimating to keep a policy promise to new outlets added to that burden.

The vice-president in charge of sales and the comptroller differed strongly about:

1. The value of the policy in getting new outlets
2. The degree of company obligation to ensure availability of these obsolete parts to new outlets

The comptroller favored conservative final-run estimates even if sometimes old-model parts would be unavailable for a new outlet. The sales vice-president felt enough should be produced always to *ensure* availability for a new outlet. The availability, he felt, was a promise.

A study by the comptroller revealed eventual scrapping of thousands of dollars worth of obsolete parts. The cause, the comptroller felt, was the liberal end-run production estimates made to protect the sales vice-president's "policy" promise.

Considering a recommendation to the executive vice-president, the comptroller knew the only final "cure" was to change the policy. But, practicing the art of the possible, he wrote a three-part memorandum.

Part 1 suggested an immediate, limited action to ensure less scrappage, but involving no change of current estimating procedures.

Part 2 suggested radical changes in the estimating procedures —and responsibilities. Adoption would involve considerable discussion and a meeting of several minds.

Part 3 recommended abolishing the policy in addition to sharpening the estimating procedures as suggested in Part 2.

Result: Since only the sales vice-president felt strongly about occasional unavailability, the executive vice-president (following conversation with the president) himself authorized adoption of the Part 1 recommendation. (Part 2 was discussed actively for several months. Part 3, when last heard of, had been tabled "for more serious consideration at a later date.")

This comptroller got approval of one important step by breaking his proposal into three parts. He would have been turned down if the three steps were integrated in a single package or if a single approval or disapproval were required of all three.

He feels sure that writing *through,* as well as *to,* the executive vice-president unlocked approval of Part 1. Without taking action of his own, the executive vice-president was aware that the president and others involved knew about the proposal. He could check their reactions casually with a minimum expenditure of time or effort. The writing-through communication had sold everybody except the sales vice-president. Even he was resigned to some limitations. So the executive vice-president could approve and implement the decision with a minimum of personal effort.

Recognize an Approver's Limitations

Whether writing through, or just to, someone, preexamine the environment in which approval may take place. Each person approves or disapproves in terms of his own experience, ability, and taste.

An art critic judges a painting in terms of his sophisticated knowledge of many other paintings and kinds of painting. You and I may just "know what we like."

An executive may disapprove a suggestion because he's bound to stay within a budget or because he can't see available personnel needed to execute it or because approval would add one more thing to worry about, when he's already overburdened.

Your approver may be hemmed in by limitations. His decision may be influenced by rules, regulations, laws, or policies. These impersonal limitations would affect anybody in the same position as your approver, and in somewhat the same way. If you were in his shoes, you would have to accept them.

So find out what the important limitations are for the person to whom you write for approval.

Then write in full knowledge that your reader will insist on being the interpreter of regulations that limit *him*. He's unlikely to take action based on *your* interpretation of limitations on him.

Timing for Approval Communications

Timing influences approvals greatly because it has much to do with the comfort or discomfort of the reader-approver. To make a fast decision is painful for many. It's impossible for some. Faced with deciding "yes" or "no" faster than is comfortable, a majority will say "no" because they think it's safer. So allowing your reader less time than *he* would like is a barrier to approval.

Occasionally, less than no time is allowed. Some misguided askers favor facing a reader with a *fait accompli*. They think that is the surest way to get an approval. Most experienced executives have faced and bridled at such situations. Typical was the department head who asked approval for an unbudgeted expenditure to execute a research project.

> Three people have already been working on this project for the last four months. We have already reallocated some $3,500 of other departmental funds and will need $10,000 more to complete the project. . . .
>
> This, you will recall, was one of eight projects recommended by the consulting engineering firm which studied our operations over a year ago. While this project was never specifically budgeted by our operations committee, it was among the eight mentioned in the consulting firm's report, which the operating committee approved as a whole.

Typically also, this particular project was a good one, destined to bring results of great value to the company. So approval was given. The department head won the battle. But he lost the war later on when he failed to get an expected promotion.

Whether the request was submitted six months late because of laxness or on purpose, no one but the department head will ever know for sure.

"Never ask a man to break the rules for you" is practical as well as ethically sound advice. Asking him to break his rules raises the greatest possible barrier to acceptance of your ideas. Usually it dooms them to disapproval. It makes it hard for your reader to say "yes."

Knowledge of a particular reader's policy limitations, however, can guide to suitable pinpointing of proposals or recommendations. Modification of a few words or phrases may change your communication from hard to easy to approve. Particularly is this true where your reader is really on your side. Executives of a great foundation once explained to a request-asking group the "rules" governing grants. "We never finance research in any form," they emphasized, among other things. Later they approved a grant to this asker for "development work leading to establishment of a going operation at some future time." Had the request been for "research funds from which a going operation might sometime develop," the funds couldn't have been granted.

The more you know about the formal limitations surrounding your reader, the better chance you have to tailor your communication to accommodate them.

Operating Considerations

It's harder to spot operating than policy limitations. The "rules" usually are all too available for the asking. The operating "binds" involve much subtler, less apparent relationships.

When you ask for an approval, try to envision how the approver can execute your proposal. Run over whatever knowledge you have of people and operations involved. Urge only action which you see a practical chance of taking. Otherwise, ask for approval of "consideration" of your ideas or of "study of the possibilities for. . . ."

Thus your percentage of approvals will rise.

How easy must the execution look? That depends largely on whether your reader-approver has to take responsibility or do additional work. His readiness to approve may vary directly with the amount of work that approval may entail.

If approval involves additional work only for *you*, his arm needs relatively little twisting. If approval rests on some third party doing the work, it is best to have the third party in agreement—and mention that he is. A recommendation that somebody else do something has less chance for approval than any other kind.

Subjective Barriers to Approvals

The same sort of self-centeredness that makes people write to themselves (Chapter 3) is a major barrier to getting approvals. The best way to surmount subjective limitations is through sincere interest in your reader's needs and concerns. To help a particular man requires understanding him—his aims, his habitual reactions, and the way he usually looks at things.

For example, you are asking approval from an executive who has his fingers in detail. He finds himself overworked; he is never caught up and is always under pressure. Though mentally keen, he may subconsciously read every communication with one thought uppermost: "I'm not going to take on any more work or responsibility." His potential for objective thinking may be negated by this intensely subjective thought. He may be emotionally incapable of approvals which would involve his personal participation in a new project. He may not realize that "rationalization is when logic follows action instead of preceding it."

There is something of this fear of further involvement in all of us. Expect it in at least mild form in everyone with whom you communicate for approvals.

The more truly objective your own communication, the better it will overcome all subjective, self-centered barriers to approval. You can't pander to the often present pride of position, fear of competition, or desire for power. But you can avoid irritating known tender spots. You can think and write objectively yourself. You can exorcise subjective reactions and concepts from your own thinking.

As you improve understanding of your reader, your writing-for-approval communications will improve.

Asking Approval of What You've Written

Sooner or later you will be asking someone to approve something you have written. It may be a letter you have composed, some minutes you have drafted, or a memorandum you plan to send. You may want an associate or your boss to check over a report before it is issued in multiple form.

Whatever the occasion, you hope your checker will say: "OK, I think it's all right as it is." The intensity of your hope will vary directly with the degree to which, in your own eyes, the job is completed. So do make whatever checks are necessary on the very first draft of what you hope will be final.

Then submit it as a first draft—and expect to make changes. But have it *look* like a final draft—clean copy; neatly typed pages; and few, if any, inserts or crossed-out words or sentences. Only a professional writer or editor (and not all of them) keeps his mind on the meaning of a mechanically sloppy text.

"Will you read this please, and see if you think I have arrived at the right conclusions?" How often has your associate's first comment following such a question been: "How do you spell 'salable'? Isn't it 's-a-l-e-a-b-l-e'?" or "In this third sentence, does the word 'he' refer back to John Stanning or to Arch Mester?" or some similar comment which has nothing whatever to do with the point to be checked? You planned to iron out those details in your final draft. But your associate let them interrupt and prolong the distance to your main question.

The average reader is inevitably diverted by errors in spelling, typing, punctuation, or grammar. He shouldn't be, but he is. Believe that!

Covering Notes Should Guide

Send a brief covering note or letter asking the reader to check your material. *Ask* him to do so, even when you know he has demanded the right. "Appreciate" his willingness to give you his comments and suggestions.

But guide him toward making comments which:

1. He is particularly competent to make
2. You really would like to get from him

To illustrate, a sales manager includes some technical material in a memorandum to dealers about a new product. He wants the chief engineer to check the accuracy of his technical statements and references. He will appreciate having errors pointed out. Then he can correct them before the memorandum goes out. But he has little stomach for the engineer's views on the memorandum's organization, sentence structure, and wording. So he doesn't write (or say, for that matter): "Bill, I'd appreciate your looking over this memo before I mail it and giving me any thoughts you may have." That would be leading with his chin. Instead he writes (or says) in effect:

> Bill:
>
> Will you let me know if any of the technical references are incorrect or inaccurate in the attached memorandum, which is going to dealers next week? Or better still, will you just correct them and send the correct copy to me? (I've double spaced, so there's room for correcting.)
>
> Thanks greatly for your help.

Unless Bill thinks the entire memorandum is a howling mistake, he'll do only what he's asked to do. To do as he is asked is easy. To make other criticisms would be work.

Finalizing a written communication which requires multiple approval can be a painful and irritating process. But strict observance of two rules will alleviate the pain and reduce the irritations:

1. Never ask anyone's opinion on what you have written unless you really want it. Be eager to make changes, or don't open the door for them to be suggested.

2. "Pretend" that compulsory submissions are voluntary. Take the occasion to ask each "checker" specifically for the kind of check he is most competent to make. Help thus to channel his reactions in the areas where he actually is competent. Get the best you can out of each checker.

Observing these maxims, you will face a minimum of impractical or inadvisable suggestions. Most frustrating suggestions arise when sales executives suggest changes in technical content, when lawyers try to change the wording for a publicity release, when accountants make other-than-financial suggestions for revision of the company's annual report, or when general company executives say how the advertising copy should be written.

Each person who checks your writing has something to contribute. Try actively to get the best of what he has. Then you won't be faced as often with having to accept the worst. Take the initiative in seeking even compulsory help. Thus, you will go far toward staying in the driver's seat on the way to your final draft.

Summary

When writing to get approvals, your chances of success will be high if you:
- Write through, as well as to, the approver.
- Ask approval for what you think is possible.
- Don't expect the approver to disregard built-in limitations that surround him.
- Allow the approver more time than he needs to make up his mind.
- Never ask for an opinion of what you have written before releasing it—unless you really want it, good or bad.
- When compelled to get approval of your writing before release, "pretend" that your submission is voluntary. Get the best each reviewer has to offer. Then use it to the best advantage.

13

Writing
Reports to Be Read

REPORTS SHOULD BE written to be read. The body of the report itself should be as stirring, informative, and easy to read as the report writer can make it. The text should get as much information as possible off the page and into the reader's mind.

In writing a report, you should emphasize the conclusions, the recommendations, the implications, and the significance of what you are reporting. Tell these things immediately—at the beginning of your report.

Your relationship to the report's recipient will dictate to some extent the "tone of voice" in which you write. More importantly, your relation to the problems with which the report is concerned will suggest the most appropriate tone.

Only when final decision making is clearly yours, for example, will you say: "We plan to do so-and-so." Even then, try to deliver your report far enough in advance of the required action time to permit reactions and modification before implementation begins.

When reporting to an associate or superior, a suggestion will usually be accepted more readily than an urging. "You might want to do so-and-so" has a better chance of sparking action than "I would advise you to do so-and-so." It's even better than "I suggest you do so-and-so." (Use of the word "suggest" doesn't prevent this phraseology from being an urging.)

Your associate or superior can feel he's making his own decision after reading: "You might want to do so-and-so." He's more likely to balk at accepting *your* implied decision in: "I suggest you do so-and-so."

Most people like to make up their own minds, just as you do. Urging as often as not raises hidden barriers to acceptance of ideas. "Pressing" sends reports into the rough as often as it does golf balls.

So word your report to permit the receiver to agree without losing credit for making the decision. Every time you write a report, review mentally the psychological barriers to reception (Chapters 4 and 5). See which ones probably are involved in each particular report.

Work on Problems, Not Reports

Think of yourself as working on a problem, not a report. Aim to get down on paper the data and ideas you think will help most to solve the problem.

To do this you must, of course, know what the problem is. If your own initiative has generated the report, you will have to define both purpose and objective for yourself (Chapter 6). If it has been requested by someone else, delay writing until you are clear about (1) what the requester thinks he wants and (2) the use he plans to make of the data and/or the report itself.

Clarity about his plans for use is the more important of the two. Your knowledge of the available material often will enable you to produce it in more applicable and usable form than the requester can conceive. You can afford to take literally his statement of his plans for use. You should be alert, however, to interpret in terms of those plans the receiver's statement of what he wants.

When a report requester fails to make clear his plans for use (which is usually), the wise report writer will speak up.

"It will help me to give you more exactly what you need on this project if you will fill me in a little on how you hope to use the material. Is this just material that you want for your own information, or is it likely to be passed along to others? If it's to be passed along, I'd like to have that in mind while I'm putting the report together. If I know who's going to see it and why, I think I can present it so as to get the best results for you."

Most report requesters are reasonable men. Most will commend you tacitly for your interest. Some will open up faster than others because by nature they open up readily to anyone on any subject. Only a few will resent being questioned.

In any case, find a way to be clear about the use to which your report will be put. Whatever the hazards or difficulties of achieving advance clarity, they are less than when you go ahead in a fog. "Careless preparation can spoil any report," warns Jay R. Gould, of Rensselaer Polytechnic Institute, with many years behind him of RPI's Technical Writer's Institute—where professional problems are discussed and solutions attempted. He adds that the report writer "should understand the situation, involving such points as the intended audience and the length." These matters, he urges, should be "discussed and thought out before the writing begins."

It's worth chancing a few turndowns to achieve so great a difference in impact and fruitfulness for your report. Besides, it is satisfying to work toward clear ends; frustrating to mill about without them.

Writing Reports to Be Read

The body of your report should contain no barriers requiring supplementary devices to complete the process of communication. Tables of contents, appendixes, abstracts, synopses, bibliographies, letters of transmittal, letters of authorization, and other elements common to modern report formats can be excellent helps to a reader. But you should never use them as crutches. Do not expect them to make clear an obscure text. Don't hope they will compensate for mediocrity of writing or research.

That you expect the body of your report to be read should be reflected in your organization of ideas and selection of data. It should be reflected also in your writing and in the shape, size, and general makeup of the report.

The main ideas and/or information you want your reader to have should come first. Those first sentences will guide and limit the data to be included. (Irrelevant material, however good, should be excluded; tangential material should be too, in most cases.)

The material will be presented in the order that your opening paragraphs have led the reader to expect. You will write in terms of the reader's interests as well as in terms of his needs. You will use words that are meaningful to him. You will write to scale the psychological barriers to communication, just as carefully as if you were writing a sales letter.

When finished, the text of a report so written embodies its own format. You could set apart (by indention and line spacing or by italics or boldface type, if the report is printed) the main ideas of your opening paragraph or paragraphs—and your "abstract" or "synopsis" would turn out to have been incorporated [Exhibit 8(A)].

Next, you could write a heading for each major division of your text or underline or set in italics or boldface the first sentence or two beneath—and your skimming reader will have run through the text while reading what amounts to a table of contents [Exhibit 8(B)].

At the end of the report, you could set apart a reprise, in more comprehensive and specific form, of the main ideas, information, or conclusions carried in your opening paragraphs [Exhibit 8(C)].

EXHIBIT 8   *Pro forma text of a report so written that it embodies its own format. By scanning the opening sentence and subsequent italicized sentences, the reader learns the report's main ideas and can decide whether he wants or needs to read more.*

FOOD FREEZER RECOMMENDED
TO IMPROVE CAFETERIA SERVICE
WITHOUT AN INCREASE IN COSTS

(A)   Acquisition of a 180-cubic foot food freezer for $2,500 would increase the quality and slightly decrease the cost of Our Own Co.'s cafeteria operation.

(B)   *The freezer would result in improved quality of food served for several reasons.* Notably, it would permit our buying most vegetables from small farmers in the area of our industrial park location. Freezing these vegetables immediately would give us year-round fresh vegetables, a treat rarely available even in a small-company cafeteria such as ours. Also, the freezer unit would permit more selective buying of meats, with resulting improvement in the average quality served throughout the year. . . .

The cost of this improved food quality, including that of maintaining the freezer operation, should be at least as low as our present costs. This conclusion is based partly on the following projections for freezer-operation cost, including net depreciation (15 years of expected life, 3 per cent interest compounded annually), return on investment foregone (3 per cent interest compounded annually), repairs (2 per cent of purchase price), electricity for freezing (0.1 kilowatt-hour per pound at 2½ cents per kilowatt-hour), electricity for maintaining the freezer (0.25 kilowatt-hour per cubic foot per twenty-four hours at 2½ cents per kilowatt-hour, and packaging (2 cents per pound). . . .

Sudsidiary benefits also may accrue. Local purchase of food-stuffs might be good civic and public relations. Also . . . .

(C)   To achieve these benefits, the plant service department requests permission to buy a freezer of the following specifications at a cost not to exceed $2,500. . . .

> Austin Heffner
> Manager, Plant Service Department

Some such handling of the body (text) of your report will:

1. Ensure the best possible presentation of the main body of information

2. Invite reading of the full text better than any other method

3. Embody the age-old rule that what you put at the beginning and at the end of your writing leaves the strongest impression on the reader

In addition, emphasis on presentation of the text itself ensures appropriate and effective use of the additional devices now common. This approach keeps clear in your mind the fact that you are designing a report primarily for reading. Even if filed for future reference, it will be readable when pulled out later on.

It's particularly important that a reference report be easy to read. When a reader reaches into a file, he is almost certain to skim, rather than study, whatever material he pulls out.

Plus-value Devices Help Readers

Plus-value devices should be so handled as to support, but not supplant, the body of the report. They should illuminate, not detract from, the text. Company-standardized report formats can inhibit maximum communication, though they ensure a satisfactory minimum. Established to throw light on the text, such formats sometimes create substitutes for the text; they may turn readers from it, rather than lead them into it. Aimed at making text reading easy, they sometimes discourage text reading at all.

A modern report format, for example, widely approved by industry and taught by business communications educators, runs something like this:

Title page
Letter of authorization
Letter of transmittal
Table of contents
Table of graphic illustrations
Synopsis
Body
End section
Appendix
Bibliography

So listed, the body or text appears as one of ten elements. When worked out physically, the body of the report isn't buried as deeply among these other elements as it is in the format listing. But it *is* buried. Rarely does this body—which has cost its writer time, tension, and perhaps tears—stand out as the gem of the collection.

Reports so enfolded in helping hands sometimes look more like the sweetheart of an octopus than like a Koh-i-noor diamond among crown jewels. Each device in this list, however, is a potential help to the report's effectiveness as a communication. Developed and presented as illuminators, each is of great value to both report readers and report writers. Specific situations make it possible to use these devices in special ways. A few widely applicable suggestions follow.

One, Two, or Three Documents?

Using two or even three separate documents may help to keep the body of the report the centerpiece of the presentation.

Sometimes you know that the single recipient of your report has no need for background or use for supplementary information. His plans for using the report require no history and no details that can't readily be included in the text. No official letters of authorization are wanted. Then, you might best incorporate on a single title page the few facts necessary—the date, your name and title, the title of the report, and perhaps a paragraph down in one corner telling why the report has been written (Exhibit 9 is a sample).

When the report deals with complex matters, little understood by the recipient, however, extensive plus-value devices are likely to be needed. Here it may help to highlight the report itself if supplementary data are conveyed in separate, but attached, documents.

Background Information

Suppose your report reader needs full background on the problems with which the report is concerned. How did the report come to be written? What might it be used for? How? Why? What about the reliability of the sources tapped for information?

Conveying such background information is a communications job separate from writing the report. Its purpose is to inform *about* the report, not to impart information *from* it. Making such a communication separate permits readier interpretation of data significance in the report itself.

Communication of background data frequently is best done in an attached letter or memorandum. There, you can speak more informally and more personally—and hence more effectively— than in the formal report itself. Instead of burying your report behind pages on which are printed "letter of authorization," "letter of transmittal," and other explanatory matter, how much better it might be to write a note which says:

Dear Mr. Harper:

Here's the report about service complaints on our hydraulic pump during 1965, for which you asked me last month [or "on March 25"].

I think you'll be interested to learn that this is the first year since the pump's introduction in 1961 that service results have improved. Both the number of complaints and the dollars spent to satisfy complaining customers are less than in the preceding twelve months. (Copies of similar reports for 1962, 1963, and 1964 also are available should you wish to see them.)

Should you have any special questions after reading the report, I'll do my best to get you prompt answers.

Sincerely,

Such a note opens the way to presenting as much or as little surrounding information as you think desirable. Also, it communicates tacitly impressions of, and information about, you—about your intelligence, your imagination, your approach to your job, and your understanding of related problems.

The bibliographies and reference material so often required also are often most effective when presented as a separate document.

It is the exception when the original recipient of a report uses the bibliographic and reference material immediately. More likely, he will want it at a later date—if ever. Yet its presence is necessary to authenticate the scope of the inquiries behind the report. It is also possible to note its availability in the covering note or letter.

Advantages of Separate Handling

Separate handling of supplemental data makes for slim and svelte-looking reports—which are easier to handle. Both these qualities have practical importance.

No isolated instance is that of the technical report brought to an automobile company president by a young engineer. Though technically trained, the president failed even to glance through the report for several weeks. Finally, the engineering vice-president through whom the report had been transmitted asked the president: "Have you had a chance to read that report yet?"

EXHIBIT 9   *A simple title page. It gives all the information necessary for many reports and makes unnecessary extra pages for a letter of authorization or a letter of transmittal.*

FOOD FREEZER RECOMMENDED
TO IMPROVE CAFETERIA SERVICE
WITHOUT AN INCREASE IN COSTS

A Project Proposal Report to
Vice-president, Operations,
from Manager, Plant Services

April 20, 19_____

This report responds to a January 10,
19_____, request from Vice-president,
Operations, for "Information on Possible Means
of Improving Employee Satisfaction with
Our In-plant Cafeteria." Additional response
will be made as practical possibilities
are developed.

"Read it?" the president exclaimed, pointing to where it still lay on his desk. "Read it? Hell, no, I haven't read it. I can't even lift it!"

Title-page Usages

A title page is almost always necessary and desirable. But omit it if it merely repeats what is on the cover of the report. If all necessary information is placed on the cover, a title page adds only paper.

All unnecessary pages should be eliminated, especially if they are destined to appear ahead of the report proper. The only pages included should be those which actively help to move the reader into the text.

So, when included, the title page should be used for additional routine information (and should eliminate other pages ahead of the text) when this can be done without crowding. (Exhibit 9 gives one example of this.)

Table of Contents

The table of contents of a report, like that of a technical or business magazine, should give the reader a two- or three-line picture of the information that each listed chapter or section contains. It should relate directly and dynamically to the text of the report. Its listings should consist of statements rather than topic words, though the topic word (or index word) makes a good start for the statement. (The table of contents of this book is an example.)

This kind of table of contents is easy to assemble when the report has been written as suggested earlier. The headings of the report can be the headings of the table of contents. And the first lines of text under each heading in the report will be the basis for the briefer lines in the table of contents.

Such a table of contents, in other words, practically makes itself. It consists of the headings of each division or section of the report, with a brief statement reworded from the first paragraph of each division or section.

Reports That Management Wants

Experienced report readers, among whom are the nation's leading executives, are no longer willing to settle for standardized mediocrity in reports. Mediocrity, they say, prevents the best as well as the worst; it is clear but not thought-provoking, brief but never brilliant.

These report receivers are today's *avant garde* in report writing. They look to reporters—not standardized formats—to produce reports which do provoke thinking; reports which are brief but also interpretative.

Recent research has brought to working focus what management is looking for in reports. Commenting on its new *Practical Guide to Management Report-writing*, one company says significantly: "It does not establish rigid formulas for such things as format and content, because these factors depend to some degree on the nature and purpose of the report and on local requirements."

To produce what modern managers (and others) want, a report must touch specific people and face the specific problems. Meeting requirements of a standardized format—though required—is no longer satisfactory in itself.

There is remarkable agreement among the managers at Westinghouse Electric Co., for example, on what they look for in techcal reports. They agree though, as is the case in other organizations, that informal needs of each manager vary. Each has a personalized job responsibility, supervisory experience, and educational background.

Despite these variations, research revealed, they all:

• Look for pertinent facts and competent opinions to help in decision making

• Want to know quickly whether to read the report, route it, or skip it

• Want—to determine this—answers to some or all of the following questions:

What's the report about, and who wrote it?

What does it contribute?

What are the conclusions and recommendations?

What are their importance and significance?

What's the implication to the company?

What actions are suggested? Long range? Short range? Why? By whom? When? How?

• Want this sort of information in brief, concise, meaningful terms, *at the beginning of the report,* and all in one piece

So when a standardized format discourages prompt presentation of such information, it doesn't help report writers to meet management needs.

The wise report writer, however, will find ways to write in terms that management wants. Yet he'll also find ways to force the final result into something resembling the standardized format— if one exists in his company.

Few report readers resent departure from standard format if they get exactly what they need, in the form in which they can use it best.

At the University of North Carolina, Prof. Arthur M. Whitehill developed an individual rating scale for student reports on business case problems which gives a basis for practical self evaluation of your report before you submit it. The factors the scale evaluates (in addition to grammar, spelling, and punctuation) are use of data, organization, perspective, presentation, decision and/or recommendations.

Characteristics required for what the university calls a "high pass" (Exhibit 10) constitute a practical guide for any report writer. Study of them should aid in execution of the methods outlined in this chapter.

Good Report Writing Gets Results

Every time you write, your reader learns something about you. He finds out how you organize your thinking and something about your reliability. He gets some idea of your approach to relations with others. Every chance to put something in writing is a chance to impress others favorably by helping them to solve their problems or reach their goals.

There are few better opportunities than writing a report.

One time I asked a promising young junior executive to write down on paper a "program" for development of his department's

EXHIBIT 10 *This rating scale can be used by a report writer to evaluate his own report before he releases it. The scale was developed at the University of North Carolina for application to student reports on business case problems*

INDIVIDUAL REPORT GRADING SCALE

Rating Factor	P+ High Pass	P Pass	P− Low Pass	F Unsatisfactory
1. Use of data	Very skillful selections and use of facts and figures. Comprehensive survey of useful sources. Complete documentation as required. Well-balanced pros and cons. Skillful relation of exhibits to text.	Most facts and figures are recognized and used. Gives most of the arguments on both sides. Is accurate in almost all instances. Quite good coverage of sources.	Turns to facts and figures but does not give them full significance in analysis. Fair use of exhibits. Figures usually correct when precision required. Only fair coverage of sources.	Weak in relating data to analysis and conclusion. Use of data scanty and indiscriminate. Relies on generalization with minimum use of factual evidence. Incomplete source coverage.
2. Organization	Extremely logical, consistent development. First things come first. Argument moves ahead to conclusion. Realistic relationship between pieces of evidence. Clear synthesis of all data.	Report moves ahead but leaves a few loose ends. Sequence is logical in most instances. Evidence is well sorted and arranged.	Reasonably good fitting together of pieces. Fair forward motion. Only average synthesis and progression.	Some jumbling of parts. Progression of argument is bulky. Reader would like to reorganize.
3. Perspective	Clearly understands overall situation. Outstanding weighing	Nice sense of balance and focus with quite good treatment	Fair sense of balance. Glimpses major consideration	Minor considerations mistaken for major

	of parts. Major consideration recognized and stressed. Completely unbiased, penetrating analysis in clear focus.	Free from bias and generally sees problem in clear relationship to others.	establishes proper relationships. Some bias or lack of objectivity.	and poor balance among those recognized. Lopsided argument with preconceived notions sometimes showing through.
4. Presentation	An extremely neat, orderly presentation. A polished, clean final copy. Clear charts, graphs, and tables. Required length. Outstanding lucidity in style; care in grammar and spelling. Easy to read and understand.	Clean copy with orderly appearance. Within required length. Very few mistakes in grammar or spelling. Exhibits well done. Generally good appearance.	Fairly clean, neat report. Charts and exhibits adequate but not outstanding. Within required length. Average number of mistakes in spelling and grammar. A number of obvious possibilities for improvement.	Barely acceptable in appearance. May be somewhat overlength or unreasonably short. Charts and graphs poorly drawn. Quite frequent errors in grammar and spelling.
5. Decision and/or recommendations	Reaches clear, definite decision which follows careful analysis. Considers all sensible alternatives; gives sufficient detail. Recommendation is unambiguous, and principal consequences are foreseen.	Decision and/or recommendations are sound. Most alternatives are at least recognized. A better than average feel for consequences of decision.	Comes to a fairly definite decision which shows a minimum of supporting details. Makes recommendations which are plausible but not exciting or compelling. Sees some, but not all, consequences of decision.	Weak, inadequately supported decision with a minimum of detail. Consequences not clearly seen. Partial and inconclusive consideration of alternatives.

immediate future. "Your comments make it quite clear," I told him, "that you have done a good bit of thinking about what ought to be done. It's clear, too, that you have a good many ideas for improvements. But I wish you would put in writing a 'program,' so I can see how your mind works."

"So you can see how my mind works!" he bridled. Surprise, incredulity, and a touch of just plain disbelief crossed his face. "Do you mean to tell me that just by reading what I put down on a piece of paper, you would have the nerve to try to say how my mind works?"

"Yes," I responded. "I mean just that. I don't say I can determine exactly, of course. But I can determine better than I can by any other process available to me."

Somewhat unwillingly, but in good spirit and with determination, he accepted the suggestion. A month later he got approval from his superiors for his written-down program—which contained (differently expressed) at least one major idea previously rejected by the same superiors. Now he seeks and finds chances to write reports—whether requested or not. He knows from experience that a well-integrated report is his most moving method of communication with his superiors and associates.

Reports Are Ambassadors

Reports act as ambassadors *in absentia* to associates and superiors. Yet writers often dispatch them unmindful of their forbidding miens, their unkempt appearance, their complicated jargon, and their awkward manners. Any wonder that their recommendations so often are dead-ended rather than released? "Books and magazines," an upper-echelon executive says, "are designed to attract attention, so they will be picked up, not passed by. But most reports that come to me are designed for overlooking, not for looking over."

A chief engineer's experience points up the power of good report writing and presentation to achieve practical ends. He tells the story as follows:

"For some time we had wanted a rather basic piece of equipment for one of our laboratories. To us the need seemed quite obvious. So we gathered together a few interdepartmental letters, attached a catalogue page of the equipment we wanted, and sent it along—with the usual purchase request—through regular channels.

"It bounced.

"Later we tried again, with a little more correspondence, a little more literature, and another request.

"That bounced, too.

"Yet we wanted and needed that apparatus. We felt sure the purchase would be authorized if management had all the facts. So we made another try, a real one this time. This presentation was designed (1) to secure the necessary attention, (2) to indicate the importance we attached to the subject, and (3) to provide enough of the right kind of information to justify the rather large expenditure involved. Of equal importance, it was beamed directly to the men whose approval was needed. It talked their language and emphasized advantages they would be interested in—and it was brief.

"Altogether, this brief presentation took quite a little time, thought, and effort. But it worked—and in record time! What's more, our management not only bought our piece of apparatus for us but also bought two more for themselves!

"Once attention was attracted and the right information effectively supplied, the rest was easy."

Most top managers today recognize the need for creative, imaginative, interpretative report writers. When they get a creative, imaginative, interpretative report, they figure it came from that sort of person.

Write through Your Reader

A report written to achieve the reader's purpose is the best possible showcase for the creative, imaginative, report writer. Successfully executed, a writing-through-your-reader report (Chapter 12) is a supreme achievement in communications writing. Writing through your reader gives a report an easy-to-use quality that will endear you to its recipient. Armed with a clear knowledge of its purpose, you can design a report to move *through* a reader, so that he can pass it along without essential change to those *he* must influence or inform. The more complex the situation, the more appreciative he will be.

Suppose your boss, the personnel manager, asks for a report of your study of suggestion-system possibilities for your 300-employee company. "What do you hope to do with this report?" you have asked, seeking a specific purpose beyond the obvious one of getting information.

"Well," your boss replies, "our general manager came home from a Manufacturers Association meeting last fall all hepped up on suggestion systems. He's been at me ever since to see what there might be in the idea for us. That's why I put you on this study. Based on what you come up with—and, I suppose, on my own predilections—I'll probably recommend to him that we go ahead with developing some system or that we forget it."

"What are your predilections?"

"I'd rather not tell you at this point. I want the facts as you see them, not as you might think I want them to be."

So you made your study. You were careful to review Manufacturers Association papers which originally stimulated the general manager to urge inquiry about suggestion systems. You did thorough library research on experience of various companies with suggestion systems. Also, you got casual luncheon-table reactions to the suggestion-system idea from several key supervisors. In addition, you talked with supervisors operating successful suggestion systems in several other companies.

Then, having studied your summarized data, you sat down to write your report. "If I were the general manager," you said to yourself, "would I set up an employee suggestion system in this company?"

Then (still supposing) you answered: "No. I don't think I would. It would have some advantages, but in our particular case I think the disadvantages outweigh them, particularly in light of the trouble of setting up to begin with and the cost plus continuing work involved in making sure it would work. For us, in fact, I think there may be several better ways of accomplishing the same results."

You know your personnel manager will use your report as a basis for *his* recommendation to the general manager. So you decide to write *through* him to the general manager.

If your boss agrees with your studied conclusions, he can put his name on them. Then he can pass them along eventually to the general manager, probably as a follow-up to an oral recommendation.

(If, by chance, he doesn't agree with your conclusions, you may have written the bulk of his memorandum to the general manager anyhow. In either case, the "facts," the points you make, will probably be the same. He would simply have drawn different conclusions from them. So he would have only to rewrite completely your lead paragraphs and your conclusions—and perhaps rearrange for different emphasis some of the other paragraphs.)

But the chances are that he will see the "facts" the same way you do, assuming that you have reasoned cogently and have weighed the evidence fairly—assuming, for example, that your report is the one reproduced in Exhibit 11.

EXHIBIT 11   *A report successfully and helpfully "written through" its reader*

TO   Personnel Manager
FROM   Research Assistant

How to Get Employee Ideas into Use in Our Own Co. Operations

Active suggestion seeking by supervisors probably could stimulate more practical employee ideas for improved operation in Our Own Co. than a formalized suggestion system. A program for training supervisors how to seek suggestions would cost less to establish and maintain. Also, it would avoid the friction-producing dangers inherent in even the most successful conventional suggestion system. These are the chief conclusions of the study of OOC suggestion-system possibilities just completed at your request.

Information was gathered on types of suggestion systems, on problems faced in setting up and operating such systems, and on results obtained by hundreds of companies operating successful suggestion systems. These data came chiefly from (1) library research of articles and books, (2) special study of the papers presented at the Manufacturers Association meeting in Oshkosh last fall, (3) informal reactions and opinions from twelve of Our Own Co. supervisors (supervisor comments were gathered because most suggestion-system case histories emphasize supervisor attitudes as a key to operational success or failure) and (4) personal interviews with five supervisors of successfully operating suggestion systems in five different organizations (the largest of these organizations employs 10,000; the smallest, 150).

PURPOSE OF SUGGESTION SYSTEMS

Our Own Co. would set up a suggestion system presumably as a means for getting into the open employee ideas for improvement. Then management could inspect, select, and benefit from those it considered useful and practical. More generally, such a system might aim to improve communication about methods and procedures between employees and management.

Some 90 per cent of the suggestion systems initiated in United States industry, authorities seem to agree, have been productive as upward channels of communication. But I have been unable to find quantitative data bearing on the question: "How productive?" Especially lacking are data on how productive they are as compared with other methods of achieving the same end.

The considerable qualitative data available, however, indicate that suggestion-system productivity is greatest in companies where size necessitates almost completely formalized contacts between rank-and-file employees and middle or top management. There, most employees have no ready means (or perhaps no means at all) for communicating ideas to decision-making management levels. A suggestion system provides such a means. And, experience proves, employees in almost every company have countless ideas for worthwhile improvements.

Most *usable* suggestions relate to minor details of operations with which the employee is familiar. But the total of suggestions made usually covers a wide range. Yet experience indicates that prompt investigation of, and decision and report on, *all* suggestions are essential. Otherwise friction and dissatisfaction arise quickly and strongly.

Companies with successful suggestion systems say that establishment must incorporate five elements: (1) a basic policy statement establishing the system, (2) a designated organizational unit to operate the system, (3) a body of operating procedures, (4) an award program, and (5) a program of employee information.

This usually has meant a separate organizational unit devoting either part or full time to administration of the suggestion system. This sort of efficient, continued handling, many case histories suggest, is essential to:

1. Selecting useful suggestions and integrating them into company operations

2. Avoiding the frictions and kickbacks which seem always to occur when administration is lax, purely routine, or insensitive to employee reactions

SHARP ADMINISTRATION ESSENTIAL

Sharpness of administration influenced success or failure far more than the format of the system itself in practically all companies studied. Experiences related by Manufacturers Association speakers last fall are among those supporting this conclusion (though most of those papers were concerned primarily with the somewhat differing formats of various conventional systems). So, Our Own Co.'s consideration of a suggestion system might well examine particularly (1) the psychological "climate" with which a new suggestion system might be surrounded and (2) the probable effectiveness as well as cost of the administration likely at OOC.

Six of the twelve OOC middle-management supervisors with whom suggestion systems were discussed said something like this:

I think they are more trouble than they are worth. If one of my employees has good ideas about changes, I'd like to know about them directly. I've got responsibility for doing a job in my area, and I can't be expected to do my job if somebody else is going to expert on what's a good idea and what isn't.

Comments from the other six were varied. One said: "If management thinks my employees won't open up to me, but will to a suggestion box, they should tell me what I'm doing wrong—not encourage my folks to go around behind my back." At the opposite pole, another said: "I'd like to see us put in a good suggestion system. We had one where I worked before I came here, and it worked fine. Saved me having to listen to a lot of impractical, screwball ideas and trying to dump them without upsetting the guy who suggested them."

While trying to integrate the somewhat voluminous notes resulting from this study, I found one chapter in a book called *Communication in Management,* by Charles E. Redfield, that influenced me greatly. "Communicating Suggestions and Complaints" was the title of the chapter. It seemed to me a good objective summary of all the suggestion-system pros and cons I had been collecting. One thing it said,[1] for example, was not far out of line with what I got from OOC supervisors:

Suggestion systems originally were, above all else, means for bypassing hostile or inadequate supervisors, and this early objective generally persists.

and

Suggestion systems have traditionally ignored the two basic social relationships in which an employee at work is involved; worker-and-supervisor and worker-and-worker.

and

If suggestions were transmitted through the formal hierarchical channels promptly and without distortion, and if the design of a formal organization gave each employee a wide rather than a narrow horizon, elaborate suggestion systems would not be necessary.

But I think the editors of *Fortune* put the clincher on my thinking about my findings when they wrote: "If business has a new motto, 'Communicate or Founder' would seem to be it."

Effective communication is impossible, it now seems to me, without active participation by supervisors. Any communication attempt—such as a conventional suggestion system—which bypasses them would seem to be doomed to limited productivity at best. But a program for training supervisors to stimulate employee suggestions and make the best use of those obtained would seem to be rooted in more fertile soil.

RECOMMENDATIONS

Analysis of study data, in short, leads to two suggestions for Our Own Co. consideration:

1. Develop and initiate some reasonably formal program to ensure stimulation of employee suggestions—and use of those suggestions —by OOC middle-management supervisors.

2. Refrain from establishing a conventional suggestion system unless at some later date a group of middle-management supervisors themselves suggest and participate in initiating some formal system.

(Attached is a reprint of the chapter referred to: "Communicating Suggestions and Complaints." A copy of the book itself—*Communication in Management,* by Charles E. Redfield, published by The University of Chicago Press in 1953—is available in Our Own Co. library.)

---

[1] Charles E. Redfield, *Communication in Management,* The University of Chicago Press, Chicago, 1953.

The Power of Writing-through Reports

To recognize the power of this writing-through-your-reader report, go back to your original search for purpose. Play back your question-and-answer exchange with your boss, the personnel manager. It's recorded on page 152.

The whole approach to this report is predicated on your boss's statement that he's planning to make recommendations to the general manager. Knowing that, you could write the report *you* think would be the best recommendation to the general manager —if you were the personnel manager. That means that you have given maximum service to *your* boss. In the Exhibit 11 report you have:

• Brought to focus in terms of the general manager's needs your considered thoughts about the voluminous data you gathered. (That's what your boss would have had to do before he made recommendations to *his* boss, the general manager.)

• Supported that focus with *summary* facts and data. (That saves your boss doing the hard work of summarizing the data; like you, he would have had to bring thoughts into focus.)

• Written sentences that march, using words that live. (Your boss can be proud to make them his own, to sign his name to them. *That's what you hope he will do!* You don't want the credit for being a good writer and not immediately even for being a good thinker. *You want long-term credit for being a fellow who helps the boss to get things done.*)

• Indicated that you have piles of notes and data which your boss can plow through if he doubts what you say. (The chances are 1 in 1,000 that he will doubt you, but he might. So be sure you have the data.)

"But," some will protest, "isn't it wrong for me subtly to foist my conclusions on my reader—be he boss, associate, or employee? Isn't it unfair? Shouldn't I give him the facts as objectively as possible or present both sides of the case with equal emphasis? Shouldn't I let him make up his own mind?"

"No" is the right answer, if you want to help him achieve *his* purpose. Sifting and evaluating evidence is work, just as gathering evidence is. When you stop with gathering, you are leaving to your reader all the work of sifting and evaluating. He has to do this before moving toward achievement of his purpose. (Unfairness enters only when you evaluate in terms of some selfish purpose of your own. Then you *are* foisting conclusions and also destroying the foundations of your communication.)

Other, more pragmatic protesters may worry about the reader's reactions to a writing-through type of report. They may ask: "Suppose my boss doesn't agree with my conclusions? What if he thinks I'm cockeyed? What if he resents my trying to put words in his mouth? Maybe [in the case cited] he thinks suggestion systems are great. Or maybe—because he knows the general manager thinks they are great—he wants a report to agree with *his* boss's predilections. Why should I stick my neck out—and maybe get my head chopped off? This writing-through-your-reader technique may be all right, but it seems to me it might backfire—badly. Where am I if it does?"

To answer the last question first: If you get an unfavorable backfire from your boss, you did a poor job of finding out what he was up to before you started to write. If he definitely planned to recommend a suggestion system no matter what your report revealed, you should have been sensitive enough to get some inkling of this from his tone of voice or the expression on his face, if not from his actual words. (Both tone and expression are normal, integral parts of face-to-face communication. Just so are spelling and organization normal, integral parts of written communication.)

Had you sensed such a predetermined action, your conclusions would have remained the same, but your handling of them might have altered appreciably. You might have given more detailed proof of your conclusions. You might have included a fuller and excruciatingly fair presentation of suggestion-system advantages. And both your conclusions and your recommendation might have been stated less positively, more tentatively. You might have given the impression that it was a close decision. You might have made it easy for him to change his mind without going back on everything he previously thought. Make it easy for him to agree without losing face with himself.

You couldn't reach opposite conclusions or make opposite recommendations, of course. Writing-through philosophy envisions helping the boss to help his boss to do what is best for the company. Presumably, your recommendations were the result of your sincere, competent, honest, and objective thought. So make only such recommendations and reach only such conclusions. Then unfavorable backfires will come only from bosses you probably should change at the first good opportunity anyhow.

Summary

Your reports will be read and will reflect favorably on your career when you:

* Emphasize the conclusions, the recommendations, the implications, and the significance of what you are reporting
* Put first the main ideas and/or information you want your reader to have
* Present the material in the order indicated by your opening paragraph
* Deliver your report far enough in advance of the required action time to permit reactions and modification before implementation is scheduled to begin
* Make suggestions and shun "urgings"
* Word your report to permit the receiver to agree without losing credit for making his own decisions
* Write a report that helps to solve problems with which its text is concerned
* Write the text so that it embodies its own format
* Make certain that title page, table of contents, transmittal letter, appendixes, bibliographies, etc., illuminate the text and never supplant it
* Write through, as well as to, a particular reader when that will help him achieve his ends
* Recognize your reports as your ambassadors to associates and superiors

14

Writing
Interoffice Memoranda

INTEROFFICE MEMORANDA CAN (and probably will) establish the image associates hold of you. Your clothes and your manner give them a physical image. Your interoffice memoranda give them a picture of how your mind works.

Some men regularly put goodwill into their out baskets. Others spread friction. Some distribute information useful to the memo receivers; others, self-serving data from self-centered minds. Some habitually respond to ill-tempered, critical memos from associates with snappy defense logic. Responding memos from others are regularly patient and courteous. Some write interoffice memoranda that cast light on whatever subjects they treat. Others meander and drift to uncertain ends.

Over the years, a man's interoffice memoranda *tend* to reveal the quality of his business thinking. They *do* establish what his memoranda receivers believe to be the quality.

Seen in this context, an interoffice memorandum becomes a major opportunity for achieving in business and in industry. The man who uses it will have overcome a common misbelief that effective writing isn't worth the work it involves. He will recognize that ineffective writing brings intracompany confusion equal to that of a loosely run accounting system. He will see that writing is an integral part of almost every job, so that everybody has to do the good writing. An accountant can be hired to run the good accounting system. But professionals can't do a company's everyday writing.

The interoffice memorandum gives chances for personal achievement through varied channels. Chiefly, it is likely to be concerned with:

- Instructions
- Recommendations or suggestions
- Information distribution
- Responses to others' memoranda

In each case, the necessary effort to write movingly is worthwhile. All principles and practices outlined for good communications writing in general are fully applicable to the interoffice memorandum.

Instructions

Clarity and accuracy, of course, are prime requisites of interoffice memoranda written to convey instructions. But the relation between the writer and the instruction receiver should influence both texture and pattern. Two elements determine what actually is received: (1) the sender's emotional impact and (2) the message and the receiver's emotional predisposition. Exhortation to accept instructions seldom stimulates action as well as completeness and clarity in the instructions themselves do.

Urging, when necessary, can often be best given orally—along with an outline of the instructions. Then a written memorandum following ensures a common understanding of what is required. It becomes the result of implementing instructions—not the implementation itself. Often this is the best use of the written instruction memorandum.

Memoranda detailing "procedures," a seminar of mid-management executives has agreed, should be confined to low-level routines. "We didn't get the word" is a common excuse for failure to follow instructions. Often it is a good excuse. Too many supervisors equate dictating a memorandum establishing a new procedure with having put the procedure into use. They can prove the memorandum was received by the instructed employee. So they assume his mind received and acted on the ideas they meant to dictate. They rely on "ought to" as the receiver's motivation to act.

Yet experienced mid-management executives see implementation by memorandum alone as always difficult and often impossible. To be successful, such a memo has to pass along the reasons for the new procedure, not just the procedure itself. The reason for change must be explained in terms that make sense and have meaning to the receiver. Otherwise, the communication is fruitless at best; confusing at worst.

Instruction-type memoranda should contain statements that can be interpreted in only a single way.

Precision is the heart of the instructional problem. "Nobody can write a specification that doesn't leave room for interpretation of its meaning," a cynical vice-president in charge of production once said. But the interoffice memorandum writer can't accept so discouraging a dictum. A carelessly or loosely given assignment can result in too much fruitlessly spent time and, more importantly, in unachieved opportunities.

Interoffice Recommendations or Suggestions

To interoffice memoranda which recommend and suggest, the "writing-through" technique (detailed in Chapters 12 and 13) is specially adaptable. Every changed or new action requires more than a single person's participation and usually more than a single group's. Before a receiver approves, he is likely to seek the ideas and comments of others. Certainly others will be involved before implementation can follow approval.

So, the suggestion-bearing memorandum should be suitable for reading by anyone who might sooner or later be involved. Most suggestion memoranda are to organization superiors. They should be written to permit distribution by the receiver to the writer's associates. This saves the receiver work and increases the likelihood of his taking some action.

Sometimes the writer can properly and profitably send copies to associates at the same time the boss gets the original. He can do this when the writer is certain the boss won't reply before checking with the particular associates or when the suggestions directly relate to an associate's area of responsibility. Here, failure to inform the associate smacks of going behind his back on matters of his primary concern.

When in doubt about secondary distribution, don't make any. Instead, send an extra copy or two to the boss along with the original. Tacitly, this leaves the decision to him. At the same time, it facilitates his passing along without delay.

It's never wise, in any case, to make secondary distribution of a suggestion-type memorandum to:
- Promote or publicize either your suggestions or yourself
- Present associates with some form of *fait accompli*
- Put associates on the spot by waking up sleeping dogs they clearly would like to let lie

Make secondary distribution, in other words, only to people who you are positive will benefit. Base your judgment on how helpful the extra distribution will be (1) to the boss to whom the memorandum is addressed and (2) to the individual associates likely to be involved.

Make Suggestions Easy to Accept

The writer of suggestion-type memoranda is responsible for making his ideas easy to accept. How easy may well determine approval or rejection. Too few writers see their responsibility this way. Half of a large employee group surveyed by a consulting engineering firm complained: "The usual management reaction to my suggestions is negative. Either I hear nothing after I make a suggestion, or I get some runaround about why it isn't practical."

Your personal experience may bear out the accuracy of this survey. But the available survey report didn't reproduce the *form in which the suggestions were made.*

Any suggestion clearly unrelated to the environment in which it must function has a good chance of being turned down. Chance of acceptance is bettered when the memo gives answers to questions certain to be asked. ("How much will it cost?" "How much current practice has to be changed?" "Do people have to be trained or retrained?" "Has it been tried before; if so, what was the experience with it?" "How soon could it be readied for use?") Depending on the particular suggestion, one or a score of such questions should be thought through by the suggestion writer. He should give some semblance of significant answers in his suggestion memorandum; that's what makes a communication whose suggestions are easy to accept.

It's useless to say: "Well, those answers are the boss's responsibility, not mine. To be fair to my suggestion, he ought to do the work of checking it out. That's what he's paid for." Granting the suggestion maker is right, "ought to" is a depressant—not a stimulant—to acceptance of ideas or recommendations. It is the weakest possible crutch upon which a writer can lean for reader acceptance.

To communicate suggestions well requires surmounting barriers in the receiver's mind, which is rarely "doing what comes naturally" for the writer. The writer must decide whether he wants more acceptances or less communications-writing work. Only he can know in each case whether pain of bursting the bonds of self-centeredness outweighs the satisfactions of creative accomplishment. Often, that's the choice facing the interoffice communications writer.

Information Distribution

Many interoffice memoranda carry information about the writer's area of responsibility to superiors, associates, or subordinates.

Information-bearing memos in most cases should carry material needed by, as well as useful to, the recipient. Most receivers are too busy to be stimulated (or benefited practically) by information, however good, which they don't really need. The volume of interoffice data on most desks precludes active interest in it-might-be-useful material.

But each receiver's situation is different, and the same receiver's situation differs at different times. So the sender should examine the reception environment each time he thinks of writing an information memo.

Where he is sending routine information automatically, he should check periodically on the use the receiver is making of it.

Perhaps its form or character should be changed, or perhaps it shouldn't be sent anymore. Such use-checks by information senders are appreciated by overloaded receivers. These checks are certain to improve reception of whatever *is* sent.

"For information" penciled in a top corner will tell the receiver that you don't expect a reply. Also it will make for relaxed acceptance of it-might-be-useful material—when you do send it.

Responding Memoranda

When answering a memorandum, your reply should be clearly and specifically responsive. Usually it needs neither introductory nor concluding phrases. A prompt, brief-as-possible response will build goodwill and speed action. Usually it does better alone than with added courtesy phrases.

If, for example, the personnel manager has asked how much office-temporary help your department may need in the next six months, tell him. Don't discuss the possibilities and then tell him. Say, for example: "Our office-temporary needs from July 1 to January 1 should not exceed 35 man-days or $650. All such help needed will be for typing and clerical assistance."—and let it go at that. (If personnel wants reasons, it can be expected to ask for them. Or if you want personnel to have reasons whether asked for or not, initiate a separate memorandum. In it, focus on whatever may be your specific purpose in giving the added information.)

Sometimes a "for-information" memorandum may be a response to many casually expressed desires from many associates. Your department may be engaged in a long-term project likely to affect many other departments. *You* understand clearly your aims and the logic of steps to realize them. Everybody else is slightly confused, a little apprehensive, or completely uninformed.

This not uncommon situation once existed in a leading engineering society. For two years, the publication division manager had been developing and implementing better ways to make available the society's constantly growing store of technical information. Concurrently, other engineering societies, industrial organizations, and abstracting services were working toward similar ends for information throughout the engineering world. This publication manager was trying so to improve his own society's data retrieval that it could be melded with other developing, but not yet fixed, systems. No society division manager except the centrally concerned publication manager vaguely understood what was going on. Each had been more confused than enlightened by technically detailed oral responses to casual questioning.

Finally, a for-information memorandum from the publication manager gave them good orientation for following the program's future progress. Dealing with complex interorganizational relationships as well as technically complicated implementation, this memo illustrates the most difficult and useful kind of for-information interoffice memorandum. Exhibit 12 reproduces it in full.

EXHIBIT 12 *A well-done "for-information" interoffice memorandum. Written by an engineering society's publication manager, it orients staff associates on a continuing program involving complex interorganizational and technical problems.*

TO Technical Society Staff
FROM S. G. Laider
Publications Manager

OUR TS INFORMATION-RETRIEVAL PLANS

OUR AIMS are:

1. To equip ourselves so that our members and industry can make use of the new retrieval techniques now available when they need TS information

2. To so design our services that they'll be comparable and compatible with those of information centers, so that TS information will be useful to a broader group of engineers than the society itself can reach

THE NEW TECHNIQUES

Information retrieval is no longer merely two words describing a complex activity. Evolutionary and revolutionary technology developments—as well as information-retrieval changes—challenge TS to integrate itself into the changing information-retrieval picture. We aim to do this by the way we put our own house in order.

A new type of organization, called the "information center," is growing up to do the information-retrieval job.

INFORMATION CENTER

Right now there are 200 to 300 information centers in the United States. A simple way to define them is to say they're the next step after a library. They act as exchange *networks* for information. They are more concerned with finding where data are located than with acting as a document supply source.

This change of emphasis in data-retrieval service has led to the development of six new approaches to an old, yet new, science of making use of information. These are:

• Interdisciplinary common language.
• New indexing techniques.
• Faster finding systems. (The computer is king.)
• Better supply of documents. (Microfiche or microfilm and Xerox-type copies are now cheaper per page than some printed books.)
• Personal technical profiles for engineers. (Prescreening of each user is part of the function of an information center.)
• Evaluation of technical material.

Examples of information centers now operating and performing some of these new functions include *Engineering Index,* Referral Bureau of the Library of Congress, *Chemical Abstracts, Chemical Titles,* Research Triangle Institute, and others. As yet, no information center or group of them comprehensively covers the technical literature or performs completely the six items listed above.

FACTORS INFLUENCING INFORMATION SERVICE

In addition to the functions outlined for information centers, two other factors influence the service:

1. Finding old versus new material
2. Supplying documents or data

Old versus New: Suppose you want all the information on a subject you can get—perhaps to help you start a new project. The service that gets it for you is called a "retrospective search." Retrospective searching is almost always done on large computers—at an information center. It may involve the computer's looking at millions of documents.

Documents or Data: Most information centers tell the reader the book, paper, report, or other document that contains the facts he wants. (In TS this would be appropriate for the technical papers presented at our meetings.)

Some services, however, try also to give actual data. If, for instance, you ask for the tensile strength of a TS 1010 cold-drawn steel bar, these services would give you back "53,000 pounds per square inch," not just "Look in the TS handbook." (This data service soon may have a profound effect on our TS standards program.)

Right now, I'm glad to report that TS is actively doing work in all six functional categories essential to an information center. Attached are samples of some of the work going on. They are:

1. Common language

    A few pages of the interdisciplinary thesaurus produced by the Engineers Joint Council are the first attachment (TS cooperated with fourteen other societies to make this possible, and it's a "first."

2. New indexing

    No sample is needed; just look at the "yellow pages" of any TS journal.

3. Faster finding systems

    I can't attach a computer, but have shown a typical work sheet that gets fed into it.

4. Better document supply

    Clipped together are a TS paper, a microfiche of the paper, and a print-out copy of a typical page. On microfiche, 100 papers fit into about 1 inch of space in a small desk file. We also supply Xerox copies of any past TS literature.

5. Personal technical profile

    Members tell us broadly of their technical interests each year when they get the attached dues bill.

6. Evaluation

    Each TS paper gets one of the most thorough evaluations going via our Readers Committees. A sample of the vote form used by the 414 experts serving on forty-six committees is attached.

On Being a Ghost

A superior's request to write memoranda (or letters) for his signature is a chance to express *your* understanding of *his* problems. Ghosting for the boss reveals sharply your sensitivity to all aspects of your business environment. It tests quickly your ability to think objectively—to see business problems through others' eyes. It gives you a taste of how the boss's job differs from yours —in ways besides salary.

A request to ghostwrite rarely means the boss is too lazy to do his own work. More likely it means he needs skilled assistance. Smart supervisors, in fact, recognize ghosting as a ready means to check an employee's current potentials for advancement. Sometimes they give chances to ghostwrite for just that reason.

So a request to ghostwrite will be an opportunity for some, an exposé for others. Faced with a request, grasp it as an opportunity. Do the writing in three steps:

1. Be sure to know all the surrounding circumstances—as well as the necessary facts.

2. Apply all the principles of creative communications writing reviewed in Chapters 2 to 6.

3. Apply all the techniques of clear writing for easy reading reviewed in Chapters 7 and 8.

Remember that on trial is your ability (1) to analyze a problem, (2) to decide what ought to be done about it, and (3) to express the decision in terms of the analysis. Your skill with words is important, but secondary.

To be sure you know the surrounding circumstances, don't hesitate to ask questions—as many as necessary. But ask for information to help you to decide what to write. Don't ask the boss what he thinks ought to be written. For example:

Ask: Does the personnel manager have final say on how many office-temporaries our department can have? If not, who does? Or does it really matter? Isn't it always a matter of a "mutual-consent" decision?

Don't ask: Do you think we should reply to the personnel manager's memo with a strong, positive pitch for more office-temporaries than he says we can have? Or do you think it would be better to take more of a selling-our-needs line?

The *ask* questions call for factual answers—which the boss can give without reasoned thought. Answering the *don't ask* questions is to do the main work involved in writing the memorandum. It's easier for the boss to write the memorandum himself than to ghost for you. Don't try to turn the tables on him.

Interoffice Memoranda Mechanics

Form and styling influence the degree of interoffice memoranda's help in establishing a good image of how your mind works.

Your memoranda's look should reflect you at your best, not at your careless or casual worst. Even in a big corporation, where format comes in pads, your memoranda can reflect an attractive individuality. (When a secretary sets up the format within the company form, her individuality may be reflected—but it will be seen as yours.)

However strictly you must conform to the organization form, the following mechanical aids can be used:

- Typing can be neat and accurate.
- Ample white space (including margins) can be characteristic.
- Single-spaced text can have double spacing between paragraphs, and paragraphs can be numerous.
- Double spacing can be used where material is complex and long.
- Every opportunity can be grasped to use tabulations and indentions.

These devices, useful in all communications writing, are especially effective in interoffice memoranda *because* so few writers bother with them.

Writing to other members of one's business family breeds carelessness rather than informality in most of us. We tend to rely far too much on "ought to" as a motive for readers to read. Each of these devices, suitably used, makes interoffice memoranda easier to read and more welcome on associates' desks.

Neat, accurate typing assumes, of course, that there will be an absolute minimum of hand corrections on the finally dispatched memorandum. When dealing with any but the simplest topic or problem, most successful communications writers make a double-spaced first draft routine. To them, editing a first draft is just as much a part of memo writing as dictating or writing the words originally. Usually, rather than occasionally, they change the order of the material, reword sentences, and inject new data or ideas. Doing this, incidentally, reduces the need for handwritten corrections on the final copy. (If you are a dictator, your transcriber-secretary will thank you for this practice. Chances are she'll do less—not more—typing in the long run.)

Ample white space, more than any other single thing, is the key to good appearance in an interoffice communication.

Note that almost every good writing practice—like short words and short sentences—tends to force more, rather than less, white space. Short words make white spaces come oftener in each line and make the memorandum fit into one or a few pages, even when wider margins are included. Plentiful paragraphing also helps to "open up" otherwise discouraging solid blocks of type.

Single or double spacing should be decided in respect to each memorandum (at least in respect to each kind of memorandum) you write. Most interoffice memoranda will be single spaced. But single spacing is harder to read than double spacing. So the white space lost between the lines should be added elsewhere—more paragraphs, indentions, or tabulations, where feasible; plenty of margins all around the page; and so forth. Large solid blocks of type should be avoided at almost any cost.

Tabulations and indentions often improve clarity of memoranda, make them easier to read. The longer the list, the more useful an indented tabulation.

Compare, for instance:

> The personal-appraisal report is intended to give the individual a reading on himself, facilitate employee counseling, identify training needs, and provide the basis from which future progress can be recorded.

with:

> The personal-appraisal report is intended to:
> 1. Give the individual a reading on himself
> 2. Facilitate employee counseling
> 3. Identify training needs
> 4. Provide a basis from which future progress can be recorded

The visual change (from a straight sentence to tabulation) makes the points easier to grasp mentally. Sir Francis Bacon wasn't composing an interoffice memorandum when he wrote the second of the following sentences. But its fifty-five words are easier to understand with indentions (than without, as he wrote it):

For what a man had rather were true he more readily believes. Therefore he rejects:

- Difficult things, from impatience of research
- Sober things, because they narrow hope
- The deeper things of nature, from superstition
- The light of experience, from arrogance and pride
- Things not commonly believed, out of deference to the opinion of the vulgar

It is hard to overuse the indented tabulation device in interoffice memoranda. Besides giving visual clarity, it almost forces a writer to think through an outline before writing. The listing almost automatically becomes the outline for what follows.

Attempts to tabulate reveal confused outlines. Also, they bring to light tendencies to add apples and oranges and express the result in grapefruit, and other common inconsistencies.

For variety, dots may be used instead of numbers:

Please remind me to:

- Answer the Wilkins letter the day it arrives
- Call Aiken to discuss the catapult deal as soon as you can locate him
- Get a birthday present for my wife

The tabulating effect is about the same whether numbers or dots are used.

Summary

Your interoffice memoranda convey the image associates are getting of your business thinking. The image is likely to be progressively better as you incorporate these practices into your memoranda writing:

- Make your instruction memoranda clear, accurate, and specific.
- Confine to low-level routines memoranda detailing procedures.
- Don't write a memorandum to avoid face-to-face communication.

- Write through, as well as to, a reader when that will help to speed up or improve subsequent communication he must have with others.
- When in doubt about sending extra "copies to," don't. (Send extra copies to the memorandum's recipient.)
- Include only information needed by, as well as useful to, the recipient.
- When you answer another memorandum, make your reply specifically responsive and as prompt and brief as possible.
- Do a particularly good job when asked to ghostwrite for your boss.
- Be sure your memoranda's look reflects you at your best, not at your careless or casual worst.

15

Writing
to Congratulate
or Console

A FRIEND or acquaintance or business associate has had some good fortune or some bad luck. He has been promoted or has lost his job. He has surmounted a difficulty or has been buried beneath it. He has grasped an opportunity or has missed an easy chance. On these and scores of other occasions, you may wish or be required to drop him a line. You may want to express your sentiments about his situation—or you may feel you should do so.

Your communication will be most satisfactory to you and to your friend if it reflects to a high degree:

- Sincerity
- Appropriateness
- Brevity
- Tact
- Singleness of purpose, expressed in terms of a single idea

Sincerity, needed to make any communication effective, is a must for a letter in which *you* comment on *another's* situation. Such a letter is, by definition, a highly personalized expression. Lacking sincerity, it is almost certain to sound pretentious, specious, or artificial. Written sincerely, its message will get through even though carried in trite words and somewhat hackneyed phrases. So to congratulate or condole, let your heart speak in whatever words come to mind. This advice holds whether you are addressing a friend about whom you feel deeply or a business acquaintance to whom duty dictates you write. Let the warmth that you feel flow into the first, and a tactful decorum characterize the second. In either case, express what you feel.

Too many letters of congratulation and condolence never get written because the writer thinks right words are more important than right sentiments. So often, when we sit down to write, appropriate words don't seem to come. So we wait to congratulate or condole until we see our friend in person. Then we don't see him for many moons—and it's too late. The purpose of communications which congratulate or condole is usually best achieved by expressing some one idea—briefly. Brevity reduces to a minimum our chance to make psychological mistakes.

We dare comment extensively on another's joy or sorrow only with fullest understanding of his emotional needs. In large measure, such understanding is rarely available. So the more we say, the greater the chance we will intrude instead of help and will spark reactions we don't expect.

A one-word message—"Congratulations"—may carry the utmost of warmth and sincerity. "My heart goes out to you!" may express a depth and breadth of sympathy. To congratulate or condole is an exercise in expressing briefly one's freed emotions —which, once freed, tend to overflow.

Letters of Congratulation

Actually, the congratulatory letter is relatively simple, when congratulations come from the heart. If a friend has been promoted, why not write as well as think to yourself:

Dear Arthur:

The good news just reached here yesterday. You're just the sort of fellow that deserves a chance at so challenging a job as your new one seems to be.

Here's wishing you the continued success I know you're going to have.

Best regards.

Sincerely,

Even if Arthur is an acquaintance, rather than a friend, an easy, relaxed expression of what comes naturally should not be too hard to write. Routine, but satisfactory, might be:

Mr. Arthur Potts
Treasurer
Olympia Fisheries, Inc.

Dear Mr. Potts:

It was a real pleasure to learn yesterday that you have become treasurer of Olympia Fisheries, Inc.

I want to add my congratulations to the many I know you are receiving.

Sincerely,

Many letters of congratulation will express approximately the same thought. But this very personal communication form should never be standardized. Both the examples cited, if actually used, should be personalized to the particular recipient. The second paragraph, or an additional paragraph, for instance, should contain some reference which is:

• Appropriate for you to write to this particular reader
• More or less meaningless and inappropriate for any other letter from you to any other friend

What is tactful and appropriate, of course, depends on your relationship to your prospective reader. Suppose the man promoted is many years your senior. He works for a company in another city and occupies a much higher-ranking position than you do in your company. You write paragraphs which are appropriate for him but which might be inappropriate for a younger man, in a lower-ranking position in your own company.

To illustrate, suppose the older man is Arthur Potts, of Olympia Fisheries, Inc. (see above). And suppose you are on the staff of Higgins & Hopewell, who have been auditors for Olympia. You worked personally with Mr. Potts on Olympia audits while he was assistant treasurer. A personalized second paragraph would improve the impact. For the impersonal

I want to add my congratulations to the many I know you are receiving.

you might substitute:

> I hope your new responsibilities may result in our paths crossing more frequently in the future. I shall always enjoy any opportunity to work with you.

Suppose, on the other hand, you are the retired board chairman of Olympia Fisheries. You are congratulating young Mr. Potts, whom you hired ten years ago, when you were general manager. Then a personalized note like the following might be more appropriate:

> Dear Arthur:
>
> Your appointment as treasurer gives me almost as much satisfaction as I know it does you. It marks the most important step so far in the steady progress you've made ever since you joined Olympia ten years ago.
>
> You're going to meet many new challenges as part of your new responsibilities. But you've always seen challenges as opportunities, and I'm sure you'll continue to do so.
>
> Congratulations—and best wishes for your continued success.
>
> Sincerely,

Suppose, however, that Mr. Potts isn't so young. You hired him as assistant treasurer ten years ago, and he hasn't had a promotion since. He plugged along faithfully and finally became treasurer at the death of a thirty-year incumbent. Then the previous congratulatory note would be both inappropriate and patently insincere.

In this latter situation, a totally different expression will be sincere, tactful, and appropriate. This different expression, beginning with the same words as before, might read:

> Dear Arthur:
>
> Your appointment as treasurer gives me almost as much satisfaction as I know it does you. Your consistently sound performance since joining Olympia assures that our treasurership will continue in highly competent hands.
>
> Congratulations—and may the future bring you the best of everything.
>
> Sincerely,

There are hundreds of informal, semiformal, and formal ways to congratulate someone. Some ways are sincere, appropriate, and tactful when writing to almost anybody. But to use them as form letters is full of pitfalls.

You might, for example, send identical letters to two associated men at the same or separate times. "Hearty congratulations and best wishes to you in your new assignment" will sound sincere to each when he receives it. But the heartiness is much alloyed when comparison reveals it as a routine. An unusually good expression becomes unusually bad when revealed as having been sent without thought of the specific reader.

"Here's wishing you the best of success," for example, is almost foolproof for any letter of congratulation. But it may seem a sly dig to the man just "promoted sideways" because he failed a previous assignment or to an aging executive, given a higher-titled job from which to coast more comfortably to retirement.

So it is with many other excellent general-purpose expressions of congratulations. Knowing your reader—and thinking of his reactions—should be involved every time you write a congratulation. Knowing your reader is the key to saying the right thing in the right way at the right time. With this warning, here are a few letters of congratulation from the files of the men who wrote them:

EXAMPLE 1

Dear Mr. Everitt:

It is good to know that you have become sales manager at Banshee's.

May your new duties make our paths cross at least as often as in the past.

Hope you will make our office a port of call next time you are down this way.

Best regards.

Sincerely,

EXAMPLE 2

Dear Martin:

Hearty congratulations and best wishes to you in your new job. Hartshaw Co. is fortunate to have you—it seems to me!

Cordially,

EXAMPLE 3

Dear Mr. Eden:
Congratulations and best wishes to you in your new work with the Crenshaw Foundation.
Hope your new duties will bring you down our way often.
Best regards.

Sincerely,

EXAMPLE 4

Dear Tom:
A salute to the new advertising manager of the Ernton Iron Works. According to our best information, there isn't a better advertising manager in the business.
Hearty congratulations!

Sincerely,

EXAMPLE 5

Dear Edward:
This note is to congratulate the Orpheum Corporation on your promotion to the general sales managership. It was a real thrill to get the good news.
Here's wishing you the best of success.
Best regards.

Sincerely,

Letters of Condolence

Letters of condolence involve the same problems—and the same solutions—as letters of congratulation. Sincerity, however, is even more important—if that is possible.

The biggest problem is that all the suitable words seem to have been used so often that they are worn out. "Sympathy" has become trite, and yet its synonyms seem pretentious or inaccurate. If you feel incompetent to write an individually aimed letter of condolence, why not *select* a printed card and send that? Sentiments common to many condolence needs are well, often beautifully, expressed in today's printed cards.

The one simple idea of your condolence communication may well stem from your personal relationship to your reader. Or you may relate some personal experience to the situation into which you are writing. But the relation must be obvious. The slightest straining to force or explain a relationship defeats its own purpose.

A good example of the personalized, yet not unduly intimate, letter was written by a regional sales manager to the general manager of his company. The general manager was just back in circulation, following a heart attack. The regional sales manager, a long-time acquaintance of the general manager, wrote:

> Dear Keith:
> When I was in the office several weeks ago, I was told you were to be given the silent treatment even as to letters. Yesterday, I was in again. This time I was told you are as brown as a berry and very fit. So I guess it is now safe to write that I was sorry trouble befell you—and delighted that you are mending.
> How to satisfy one's conscience and still stay on an even keel seems to be a major problem these days. I do not have the key to the solution or I would send it to you as being more valuable than a credit card.
> Instead, I send you all best wishes for a sustained recovery.
>
> Sincerely,
>
> P.S. Knowing you, I must add: "Please no acknowledgement, or I shall regret writing."

This note has several desirable characteristics. It reflects sympathy without using the word. It is optimistic, yet realistic. It is natural, not contrived. The unique postscript is especially notable. It makes its point forthrightly, yet graciously. Its clear sincerity permitted the general manager to feel comfortable, yet not obliged to respond.

So important is sincere personalization in letters of condolence that danger lurks in every attempt to copy examples. A letter that consoles in one instance might shock or disgust in another. Here are some examples, from the files of those who wrote them, which *were* helpful to the particular people who received them:

EXAMPLE 1: *to the wife of a business associate*

Dear Gloria:

You have my deepest and sincerest sympathy.

As you well know, Vic has for many years helped to make life happier and more productive for all those privileged to know him. His dedication and thoughtfulness of others set us high examples.

His constructive influence and the memories of our long association will endure.

Sincerely,

EXAMPLE 2: *to the son of a business acquaintance*

Dear Mr. Alstair:

John Alstair will be greatly missed by all of us who knew his thoughtful, friendly, helpful ways. He earned the high esteem of hundreds of those who lived and worked with him.

I want you to know how deeply we share with you in the grief your father's passing brings.

John has enriched us with his many fine accomplishments. The memory of this great and kindly man will remain with us always.

Sincerely,

EXAMPLE 3: *to a friend who has lost his wife*

Dear Harry:

Nothing can be said to lessen your deep loss and sorrow. But I do want you to know of my heartfelt sympathy and sadness. I can only hope that time and many precious memories can erase the emptiness and unreality you must feel right now.

Florence was a lovely person. She will be missed by everyone.

My kindest wishes, and my prayers for you and your family.

Sincerely,

EXAMPLE 4: *to a friend who has lost her husband*

Dear Helen:

My heart aches for you.

You and Ernest have been so faithful and devoted to others in trouble that many, many friends are now sorrowing with you.

May the mercy of God's wings uphold you and bring His loving care very close.

Sincerely,

EXAMPLE 5: *to the wife of a business friend*

> Dear Mrs. Golden:
> We have just heard that Everett has passed on, and I want to tell you at once how sincerely we feel the deepest sympathy for you and those closest to him. We share your grief and are thinking especially of you in these trying hours.
> Now that he will not be among us, we shall miss Everett greatly. The memories of our pleasant and helpful association will be enduring.
>
> Sincerely,

No Middle Ground?

Perhaps there is no middle ground between a highly personalized condolence communication and the printed card. "Ringing with true sincerity and emanating from a warm heart," says an executive who has written hundreds of condolence letters, "such communications, no matter how crudely written, can rank high in human values. Ground out as office routine, they simply fill a file marked 'Death-time Amenities.'"

When duty rather than desire dictates a condolence, the printed card is almost always preferable. Creative energy is used up trying to write as though you were emotionally concerned when you're not. Better to put it into sincere selection of a suitable card.

Condolences aimed solely to fulfill a duty often are best left unwritten. Otherwise, they may sound like a duty letter—and thus negate the good it is hoped they will do.

But *where you have a sincere desire to write, don't let seeming lack of the right words stop you. Sincerity will make itself felt, however timeworn the words.*

A Single Theme

However short, a letter of condolence needs a single theme idea. It should give a sense of movement, of life. Life and movement are the qualities most characteristic of the warmth you so greatly wish to convey.

16

Writing
Minutes to Move
Groups Forward

MINUTES OF MEETINGS, like other communications, are best written creatively. Creative minutes can guide programs and point out needed action. They can ensure common understanding on the part of the meeting's participants. "The official record made of proceedings at a meeting" should be a living document, useful when read before or at a following meeting.

Only tradition decrees inert thoughts, dead words, and pointless paragraphs as characteristic of minutes. Tradition sees minutes chiefly as legal necessities or formal requirements. As traditionally written, reading of the minutes is properly "dispensed with," as is customary. Little useful purpose is served by reading them, thousands of committees and boards solemnly agree every hour of every day throughout the United States. The wonder is that so few question whether any useful purpose is served in *writing* them. The time wasted per reader in reading minutes is more than matched by the time wasted writing them in traditional form.

Ineffective minutes writing stems from failure to define specifically the purpose of the writing. (This same failure is responsible for most relatively ineffective communications writing.) In only a minority of cases is necessity for a legal record either a conscious or a required purpose. Yet only when a legal need may be acute is writing with blinders as regards other purposes justified. Because legal requirements sometimes must dominate is no reason to so structure all minutes that they are hard to read.

Traditional minutes are a natural outgrowth of accepting a dictionary definition as a main purpose: "the official record made of proceedings at a meeting." Many tacitly assume that a perfect set of minutes would result from accurate transcription of a tape-recording of a meeting. So they do their inept best to approach such a transcription as nearly as possible. Most agree, though, when asked, that a complete, unorganized, unedited transcription would be a poor "official record of proceedings." And it would be. Yet a creative, imaginative, purposeful synthesis of ideas and actions *is* a useful, pertinent official record. Besides, it can be made accurate psychologically as well as factually.

Minutes Can Speed Committee Action

Business, industrial, and technical committee meetings make up a majority of all meetings for which minutes are written. Tens of thousands of such intracompany or association-sponsored groups form the mainstream of modern industrial and technological movement. At meetings of such committees official votes on formal motions are an occasional part of an occasional meeting. Most decisions are reached by a consensus; the group may have no formal voting procedures.

Many such meetings are adjourned as soon as a *feeling* of agreement is evident, long before any specific expression of the agreement is made. Unless chaired by a very skilled and ready summarizer, expression of the felt agreement is left to the minutes writer. So the way usually is open for minutes writing to serve ultimate group aims dynamically.

Left in a haze at the end of the meeting about what a committee wants done, the alert minutes writer will project what he thinks the committee probably wants to do. His synthesis will point toward solutions to committee problems, however far from specific solutions committee discussion ended. It will suggest lines along which the group thinking might have come to a point, had discussion not stopped short. When that isn't possible, the committee's differences can be expressed in focused form. Then the next meeting can start not where the last one stopped but where it *should* have stopped.

Good minutes, in short, can be made a dynamic part of any group's operating pattern.

If You Are a Minutes Writer ...

This report approach to writing minutes doesn't preclude the blow-by-blow account traditionally sought. If you are writing for a group which demands blow-by-blow recording, give it to them. But give them in addition your report of what happened at the meeting. Do regularly a good synthesis-type reporting job. Then the time may come when you can drop the chronological rehearsal of statements and acts. Some groups are slow to accept a new format; others reach for it. Faced with any question of acceptance, start by writing new report-type minutes, with old-type minutes appended. But never suggest or describe the new type in advance of producing a sample. Just write a set of minutes the new way. Then send it out to tell its own story.

Report-type minutes will win their way with most groups, as they did one time with four out of five committees of a national trade association. A newly assigned staff man became secretary of the five committees. He abandoned the recording-secretary type of minutes at once. Immediately he began to write reports instead of minutes. He saved hours of reading effort for the committee-men—and for himself as the minutes writer.

Two of the committees noticed the change promptly and praised him for it. Two accepted the change without comment. Two of twenty members of the remaining committee objected—following the third meeting at which report-type minutes were read. Both objectors admitted the accuracy of the summary—which reported action they had opposed. But they objected that their viewpoints, expressed in lengthy discussion, were not detailed in the minutes.

Opportunities for Committee Secretaries

Most secretaries are more capable of writing useful, creative minutes than of successfully substituting for a tape recorder. Some

80 per cent of all minutes writers are knowledgeable members of the group whose meetings they cover. They are working members of the committee or board they serve, or they are paid members of a headquarters staff of a trade association or professional society. They are employed because they can serve member committees as well as write useful, creative minutes.

In a minority are secretaries chosen for their greater ability to record words than to work with ideas. Most secretaries, in short, are competent to interpret as well as record, to summarize as well as parrot words. Such a knowledgeable secretary is competent to focus for agreement the varied, and often tangential, ideas expressed at committee meetings.

This synthesis of loosely expressed ideas and related information is the hallmark of useful, creative minutes. It is absent from traditionally written minutes—except to the extent that it is expressed in formally passed motions. The secretary who sees synthesis as the true purpose of minutes changes his task from a chore to a service.

Change Your Chores to Services

When you write minutes—and you will sooner or later—see them as a service, not as the chore your predecessor did. See minutes writing as a prime chance to play a more important role in shaping the group's course. Try to bring into focus for agreement whatever varied ideas and information came out at the meeting. Use your knowledge of the subject matter to express a consensus in terms that are clear, specific, and integrated. It doesn't matter that the meeting failed to perform this essential task. Nine times out of ten, you will be expressing exactly what each committeeman wanted to say but couldn't. Each will approve your minutes, murmuring to himself: "Yes, that's just what I meant. . . ." The tenth time, when one demurs, prompt correction of your minutes will achieve the necessary synthesis accurately.

Write Reports, Not Minutes, of Meetings

To achieve useful, maximum-value minutes, start by saying to yourself: "At this meeting, I must prepare myself to report to committee members who aren't present. I'll want to tell them (1) the actions taken, (2) the agreements reached, (3) the plans projected, and (4) enough of the reasoning leading up to the actions, agreements, and plans for them to understand, as well as know, the facts."

Use any note-taking techniques comfortable for you. Your familiarity with the group's purpose and personnel will determine how many and what kind of notes you need. The written material available at the meeting will also be an influence. (Some organizations prepare very complete agenda. Agenda may include proposed motions upon which action is expected, names of proposed appointees to subcommittees, specifically proposed programs for months or years ahead, and so forth.) Find out what is going to be available. Then plan your note-taking accordingly. The less your note-taking chore, the better your chance to participate in the discussion yourself.

In reporting a meeting (in writing minutes, that is), specific actions taken are the best things to start with. They constitute the officially completed business, as at a meeting of a company committee charged with selecting a site for a new branch factory. It was voted to:

1. Narrow selection of a possible site to Calpine, California; Liberty, Montana; and Hidalgo, New Mexico

2. Refine the scale of values for the criteria of selection before applying it again to the three towns still under consideration

3. Report to the company executive committee that a final recommendation can be expected in not less than thirty and not more than forty-five days

Significant action leading up to the actions may be summarized in the immediately following paragraphs. The secretary of this site-selection committee decided the following was worth including:

> Calpine, Liberty, and Hidalgo are the only three of the twenty-four towns investigated to score more than 85 on the criteria rating scale, developed at the start of the site search. (The scale gives weighted values to such items as tax outlook, labor availability, local wage levels, tax concessions, land values, etc.)
>
> Wide variations in tax concessions offered make the committee feel this factor, at least, should be reevaluated. Experience to date

indicates that several other factors also perhaps should be re-evaluated.

The committee is currently engaged in detailed discussion with officials of the three towns about water supply, drainage facilities, and road access to the proposed sites. Also firm tax-concession offers have been made by only two of the three "finalists." The committee believes it wise to complete these discussions in an unhurried atmosphere.

Next in such a meeting report might well come the secretary's summary of other developments of the meeting—points of view agreed upon or disagreed about, suggestions for possible future actions, subjects mentioned but not discussed, etc. In the site-committee instance appeared:

> Following Chairman Gassor's report of talks with executives of other companies with branch factories in Calpine, Liberty, and Hidalgo, the committee believes none of these sites suitable for our proposed expansion of research facilities. Members are inclined to feel that:
> - Separate search for a new research facility site should be undertaken
> - Data gathered in the factory-site search should be restudied by the committee named to do the research-site investigation at the start of their work.

The decided-upon date for the next meeting might properly complete this site-selection committee report (minutes). Then if the entire report were summarized in a beginning sentence which read:

> Three specific actions were taken, and two proposals for future action were made, at the September 19 meeting of the site-selection committee.

the entire report would be integrated. This illustrates in its simplest form report-type minutes as opposed to traditionally written minutes.

Dynamic Potentials Are Great

But this simple illustration doesn't reveal the dynamic potentials of report-type minutes. It doesn't make evident why such minutes are increasingly being written to help groups achieve their purposes faster and with less effort.

Report-type minutes can be an important dynamic of movement for groups dealing regularly with complex matters. They can suggest agenda for following meetings as well as ensure common understanding of decisions and proposals. A single-purpose committee—which is a common type—can benefit particularly from the guiding force of report-type minutes. Maximum benefit accrues when such a committee's single purpose is not specifically defined—as is often the case.

For any standing committee or board, report-type minutes guide best when they infer topics suitable for the next meeting's agenda. So written, they provide continuity for the group's thinking and are a moving focus for its actions.

Report-type minutes now perform this function regularly for the board of directors of a small nonprofit organization. The organization is engaged in cooperative, noncompetitive research. Its directors deal largely with fiscal matters, approval of proposed programs, and intraorganizational and interorganizational relationships. They rely heavily on recommendations of the managing director, who heads a paid staff serving the nonpaid working committee.

Typical of minutes once traditional with this board is the set reproduced in Exhibit 13.

EXHIBIT 13   *A set of minutes as traditionally written*

ASSOCIATION FOR TURBINE RESEARCH, INC.

MINUTES OF MEETING OF BOARD OF DIRECTORS, MAY 14, 19–

Present	*Absent*
Abbott Johns, chairman	Bertha Comiski
B. D. Ashely	Livingston Fernall
Harry F. Clarke	Abraham Rosenfeld
W. K. Graham	
Arthur Greenbaum	
Wakeland Harvey	
Peter L. O'Brien	
F. J. Wolfe	
King Hillyer, managing director	

Call to Order

A board of directors meeting of the Association for Turbine Research, Inc., was held at the offices of the association at 9967 Nosidam Avenue, Hiram, Illinois, on Wednesday, May 14, at 3:30 P.M., with chairman Abbott Johns presiding.

Minutes of Last Meeting

The minutes of the directors' meeting held on February 19, 1962, were read by the secretary and approved.

Report of Treasurer

The treasurer's report, attached herewith, was approved as read by treasurer Wakeland Harvey. Mr. Harvey stated that it would be advisable for the board to give serious thought to means of raising additional funds.

Welcome to New Board Members

The chairman welcomed F. J. Wolfe and Peter L. O'Brien, new members of the board.

Report of Executive Director

King Hillyer, managing director, reported on activities of the AWR which have been assumed by the staff in addition to the regular office activities. In 1961–1962, Mr. Hillyer spoke at, or gave the keynote speech for, research conferences at three university research centers and at four regional conferences of the Turbine Manufacturers Association. On each of these occasions he emphasized the importance of continuing research to industry progress and used recent ATR developments to illustrate current possibilities. Mr. Hillyer made two requests: (1) that a permanent Nominating Committee be appointed whose function would be to search out continuously new prospects for the board of directors and (2) that a Tenth Anniversary Committee be appointed to consider plans for a celebration in 1964. The board approved both these suggestions, and requested that the chairman appoint the above committees.

Report on Projects

Mr. Hillyer reported proposals for new projects as follows:
1. From the Lubricants Committee: a study to determine the effect of new heavy-duty detergent oils on turbine wear in space

vehicles. (Mr. Ashely said he thought too much reliance is being placed on heavy-duty detergents.)

2. From the Manufacturing Processes Committee: a study to determine probable effects of increased automation on inspection costs and methods.

The board approved both requests.

Election of Officers

Arthur Greenbaum read the following nominations for officers:

Abbott Johns, chairman

Wakeland Harvey, vice-chairman

Peter L. O'Brien, treasurer

B. D. Ashely, secretary

There were no other nominations. The above officers were elected upon motion made, seconded, and carried.

Adjournment

The meeting adjourned at 5 P.M.

Respectfully submitted,

Arthur Greenbaum

Secretary

Like the mule, these minutes display neither pride of ancestry nor hope of posterity. They record a series of seemingly unrelated events. They point up no relation with events of a previous meeting or with each other. Also, they give no noticeable indication of possible relation to events of the next meeting.

Rewritten by the board chairman as an example of the better values of report-type minutes, this set of minutes read as shown in Exhibit 14.

EXHIBIT 14   *Report-type minutes permit the reader to get the same information in one-third the time it takes to read traditionally written minutes, or to get twice as much information in the same time.*

ASSOCIATION FOR TURBINE RESEARCH, INC.

MINUTES OF MEETING OF BOARD OF DIRECTORS, MAY 14, 19–

MEETING at association headquarters on May 14, 1962, the board of directors of the Association for Turbine Research, Inc., took the following actions:

- Set up a permanent Nominating Committee to search continuously for suitable nominees for the ATR board of directors
- Established a Tenth Anniversary Committee to develop and recommend plans for celebration in 1964 of ATR's tenth anniversary
- Approved undertaking of two new researches by ATR committees: one by the Lubricants Committee and one by the Manufacturing Processes Committee
- Approved the treasurer's report—which shows income ahead of expenditures for the last seven months
- Elected officers

The permanent Nominating Committee stems from managing director Hillyer's comment that: "The kind of executive needed to direct a cooperative organization like ATR almost always feels he's too busy. But ATR can't afford to select directors on the basis of the fact that they have time on their hands. We should constantly be on the lookout for executives who—even though busy—can be stimulated to enough interest in our work to overcome hesitancy about serving."

The Tenth Anniversary Committee, also suggested by managing director Hillyer, will need the two years available to make and implement suitable plans. ATR started eight years ago with seven companies as members and a first-year budget of $30,000. Now, eight years later, it has twenty members, who provide nearly $100,000 a year to carry out their cooperative projects through ATR.

The two new programs approved are (1) for the Lubricants Committee —to determine the effect of new heavy-duty detergent oils on turbine wear in space vehicles—and (2) for the Manufacturing Processes Committee—to determine the probable effects of increased automation on inspection methods and costs.

Presenting his treasurer's report, treasurer Harvey noted that, previously, ATR income had never exceeded expenditures for more than six consecutive months.

The officers elected were those nominated by the Nominating Committee, as follows:

Abbott Johns, chairman
Wakeland Harvey, vice-chairman
Peter L. O'Brien, treasurer
B. D. Ashely, secretary

Managing director Hillyer reported that he had spoken at research conferences at Harvard, Wisconsin, Texas A. & M., and the University of

Illinois and also at two regional Turbine Manufacturers Association conferences.

At the universities, he showed how successful ATR committee techniques might be adapted to overcome difficulties met by research teams in other fields. At the TMA conferences, he emphasized the importance of continuing research to industry progress. Then he used ATR developments to illustrate current possibilities.

Arthur Greenbaum,
Secretary

Present	*Absent*
Abbott Johns, chairman	Bertha Comiski
B. D. Ashely	Livingston Fernall
Harry F. Clarke	Abraham Rosenfeld
W. K. Graham	
Arthur Greenbaum	
Wakeland Harvey	
Peter L. O'Brien	
F. J. Wolfe	
King Hillyer, managing director	

Note that this conversion to report-type minutes gives all essential information in easy-to-read, summarizing sentences—right at the start. A committeeman gets all he really needs to know in the opening tabulation. For the same information he must wade through the entire traditionally written minutes (Exhibit 13) and sort out for himself the significant from the nonsignificant.

Should he be attracted, however, to read further into the report-type minutes, he would be rewarded by *related, additional* information on each essential item. Should he finish them, he would learn what managing director Hillyer said when he spoke for ATR, not merely that he did speak.

The committeeman reading the new type of minutes has a choice; he can get the same information (as in the old-style minutes) in one-third the time or acquire twice as much information in the same time.

Exhibit 15 is also a good example of report-type minutes, though the format differs from that of the Exhibit 14 example. The information-from-minutes needs of the Exhibit 15 committee are typical of those of thousands of committees in hundreds of nonprofit organizations. This committee meets three to six times a year. It functions usually by a consensus of committee-member views and only occasionally takes formal votes. Few meetings are attended by every committee member. Absentees must rely on the minutes to keep up to date on the significance, as well as the fact, of what's going on.

EXHIBIT 15   *A good example of report-type minutes of a meeting of a technical-society committee. The committee functioning is similar to that of most committees in nonprofit organizations.*

MINUTES OF
PUBLICATION POLICY COMMITTEE MEETING,
NOVEMBER 21

I. NEW HANDBOOK "TEARSHEET" PUBLICATION SERVICE ENDORSED

The practice of printing a low-cost, advanced "tearsheet" of specific new or newly revised ground vehicle reports was endorsed by the PPC. These tearsheets are produced for approved reports in a format similar to a Handbook page and are intended as a preprint service when:

1. There is a widespread need
2. The time of report approval to Handbook publication is long enough to warrant interim publication

The service is only for single reports scheduled for future publication in the Handbook. They are identified only by their "J" numbers and will be checklisted immediately after "Handbook Supplements" as "Technical Report Preprints."

The need for a specific report in "preprint" form will be determined jointly by the responsible committee and staff.

"Handbook Supplements" will be continued for groups of reports, or reports not intended for Handbook publication.

II. DUPLICATION OF PUBLISHED MATERIAL DISCUSSED

Some "apparent" duplication of publications of other societies or groups was endorsed when this duplication meets the society's objectives. Although no firm line can be drawn on when duplication is justified, the following specific situations were felt by the PPC to be cases when duplication would be warranted:

1. When the society wishes to document a technical position that is somewhat different from other groups' standards
2. When speed or timeliness of revisions is important and can be better handled by the society's procedures
3. When the society initiative is an important factor in shaping a broader standards picture
4. When the "duplicated" material is an essential part of the work of a committee and the continuity of reports would be broken with it.

One technique recommended is that the appropriate society committee undertake the maintenance of the "duplicate" and be responsible for society revisions to it. An example is the Screw Threads reports. With this technique, the flexibility of expressing the society's position and timeliness of revisions are under direct society committee control.

III. HANDBOOK ILLUSTRATIONS SUBCOMMITTEE

Appendix II is the report on recent progress of the Handbook Illustrations Subcommittee, submitted by its chairman, D. Hoover.

IV. HENRY NEMUR RETIRES

A full and happy future was the heartfelt wish for Henry Nemur in his coming retirement. He plans to spend most of the year in Florida and the summer months at his lake cottage near Chicago.

V. ATTENDANCE

T. P. Bridge, chairman	Arthur Jaeger
N. K. Hutter	S. L. Daiger
F. R. Muir	Willis Oeder, secretary
	11/26

Use by Single-purpose Committees

Applied to a single-purpose task-force committee, report-type minutes can perform even more dynamic and creative functions. A good example was their use with a committee of ten top executives of the big Highland Tractor Corporation.

Highland directors had asked this group to study the entire organizational setup of the corporation. Then the group was instructed to recommend changes in the corporate structure and operating methods to fit the corporation to function best "in the era of exploding technology which lies ahead."

The board chairman (who was *not* an operating official) was named chairman of this progress-planning committee. A management consultant, hired to help the committee assemble and discuss data, was named secretary. Responsible for writing and circulating minutes promptly, he was told to work for the corporation, not for any individual.

Here was presented a not untypical situation. To the committee secretary would devolve most of the actual work of the committee. He was being paid to do just that. (All the operating executives were being paid chiefly for other responsibilities. The board chairman, though knowledgeable, no longer had any specific responsibility, except to preside at board meetings.)

The consultant-secretary saw that translation of the committee's general purpose into what-to-do terms must be a first step. So he jotted down before the committee's first meeting *his* idea of how the committee might proceed. At the meeting, he listened and made notes for nearly two hours.

The chairman had begun by suggesting that the committee discuss the best way to proceed. Each executive made some comment. Most suggestions were good, specific examples of the sort of thing the committee might get into. None of them was a suitable launching pad for the committee's activity as a whole. None was a statement of specific, immediate objectives.

At this point, the secretary-consultant interjected: "It seems to me everyone is thinking in about the same terms as to how this committee might best function. Almost all the various ideas expressed seem to me to point in the same direction. Aren't you all, gentlemen, saying in effect that this committee feels its investigation should cover five or six areas—and begin by developing a combination historical and current-status report on each? In other words, that we should break the problem into fiscal, administrative, product development, marketing, and manufacturing—and start by taking a look at where we've been and where we are?"

By this time, it was 4:35 P.M.—and at least half the group were commuters.

The secretary-consultant's rough summarizing had expressed accurately what the positive-minded committeemen had indicated in their comments. And it gave the less-certain-of-themselves members something quite satisfactory to claim they had in mind. So most of the group nodded agreement; no one voiced disagreement. The executive vice-president said: "Well, I've got to get back to my desk for a few minutes before quitting time." And the chairman said: "Yes, I think we'd better call it a day. Can we get together again at this same time next week? OK then, next Friday at 2 P.M."

Then is when this secretary-consultant decided to make his minutes writing a constructive force in moving the committee to its stated ends. He couldn't direct the committee's actions. But he could synthesize its members' thinking. He could focus significant, rambling comment into statements which could be followed as directives. "If I don't do this," he said to himself, "this group may take months deciding what—as a group—it can and should do."

So the secretary-consultant started immediately to make his minutes a constructive, useful committee tool. The minutes reporting this first meeting of the progress-planning committee read:

> Following full discussion of possible procedures, committee members agreed that:
>
> 1. The committee will aim to suggest "needed changes in the corporation's structure and operating methods" in six categories:
> - Corporation-as-a-whole
> - Fiscal
> - Administrative
> - Product development
> - Marketing
> - Manufacturing
>
> 2. As a basis for consideration of changes, the committee will need an interpretative, factual report on the history and current status of activities and methods in each of these to-be-studied areas.
>
> The secretary interprets this sense of the meeting to favor a start on the first of the studies as promptly as possible. Consequently, he will aim to have at least preliminary material available on the corporation-as-a-whole within two weeks.

Subsequent to adjournment, chairman Quinque set the next meeting for Friday, October 19, instead of for Friday, October 12, as he had indicated at the meeting proper. The change is to permit preliminary material on the corporation-as-a-whole report to be in committee members' hands for study prior to the next meeting.

And so it went through two years of progress-planning committee meetings.

As in the first meeting, minutes "reported" the focused essence of one rambling discussion after another. The minutes became modified interoffice memoranda, as in the first meeting, whenever modification helped toward committee ends. Always they contained the seeds (usually the buds) of the next meeting's agenda —as in the first minutes. Always they were in committeemen's hands within forty-eight hours. In this vital corporate activity, committee minutes provided continuity of purpose, consistency of movement, and focus of thinking.

Had these minutes not furnished a common dynamic for the committee membership, the job might never have been finished. Said the board chairman following implementation of the committee's thirty-eight specific recommendations: "I think I can take major credit for bringing the committee's thinking together in terms of practical and specific needs for change. But I never could have kept it together without having our consensus expressed clearly and specifically in writing—step by step. Everybody had to know at all times *exactly* what everyone else knew, and the minutes turned out to be a perfect medium for that purpose."

Any secretary who sees minutes writing as an opportunity— not a chore—can multiply his usefulness to the group he serves. The size of his achievement will vary directly with the character of his motivation. If he thinks minutes a dirty job, his satisfactions will be those of "good old Joe." ("Everyone can count on Joe, when others refuse the dirty jobs.") Thinking himself a helmsman and his minutes a rudder, his satisfactions will be those of a creative participant in group achievement. As always in communications writing, motives are more important than methods; sincerity, than systems.

Deliver Minutes Promptly

Prompt delivery of minutes is vital to their maximum usefulness. Their capacity for guiding, pointing up action, and ensuring common understanding is depleted by tardy availability. They must arrive in time to be fully effective. Speed makes sure a swordsman's thrust and a boxer's blow. And it multiplies the impact of creative minutes on group accomplishment.

Creative, report-type minutes are written to be read—like any other kind of purposeful communication. And, other things being equal, they will be read. So it is worth the effort to get them out promptly. (Traditionally written minutes are rarely read except by those who must—usually to protect a legal, economic, political, or personal position. Eight times out of ten, they are filed without reading.)

Prompt delivery of useful minutes has these advantages:

1. The reader—tipped off as to likely topics for the next meeting and made clear about results of the last—may be stimulated to more thinking in advance about committee problems. (Nothing else helps more to move committees toward their final goals—faster.)

2. The reader gets a good feeling about the "tempo" of the committee on which he is serving. Prompt delivery of minutes seems to foretell live thinking and prompt action.

3. The reader—to whose livelihood reading minutes is rarely important—is more likely to read minutes of a meeting still fresh in his mind. They are easier to discard when they arrive weeks or months later.

4. The reader has an ample chance to suggest corrections and have them promptly distributed. (The faster a mistake is corrected, the better.)

5. The minutes are better written—because the writer's notes are fresher in his mind. He more readily remembers what he can't decipher.

6. The writer's mind is freed promptly for concentration on tasks directly important to his livelihood.

Format for Report-type Minutes

To increase readability, one successful writer of minutes makes them look as little like minutes as possible. Traditionally written minutes, he feels, are presented traditionally in a format as dull as the style in which they are written. So usual is this combination, that traditional-looking minutes tend to repel reading.

The suggestions for increasing interoffice memoranda readability (Chapter 14, pp. 169–72) will also help to get minutes read. Plenty of white space, free use of tabulations and indentions and plenty of paragraphs are specially helpful to minutes. They are so often absent from this communication form.

Are Minutes News?

A few radical practitioners of the art of writing readable minutes regularly top them with headlines. They confine necessary identifying information to a brief notation at the top left- or right-hand corner of the opening page. They relegate necessary listings of committee members to the right- or left-hand corner of the last page. (Where the list is long and space-filling, they attach it as a separate *last* sheet.)

To all except those with editorial training, headlining minutes may seem to be going a little too far. And perhaps it is, although it does achieve its purpose when the headlines are good.

But report-type minutes in general do penetrate readers' minds by the same means a newspaper item does. They tell in the first paragraph the main points of the entire communication. Then they go on to explain, prove, or amplify those main points—in the order of original mention.

Such minutes, like news stories, have a good chance of interesting a reader. Besides, they give him a maximum amount of information for a minimum of effort.

17

Writing Invitations to Action

HAVE YOU EVER had to invite a speaker to address a group? Or a person to become a member of a committee? Or an officer to serve an organization? If you haven't, you will. If you belong to any business, professional, civic, religious, political, or social organization, your turn will come.

Unless you are unusual, you will regard this responsibility as a chore. Your first thought will be: "Whom can I get to accept?" As soon as he has said "yes," you will reason, your obligation will have been fulfilled. "I can forget about it," you'll say, "and get back to my regular business."

Yet an assignment to invite is actually an opportunity to serve your organization mightily.

Handled as a chore, getting acceptance may concern you most. When it does, you may or may not produce an effective speaker, committee member, or official. You may furnish merely a name for a program, a committee listing, or a publicity release. Only by chance will you provide information or inspiration for those attending the meeting, an active participant in the work of a committee, or a forceful, imaginative approach to an administrative job.

Your assignment to invite may be from the Knights of Pythagoras, the Society of Scientists, the Buggywhip Manufacturers Association, or the Ladies' Sewing Circle. It may be from any of the other tens of thousands of national, regional, or local organizations in the United States. In any case, your responsibility is to get someone to do something that will be beneficial to the organization you represent.

Getting acceptance to an invitation, therefore, isn't your main objective. It is the method by which you accomplish your objective.

Your responsibility is to get a speaker to say something your organization members will think is worth listening to, to get a committee member who will do what the committee expects of him—and perhaps provide some leadership besides—or to enlist officers who will serve the organization and not just hold office. If you are unready to see your assignment as an opportunity, do your organization a favor and turn it down. If you do see the opportunity, you will often have to force needed clarification of purpose from the assigning group.

A Familiar Dialogue

The looseness with which assignments to invite are tossed off in most nonprofit organizations is little short of frightening. It accounts for the paucity of perfect fits between speakers and audiences and between committee members and committee achievement requirements. It accounts also for the frequency with which officers do not perfectly match the needs of the offices they fill.

If you are one of the millions of Americans who participate actively in any organization—large or small, national or local—the following exchange, ending a program-committee meeting, may sound familiar:

CHAIRMAN: OK, then. We're agreed we should ask Alvin Shepard to talk at our June meeting and that, if we can't get him, we'll try next for Oscar Hammond, and then for Henry Kephardt. Now, who will take on inviting Shepard? (I have to be out of town for the next couple of weeks.) How about you, Joe? Will you do it? You haven't had this job since last year sometime.

JOE: Well . . . yes. I guess I can fit it in. By the way, what do we want

Shepard to talk about—or shall we just ask him to pick his own subject?

CHAIRMAN (after looking inquiringly around the table for suggestions and hearing only silence): Yes, that's best. Let him pick his own subject. I heard him talk over at the State Capitol to the Manufacturers Association last year. He's really good. He'll keep 'em awake all right, no matter what the subject is. And that's the main thing.

JOE: OK, then. That's how I'll handle it . . . and the same way, too, I guess, with the others in case we don't get Shepard—which we probably won't.

All too often getting a speaker is approached with this sort of nonchalance. To fill a spot on a program is its only discernible purpose. Joe will have to provide the necessary focus, or the meeting's success will be left to chance.

Exposition and Persuasion Are Involved

Both exposition and persuasion are involved in a successful invitation. Exposition makes clear to the recipient what is expected of him. Persuasion aims to get him to say "yes."

Since clear exposition is the best of persuaders, what is expected of the man invited must be in sharp focus *before* the letter is started. The best first step: Write down—in one sentence if possible—what the organization expects of the recipient, should he accept. This single sentence should state what a speaker is expected to talk about—the information or message the organization hopes he will bring. It should specify in brief detail what would be required of a committeeman. It should indicate the problems and aims of the office in which a nominee is being invited to serve.

This sentence written, you are ready to begin composing the letter. Its opening paragraph or paragraphs may well contain the ideas of that single sentence.

The exposition in the letter will express the organization's desires and point of view—*in terms of the recipient's interests.* The persuasive elements will take the "you" viewpoint entirely. They will appeal directly to the individual desires of the person invited.

The exposition will include:

- What is expected of the recipient in case he accepts
- What his speech or service is expected to accomplish
- When, where, and for how long he is expected to perform or serve
- How the organization will be served by the acceptance
- The character and size of the audience, committee, committee contacts, or organization to be served

Persuasion will involve suggestion of how the recipient might benefit from acceptance. It will imply—not state—that acceptance might bring honor, prestige, money, a chance to meet friends, an opportunity to serve others, or emotional satisfactions.

So, charged with inviting a speaker, Joe has a major opportunity to further his organization's interests. Well thought out in advance and deftly presented, his invitation will communicate feelings as well as facts. It will make acceptance seem like an opportunity. It will be a personal communication—not exactly what would be written to anyone else for any other purpose. It will radiate warmth as well as cast light. It will make the proposed assignment something to be looked forward to with pleasure.

Inviting a Speaker

Inviting a speaker gives perhaps a chance for broader results than any other letter of invitation. A letter inviting a speaker should be recognized as a form of written communication requiring great skill.

It will seek an acceptance. But it will also constitute a clear "assignment." It will let the recipient know what is expected of him if he says "yes." Tacitly, it will envision a "no," if he is unwilling or unable to fulfill the assignment.

In writing such a letter, you will be neither apologetic nor overly prideful. Actually, you should feel that you are offering your prospective speaker both a challenge and a responsibility. The challenge is to evaluate himself: "Do I know at least a little bit more than most members of this organization about the subject on which they want me to talk?"

The responsibility is to say "no" to the invitation unless "yes" is the answer to the challenge question.

Your task, of course, is to convey these important truths in your letter, without ever mentioning them . . . and that's not nearly as impossible as it sounds.

But it *is* impossible unless you yourself:

1. Know in your heart that you really are offering an opportunity and something of an honor in extending the invitation

2. Know you are after information and ideas for your fellow members who will attend the meeting. Know that you are not just after a name for a program or a body for a rostrum

3. Actually hope the answer will be "no" unless your proposed guest has something worth saying—and will do the preliminary work necessary to enable him to say it well

Writing from these premises, five aids to your speaker incorporated in your letter will help to get the right man to accept:

1. Make sure he knows he is being invited to say something to an audience of a given size and stature. Tell him how many you expect at the meeting. Include a few words about their interests and backgrounds. Be specific and conservative about both. (Exhibit 16 shows a sample letter inviting a speaker for a big meeting; Exhibit 17, a letter inviting a speaker for a very small meeting.)

2. Give him some idea of how you happen to have picked him. (Tell why what he knows will benefit your organization at just this time. Name a prominent or distinguished member of your organization as having suggested that he be asked. Mention perhaps some person or group who might be meaningful socially or commercially to the man invited.) But be specific in giving reasons for having chosen him. Be specific—or forget it entirely. Generalities will actually hurt because they sound as though there aren't any specific reasons.

3. Make sure you reflect some warmth and welcome from whatever number of people you think will be at the meeting. (Tell him specifically of some friend or distinguished member of your organization who would especially like to see him or who will be in the audience. But don't say this, of course, unless you have made sure in advance that it will be true.)

4. Tell him as specifically as possible what you want him to say;

don't just mention a general subject you want him to talk about. ("How Abex Company uses computers to speed gear-tooth design"—*not* "Something on computers" or "Something on gear teeth." "What new high school curricula have done to teen-age study habits"—*not* "Teen-age study habits.")

5. Never, never, never invite him to speak on "whatever you would like to talk about." (If *you* don't care what kind of garbage is foisted on your fellow organization members, why should he?)

Don't sit down to write your letter of invitation to a speaker until you have prepared yourself to carry out some or all of these suggestions effectively.

When you do write it (or dictate it), have the first draft triple spaced. Then, taking pencil in hand, edit into that draft all the changes needed—before you do the whole thing over again!

Taking pains with letters of invitation to speakers will bring you at least three rewarding results:

More refusals from speakers your organization members will be glad they didn't have to hear.

More acceptances from hard-to-get but easy-to-profit-from speakers your organization members will enjoy.

An increased ability on your part to get people you respect to do things for you and yours. There will be a bonus, too: an increased ability to do the clear writing for easy reading for which associates will bless you.

EXHIBIT 16   *Invitation from a large organization to speak at a big meeting. It invites a prominent official to say something specific—to an audience of size and stature.*

Hon. Wm. Xerxes
Secretary of the Exterior
Washington, D.C.

Dear Mr. Secretary:

The Industry Association of America invites you to be the principal speaker at its 1969 annual dinner in Houston next January 12.

The 2,000 industrialists attending this dinner are eager to learn the probable effects on other-than-petroleum companies of the proposed changes in oil allowance regulations. Will there be widespread effects, or do the changes affect chiefly intrapetroleum industry problems?

President H. O. Mitten, of the U.S. Turbine Corporation, who will be toastmaster, looks forward with real pleasure to the honor of introducing you on this occasion.

May we hope you can fit this opportunity into what I know is a very busy schedule?

Sincerely,

President
Industry Association of America

EXHIBIT 17   *Invitation from a small local organization to speak at a small meeting. Inviting a specialist to speak to a lay audience, it suggests specific audience interests.*

R. K. Loesser

Dear Mr. Loesser:

The Hamton Businessmen's Club invites you to be guest speaker at its monthly luncheon meeting on November 15.

News accounts of your work in powdered metallurgy have made our membership of retailers curious about its possible relation to the variety of consumer products sold across their counters. What impact—if any —will perfecting of powdered metallurgy techniques have on stores in a little town like Hamton? Will we be handling products that cost less but perform better? If so, what products, and why and when?

Almost all the fifty members of the HBC will attend the November 15 meeting, I am sure, if you can fit this meeting into your schedule. Among them, you can count on chatting with Harold Ickes and John Brown, who report having greatly enjoyed serving under your chairmanship in last year's Red Feather campaign.

We're hoping you can be with us.

Sincerely,

Chairman, November Luncheon Committee
Hamton Businessmen's Club

Inviting a Committee Member

Writing an invitation to serve on a committee involves the same opportunities and the same pitfalls as writing invitations to speakers. The aim is to inspire interest in the committee's work and to make the recipient eager to participate.

It should start with the invitation to serve on the committee. That's the main question you want the recipient to consider and respond to. It is the subject of the letter. Nothing else you may say connects with anything for the reader until he knows this. So you start with the invitation, as the example in Exhibit 18 does.

Next—in this invitation to foreign members to serve as liaison committee members for a United States engineering society—comes the specific statement of the committee objectives. This is expressed in terms of their possible significance to the recipient of the letter. It personalizes these general objectives.

Then follows an itemized statement of what will be expected of the recipient should he accept the invitation. Here again, these items are personalized in terms of potential action by the individual recipient.

The next-to-last paragraph (beginning "I am eager to man . . .") aims to position the recipient as one of a distinguished group. And the last paragraph asks for a "yes" or "no" response to the question: "Will you participate?"—*not* "Will you accept the invitation?"

Finally, the postscript alerts the recipient to an actual assignment about to be forthcoming if he answers "yes."

This letter, as a whole, invites its recipients to join a live, high-quality group of his fellow engineers—clear about their objectives and on the move toward useful accomplishments. It indicates that his participation as an individual will be sought, utilized, and recognized.

EXHIBIT 18　*Invitation to serve on a committee. It invites participation in the committee's work, not acceptance of membership.*

Dear Mr. Ellange:

This letter is to invite you to become a member of the SAE Overseas Information Committee.

In revitalizing the efforts of this committee, I am inviting to membership men likely to get personal satisfactions from:

• Assisting SAE Engineering Activity Board committees (as requested from time to time) to procure technical information from outside the United States and Canada for use in SAE meetings, literature, and committee information-development projects

• Advising the EAB and its committees (when requested from time to time) on potential engineering trends abroad

Here are some paths your participation might take:

1. An Engineering Activity Board committee (responsible for programming of SAE national meeting sessions) might ask you to check on the desirability and/or possibility of getting a paper on a particular subject from one of your countrymen. Responding, you would give us your best opinion (following such investigation as you think needed) concerning both the desirability and the possibility. (Official invitations to prepare papers would come from the Engineering Activity Board committee itself.)

2. Then you might be asked to report periodically on engineering topics or trends in your country. The reports would help our activity committees better to set up programs and might occasionally be found suitable for summarizing for publication.

3. Also, you might help your local engineering societies by serving as a technical-information-exchange liaison with SAE. If they want speakers from the United States, SAE would be glad to suggest ways in which they might be procured. SAE would be glad also to try to suggest names of potential authors and so forth.

I am eager to man this reorganized Overseas Information Committee with distinguished engineers in every part of the world.

Will you participate with us?

Sincerely,

Chairman
Overseas Information Committee

P.S. You may first be asked to help in connection with one of the eighty sessions scheduled for the 1965 SAE International Automotive Engineering Congress and Exposition in Detroit next January.

How Not to Write It

Compare the Exhibit 18 letter with the Exhibit 19 letter—of which Exhibit 18 is a rewrite. (The committee chairman rewrote the Exhibit 19 draft, which had been prepared by a secretary.) Note as regards the Exhibit 19 letter:

• The actual invitation—the main point of the letter—is buried almost exactly in the middle, where the reader might forget about it before he finished, even if he had gotten far enough in the letter to find it in the first place.

- It is entirely impersonal. Every item is presented in terms of the committee's interests or viewpoint. The recipient is left to translate the facts and ideas into what they mean to him as an individual.

- It is at least one-third longer than the rewrite.

- It goes into great detail about the *congress*—which won't concern the recipient at all unless he accepts. The promotional details of the congress do nothing to answer his question: "If I do accept, what will I personally have to do in connection with this congress?"

- It closes with an almost peremptory command to the recipient to accept.

EXHIBIT 19 *You must read to paragraph 8 of this letter to discover that it is an invitation to membership on a committee. This is chief among several faults illustrated by this letter.*

Dear Mr. Ellange:

The desire to interchange automotive engineering information on a worldwide basis has been expressed by an ever-growing number of SAE members. The SAE Engineering Activity Board has requested its International Information Committee to:

1. Assist the committees of the Engineering Activity Board in the procurement of desired technical information from any sources outside the United States and Canada

2. Advise the Engineering Activity Board and its committees of any important engineering trends abroad

To accomplish these objectives, the International Information Committee believes that SAE members living outside the United States and Canada can make a significant contribution to their society by serving as overseas members of the committee. The overseas member will perform three functions:

1. When one of the Engineering Activity Board committees which does not enjoy excellent overseas contacts desires information on a specific topic, the "overseas members" will be requested to investigate the availability of such data and suggest possible organizations and authors who could contribute the desired information.

2. Overseas members will be requested to report periodically on engineering topics and trends of importance in their geographic areas so that the Engineering Activity Board committees will be kept abreast of the latest developments and thus be in a position to consider the inclusion of papers from abroad in their planning of future SAE technical sessions and publications.

3. Overseas members, through their contacts with engineering societies in their country, will indicate the information desired by these organizations which might be obtained from the United States. The International Information Committee will attempt to arrange for the presentation of desired information by American engineers who are traveling abroad.

It is with a great deal of pleasure that I invite you to serve as an overseas member of the SAE International Information Committee, and it is hoped that you will be in a position to participate in, and contribute to, this important effort.

The International Information Committee is now rendering assistance to the Engineering Activity Board committees in obtaining and coordinating the development of information for presentation at the 1965 SAE International Automotive Engineering Congress and Exposition. It is expected that the technical program at this event will include thirty-five to fifty papers from overseas sources. Several of the activity committees have already issued invitations and have received acceptances from overseas authors. In addition, SAE president Dyment has written to the presidents and/or secretaries of the twenty-five automobile and aerospace engineering societies on the attached list informing them of next January's international meeting, and he has transmitted the attached listing of topics on which the activity committees desire information. As offers are received they are being transmitted to the appropriate activity committee for consideration.

It is anticipated that the 1965 SAE International Automotive Engineering Congress and Exposition will include approximately eighty technical sessions at which 200 or more papers will be presented. Complementing the formal presentations will be the engineering display, which will undoubtedly include more than 175 exhibits of the latest hardware and manufacturing techniques of interest to automotive engineers. Overall attendance at the five-day congress and exposition is expected to approach 25,000 engineers, of whom from 750 to 1,000 will be from overseas. As the program planning progresses, it is planned that progress reports will be prepared and distributed to keep the committee members informed. Undoubtedly, it will be necessary to call on certain overseas members to assist in finalizing details regarding specific papers or to help overseas authors in the completion of their papers.

I shall be looking forward to your acceptance of this invitation.

Sincerely,

Chairman
Overseas Information Committee

Study of these two letters reveals clearly the results of application and nonapplication of the principles given at the beginning of this chapter. The Exhibit 18 letter is certain to bring as many— and probably more—acceptances as the Exhibit 19 letter. But more importantly, acceptances of the Exhibit 18 invitation are tacitly expressing some eagerness—not just willingness to participate. Men seeking only prestige from committee membership are likely to refuse an invitation which seems to say: "You're expected to *do something*—and here's what it is!"

Invitations from the Nominating Committee

Every year, with or without formal nominating committees, tens of thousands of people are being invited to serve as officers of business, professional, civic, religious, political, and social organizations. More often than not, the person who invites them makes an apologetic approach. ("Harry, you've been nominated for treasurer of the Lodge—and I'm calling to see if we can get you to accept.") Sometimes, the desire to get the offices filled is so great that alternatives are named to begin with—and pressure results for immediate acceptance from the first-asked. (One top-of-the-list nominee for the presidency of a large national organization remarked forty-eight hours after saying "no" to a telephone call from a nominating committee spokesman: "I'm beginning to wonder if I did the right thing in turning down this office. I'd really like to serve. I've been active in the organization for many years, and I think it's a great honor. But I was taken completely by surprise by this telephone call; I wasn't positive how our board chairman would feel about my taking it on, and since my caller seemed to want an immediate answer, I just felt 'no' was all I could say right that minute.")

For even minor offices in small organizations, a brief written invitation adds to the dignity of the transaction and the prestige of the office. For large organizations, where the elements of acceptance may be complex for the nominee, a written communication would seem to be almost a must. Telephone or personal contacts would then seem to be natural follow-ups.

EXHIBIT 20   *Invitation to serve as an officer of a small nonprofit group*

Mr. Murray Lawrence
1099 Fifth Avenue
Somewhere, Oklahoma

Dear Murray:
The Personnel Guidance Foundation wants you to serve as its treasurer next year.

As a PGF director, you have contributed often and importantly to our sound fiscal thought and action. That's why the Nominating Committee suggests you be placed in a position of leadership in this area.

May I look forward to working with you during my second term as PGF board chairman?

Sincerely,

Aldous Hendrick
Chairman, Board of Directors

The letter inviting a person to serve as an officer usually can be much briefer than the letter inviting a speaker or a committeeman. Its objectives and its techniques are exactly the same. But the recipient almost always knows all about the organization—its aims, methods, and achievements. So the communication inviting him to serve as an officer needs only to be clear, sincere, and brief. Exhibit 20 is a good example.

18

Writing
to Get a Job

WRITING IS CRUCIALLY involved in four necessary job-getting steps.

The best way to bring together your thoughts about the job you want is to put them in writing. You have to write down your qualifications for use in communicating with prospective employers. You had better write down a list of prospects and approach more than one at a time. Finally, you will write letters of application and letters seeking interviews; you will also write résumés, presentations, and follow-up letters.

Writing well done, in other words, is the best and cheapest tool with which to start carving out a career. It is especially useful in taking the four main steps to a new job—or even to a first job:

1. Decide on the job to look for.
2. Prepare your qualifications.
3. Find prospects.
4. Reach and convince your prospects.

Good communications writing helps greatly in taking each of these steps.

Writing down What You Want to Do

You can say: "I know the kind of job I want" when you can describe it for yourself in a sentence or two.

So start thinking: "Exactly what would I like to do?"—with a pencil in your hand and a scratch pad under it. Just trying to write down an answer slows up the mental merry-go-round that so many ride when they are trying to decide what to do.

Let your mind go toward what you'd most like to do. There's no reason to believe you'll do best in work you dislike. On the contrary, you are almost certain to make better progress doing what you enjoy. Begin at least by trying to define your likes in terms of specific, yet broad, vocational areas. (Forget your dislikes for the moment. You're looking for desirable work to do, not undesirable work to avoid.)

Let your mind wander awhile. Then, as a variety of ideas begin to take shape, try to relate them; order them into something like:

> *I'd like a statistical job*—the kind of statistical job that would give me a chance to study the relationship between figures and to try to understand and interpret their significance. (I like to work with figures in general, but I actually enjoy using them, rather than just compiling them accurately.)

or

> *I'd like a statistical job*—the kind where precise calculations have to be made and where accuracy is necessary and appreciated. I get great satisfaction from working out simple results from a complex of detailed data. Once I've got the answers or the balance or the simplified result, I'd like to let somebody else worry about what it means and how to apply it. I want another complex to dig into and another accurate answer to seek.

Here's the way two subsequently successful job seekers defined objectives for themselves before they took the last three job-getting steps:

> *I'd like a writing job*—the kind which requires that I dig up information, bring it into focus, and try to explain it or transmit it to others. Guess I'd like a teaching job, if I didn't have to teach people in person—if the teaching could be accomplished through writing.

> *I'd like to work with computers*, probably in programming—the kind of job where you have to analyze both data and ideas and look for logical solutions to specific problems. I like mathematical

work, but I majored in philosophy. I'd like a job where I could follow both bents. (An IBM executive tells me the most important quality for a programmer is "ability to solve problems logically.")

Once your general thinking has been channeled into some such written form, you are ready to identify jobs that have the desired characteristics. And you are ready to match the particular job needs to your own qualifications—as soon as you have written the qualifications down on paper, too. To do this, you will want to ask yourself some penetrating questions and to look into yourself as deeply as you can. Ask yourself questions like these:

• What is the most interesting thing I ever did?
• Of what accomplishments am I the proudest?
• What sort of thing do I do most easily?
• In previous jobs, what did my employers most appreciate about my work? Why?

Answer these questions conscientiously and without rationalization. The answers will help greatly to focus your thinking about where you belong in business, industry, or government service. They will point to characteristic personal qualities and to talents you apply easily and well.

Write these down ("accuracy," "ability to learn quickly," "determination," "imagination," "leadership," "resourcefulness," "stick-to-itiveness," "ability to get along well with people"—or whatever). Then match these qualities with the kind of work that interests you. If you are unfamiliar with what seems an interesting field, take time out to learn about it. Ask men and women in that field what qualifications are needed. (Most people will be glad to help, even if you walk in "cold" for information or advice. Introductions from friends or business associates may smooth the way further.)

Complete your self-analysis by listing your characteristics as factually as possible against characteristics needed for the jobs you have defined. If you lack a majority of qualities needed for a particular job, your future probably lies somewhere else.

Preparing Your Presentation

A basic presentation (in writing) of your qualifications is a sound basis from which to take off in job hunting. You need to know your product (yourself) and have sales literature available (your presentation) before you go out to sell. While job hunting, this basic presentation will serve you broadly and specifically:

1. It ensures organization of your own thinking about yourself as a product to be sold. It establishes the way you are going to think and talk about yourself. It provides a full well from which to draw answers to expected or unexpected questions. It gives you a pattern for oral presentations or interviews and examples for use in letters or résumés. It gives you firm ground from which to jump into your job-getting effort. Your mind is at ease because it is ordered. Having written your presentation, you are ready for any challenge job seeking may bring.

2. It can be left with a prospective employer after an interview or can be sent to him with a thank-you-for-the-interview note. Thus used, it can be a potent help. It will nail down the main points you have made in the interview and will give additional details and examples. Its very existence evidences an organized mind. (Submitted before, or used during, an interview, the presentation takes the prospect's mind off you as a person. It reduces his chance to get to know you and depletes the personal impact—which can be made *only* when talking person to person.)

Examples Are the Heart of a Presentation

Writing this basic presentation involves several steps.

First, make a complete record of your experience, aptitudes, likes and dislikes, hobbies, and articles or papers you have written—everything you can think of. Then put with that record specific examples of past actions or situations illustrating your possession of the various qualities you feel you have.

These examples in your presentation are the heart of your job-getting campaign. You are going to sell yourself by example. You are going to prove your abilities by specific examples. You aren't going to say: "I have imagination" or "I have initiative." You are going to cite an incident in which you exhibited imagination or initiative. (If you can't think of a single case where you did exhibit a particular quality, the chances are strong that you haven't got it.)

Here's one example from a presentation by a very young man,

seeking his first full-time job. It shows how this specific-example method can relate qualities to job requirements, even without previous business experience to draw upon. The young man was interested in a trainee job in a bank. One of his examples:

> When elected treasurer of my fraternity at the University of Michigan, I inherited an unbalanced budget. The unbalance was created by my fraternity brothers' willingness to spend their parents' money rather than practice self-discipline.
>
> To alleviate this situation, I first studied the fraternity's income and expense situation carefully. Then I got approved a budget revision—from which I had pared unnecessary or exorbitant expenditures for such things as cleaning materials, preservatives, light bulbs, and other sundries.
>
> Then I enlisted the support and assistance of the other officers to institute shortcuts and dollar-saving programs to cut heating, electrical, and telephone bills. Also, by my willingness to take over duties such as collection of past-due bills, we were able to get a new auditor at lower cost.
>
> Net result of this program was maintenance of our accustomed standard of living, along with the reduced costs. Charges to members were reduced as well.

The qualities indicated? Analytical ability and initiative certainly, and perhaps imagination, ability to get along with others, and leadership too—all qualities desirable for a trainee in a bank.

The application of this same method is shown in the next example—a publicity writer's presentation. He felt it necessary particularly to prove adaptability to varied assignments and varied personnel. One of five examples used in his presentation follows:

> At Quality Stores in Buffalo, I found employees unusually uninterested in management's problems and needs. The indifference was reflected in attitudes toward customers rather than in any actual friction with management.
>
> I decided that a better feeling might be developed if employees could better identify themselves as employees of this particular company. So I originated a news column for monthly publication in the company's internal house organ.
>
> I interviewed salesclerks, buyers, packers, and executives to get the personal and other news items for this column.

Gradually, as everybody learned more about everybody else, the feeling between employees and management seemed to improve.

A year or two later, when the company had financial reverses, the employees offered to take a temporary salary cut.

Many have military experiences that can be shaped to help in presentations to get civilian jobs. Here is the story of one such experience. Sandwiched between civilian examples, it helped a thirty-one-year-old captain to a better supervisory job than he had before enlistment:

> At Fort Texas, I was given the job of revamping the Entertainment Branch. It had not been producing results on a par with other posts in the Fourth Army area.
>
> I started by examining in detail every aspect of the operation and of the branch's program, personnel, and finances. Also, I looked carefully into the handling of government contracts for civilian service and entertainers. This study revealed opportunity for many specific improvements.
>
> To achieve these improvements, I:
>   • Rerouted document flow relating to government contracts and pay vouchers
>   • Instigated a search of major command files for specially qualified personnel
>   • Revised and got approval for an enlarged budget for the entire section
>   • Began an expanded program of troop entertainment by both civilian groups and military personnel
>
> These changes resulted in a greatly improved program. The rerouting of documents eliminated unnecessary duplication and delays. The search of files yielded a more capable staff. The revised budget permitted enlarged personnel and entertainment much more pleasing to the troops.
>
> The improvements were recognized when Fort Texas was awarded the job of hosting the Fourth Army Entertainment Contest—in which the Fort Texas entry I directed took second place. Later, I was assigned as Officer in Charge of the Fourth Army Entertainment Team during its preparation at Fort Texas and during its later tour of the Fourth Army area.

Problem ... Action ... Result

Note that a pattern is common to all the illustrative examples. Each concerns a specific incident, and each is told informally. But most important is the pattern of the telling. In each the writer tells:

- A problem he found
- What he did about it
- What resulted

Whatever the experience you have to relate, it can be fitted to this mold in the telling. When it is, it is almost sure to be read clear through. Told of a problem, few can refrain from asking: "Well, what did he do about it?" And, having learned what was done, it's practically impossible to stop before finding out the results.

So you'll want to complete your presentation (your sales literature) before you start out to sell your product (yourself). In preparing it—and the letters or résumés which grow from it—you will want to follow these principles:

- Offer a service; don't just ask for a job.
- Appeal to the self-interest of your prospect.
- Be specific about the job you want and about your qualifications and your accomplishments.
- Be sincere and be yourself.

You have only yourself to sell. You can't sell what you haven't got. But by the time you've written the kind of presentation recommended, you'll see you have considerably more than you thought.

Write down a List of Prospects

Your presentation finished, you are ready to approach people who might use your services. Finding the right prospects is your next specific task. Your written list may come from many sources, including:

- Directories and rosters listing companies and company executives. (Ask the librarian in your company library or city public library for the names of such books.)
- Advertising pages of industrial, technical, or trade publications in the field of your choice.

- Help-wanted columns of metropolitan newspapers.
- Employment agencies. They have lists and will use the lists to serve you, but they won't give you the lists to serve yourself.
- Friends and/or business associates, past or present. (Be sure to give them a good written summary of your qualifications. People with whom you golf and bowl probably know little about your business performance.)
- Placement services of professional societies and trade associations.

Put your prospect list in writing. Then plan systematic use of it.

Interview-seeking Letters

Most letters of application are aimed at getting an interview. For such a letter, select from your written presentation one or two of your experience stories. They will help more than anything else to make a prospect want to talk with you.

Your interview-seeking letter should tell enough to interest your prospect in seeing you. Don't expect the letter to complete your sales job. It achieves its purpose if it gets you an interview.

How long this letter should be depends on what you have to say —and how you say it. Your prospect will keep on reading as long as the letter interests him—that long and no longer. So no words should be wasted. Don't use twenty words to say something you can say in fifteen. A 400-word letter of sentences that march may hold a reader to its end better than a 200-word letter heavy with say-nothing words.

We know of a twenty-one page letter—accompanied by a twenty-page illustrated, written presentation—that got a man a $25,000-a-year job. It contained material about an executive who had a great deal to sell—and who knew how to sell it.

But that's unusual. Most of us do best to concentrate on saying what we have to say clearly—and as briefly as possible. But if you need two pages to tell your experience stories, don't ruin the telling by insisting on a one-pager.

Open your interview-seeking letter with a statement of what you want to do ("I would like an opportunity to join the market-analysis staff of B. R. Okerage.") If your prospect isn't interested in personnel for this kind of position, you don't care whether or not he reads further. If he is, you have made the opening most calculated to lead him further.

The bulk of the letter's text should be experience stories, selected for their pertinence to qualities desirable in a market analyzer. The places and positions in which you had the experiences will be revealed as part of your narrative. ("While regional manager at Headlong Corp., from 1963 to 1966, I faced many interesting problems. Once. . . .")

Your letter should close by giving your prospective employer something to do or something to expect. You may leave the door ajar by asking for a reply or by saying you will call for an interview. This concluding paragraph can consist of one or two brief sentences. It is an important part of your letter. Make it effective.

Never use a participial conclusion, and never waste this opportunity by using some stock phrase. ("Hoping to hear from you at your earliest convenience, I remain. . . ." "Hoping you will consider my request favorably, I am. . . .")

Rather, use the last paragraph to the fullest advantage. Make it stimulate action. ("I should very much like the opportunity of a personal interview." "May I telephone you for an appointment?" "I should like a personal interview at any time convenient for you." "Will you set a time for an appointment?" "If you will telephone me at 335-6973 (Area Code 203), making an appointment, I can call at any time convenient for you.")

Writing to Follow Up

Returning from an interview, write a thank-you letter. Don't sit back and wait for results. Write an expression of appreciation for a pleasant interview—if you still are interested in the job.

Attach to this thank-you note selected material from your written presentation—perhaps even the entire portfolio. Indicate you think it "may recall some of the points touched on during our talk—and perhaps clarify others."

Such a follow-up gives you, in effect, a second interview. It ensures a common understanding between you and your prospect on mutually important points, and it refreshes his memory of you. Follow up, and you will set yourself out from the crowd.

Résumés

"Please send résumé" still is almost as common a greeting as "hello" from an employer to a job seeker. And a résumé that lists where the applicant has worked and what he was officially titled is the common response. It tells the employer nothing about what you have accomplished and gives him little to differentiate you from others of your kind.

"I once got thirty-eight letters of application and twenty-seven attached résumés, in response to a help-wanted advertisement," an insurance executive recalls. "We had advertised for recent college graduates to enter a sales training program.

"All the résumés and all but one of the letters, I remember, gave exactly the same information about the applicant: his college, year of graduation, major subject, summer jobs held, full-time jobs (where applicable), age, marital status, and permanent address. As I plowed through these applications, it became increasingly impossible to differentiate one from the other. I had hoped to select what seemed the five best prospects and have them in for an interview. But these résumés told of faceless men—all cast in the same mold. I knew there were differences—great differences—but how to clock them?"

He couldn't. The quality of the college and the neatness of the letter—the only clear differences—weren't very satisfactory bases upon which to select.

What an employer needs, of course, is information about what applicants have accomplished. Has the boy who sold soft drinks at Hoho Beach increased the sales over the previous year? Has the young man now in public relations at Nasbie and Nasbie met any problems? Has the $25,000-a-year executive shown imagination and reliability?

Whether you seek a $4,000- or a $40,000-a-year job, you become an individual capable of service—as opposed to a job seeker—only when you manage to reveal specifically what you have done and what has come of your efforts.

So when asked to "please send (or leave) résumé," consider seriously leaving a copy of the written presentation you have worked up or selections from it. In any case, if you are not required to follow a specific pattern, your format should be a clear statement of your accomplishments in logical (not chronological) sequence. The employers you want to work for will thank you for giving them the information they need—though they failed to ask for it.

When required to fill out a form, try to adapt your material to it. Regardless of the particular form, try to insert near the top of the first page a "position-desired" statement. ("*Position desired:* personnel director. Background includes fifteen years of union dealing with only one two-week strike.") If the form makes it impossible to indicate what you've accomplished, append a separate sheet at the end—a brief résumé of the kind here recommended. At least give what-I've-accomplished data in the standard résumé form. Each time you list a job and the time you held it, tell how you performed the function, not just what function you performed. Try to give a one-sentence statement of what you accomplished or encompassed in each job. For example:

> As assistant research engineer at Vacco Products, Inc., from 1965 to 1968, I supervised and reported on more than one thousand tests to pinpoint performance characteristics of Vacco oils in twenty different environments.

not just:

> 1965–1968, assistant research engineer, Vacco Products, Inc.

Modification of the standard résumé format *might* annoy an occasional advocate of strict adherence to standardization. But it will do a good job on the man who looks beneath the surface— and usually on the annoyed disciplinarian too.

A letter should cover each résumé you mail. Accompanying the modified type of résumé recommended, such a letter can be very brief:

> Thank you for wanting to see the attached résumé.
> Should you be interested in more detail on some phases of my experience, I shall be glad to supply it.

When writing to employers for jobs, list the questions you would ask a man applying for the particular position. Then answer your own questions by what you say in your presentation, your résumé, your letter of application, and your interview-seeking letters. These answers will not be too far from what your prospective employer wants to know.

Summary

Orderly job hunting, like good communications writing, gives you a chance to exercise the same talents you'll need for success on the job. You analyze, you synthesize, you decide, you act. *Pick Your Job and Land It* [1] expresses the approach to job hunting that gets the right job—for you.

Orderly job hunting is step-by-step seeking:

1. You decide what sort of job to look for by defining your likes and dislikes in terms of specific, yet broad, vocational areas.

2. You identify specific jobs that require exercise of the talents you have and like to use.

3. You complete your self-analysis by listing your major characteristics as factually as possible against characteristics needed for the jobs you have defined.

4. You look for jobs which your talents match.

5. You make a basic presentation (in writing) of your qualifications, a presentation for others to see. From it you draw material for writing application letters, letters to get interviews. Sometimes you leave the presentation with the prospect at the end of the interview.

6. In your presentation, you prove possession of claimed qualities by citing their use in some previous activity. You tell about problems you have met, what you did about them, and what resulted from the action you took.

7. You never fail to follow up an interview or a contact. You always write a thank-you letter—if you are still interested in the job.

By being an orderly job hunter, you automatically stand out in any group of applicants. Not one in fifty will have taken the attractive-to-employer steps *the way you have taken them.*

---

[1] Sidney and Mary Edlund, *Pick Your Job and Land It*, Prentice-Hall, Inc., Englewood Cliffs, New Jersey, 1963. This is the classic book on job getting. It is practical, complete, and readable.

19

Writing
to Groups or Audiences

COMMUNICATIONS REPRODUCED in quantity and distributed to more than a single person aim to reach many people with a single message. Some office memoranda have this aim, though directed to a single person with copies to others. Clearly in this category are such forms of communications writing as magazine articles, papers for professional societies, promotional sales literature, instruction books and form letters of all kinds.

Constitutions, bylaws, operational procedures, political-party platforms, and employee manuals are among the other forms of communications writing which aim to reach many people with the same message.

Traditionally most such writing has been done by experts, specialists, and trained professional writers. But progress in almost any salary-paying job today provides a chance for—or actually requires—writing to group audiences.

An Audience Is Many Individuals

Writing to a group, you still must aim at the individuals in it. You may go wrong if you envision a "typical" member of the group and write to him. The typical association member, for example (he is 37.9 years old, has 2.34 children, had 1.1 years of college, and weighs 147.2 pounds), doesn't exist, nor do either formal or informal group labels ("lawyer," "engineer," "administrator," "salesman") reliably indicate the mental interests and intake of those in a group.

Only the receiving qualities common to most human beings can safely be posited for members of any particular group audience.

A writer may go furthest astray when he imputes special characteristics to individuals because of their membership in an organization, profession, or audience. The limit of safety is to assume some undefined common interest in a particular subject. Some variable backgrounds of common knowledge also may be safe to expect. But to assume that the engineeering-society members who read your technical paper will all read as engineers is unrealistic. The engineering knowledge of some members of such an audience is wide and deep. Others have only a shallow and specious knowledge of engineering. Even wider differences will exist as regards the interest of the individual in engineering (or law or accounting or social service or any other specialty which concerns a particular group).

So single-message communications to well- or ill-defined group audiences are best designed primarily to scale the psychological barriers common to most people (Chapter 5)—whatever their specialty. The president of a leading engineering society recognized the common humanness of its members when he sent this reproduced letter to each of them:

Dear Member:

When you attend future national meetings you will be asked to show your membership card.

At first blush this may seem to be a nuisance, but there really is a good reason for it. We are one of the few engineering societies which do not charge a member registration fee. Your society feels that payment of dues entitles a member to attend national meetings with no additional charge. By the same token, nonmembers should pay for the benefits they gain from attending our meetings. Member dues shouldn't have to cover additional costs incurred by attendance of nonmembers.

The only way to ensure collection of registration fees from nonmembers is to have members show their cards when registering. So, though it's a slight inconvenience, please bring your membership card with you when you attend future national meetings.

I hope you will endorse this practice to ensure that your dues are spent wisely and for the benefit of members.

Sincerely,

President of the Society

This clear, friendly, forthright letter is suitable for any president to send to any member group. The members could just as well have been advertising men or harness manufacturers. This letter is good because it was designed to overcome the psychological barriers to be expected in *anybody's* mind. Chances are it would have been weakened rather than strengthened by an attempt to approach these members primarily as engineers instead of just as people.

Look at it this way:

Your degree of expertness and interest in a special area predisposes you to read on certain subjects. Also, it determines your intake of material coming to you as a member of a special audience. If, to reach you, my communication relies mainly on my ideas about your specialty, the gamble is much higher than if I keyed it to interest you as a person. Then my knowledge that you are a specialist can determine the factual content. But I can't assume that because you are a lawyer, I can bury my main idea in the middle of my piece. Or that I can obscure it with needless verbiage. Or that I should aim for the pettifogging preciseness of a legal brief. Rather, I'll want my communication to present the main idea in the first paragraph, to be accurate in factual detail, and to be clearly written in sentences that march. And I'll want it to be expressed in words that are readily understandable to *every* member of your group.

The form of a group-audience communication, in other words, should grow from consideration of the reader as a human being. Its content may establish relationship with him as a member of a particular group.

Writing which goes to where a specialist lives gets top communication results. Make your words clearly applicable to the particular group addressed. Failure to do so is to let slip a good chance to stimulate your reader's grabbing equipment to action. But there are dangers to be avoided.

Many will recall the speech Senator Nameless made to a national banquet of the Phi Kappa Psi fraternity—of which he was a member. His subject was "brotherhood." He made a strongly emotional address, covering all possible angles of this traditional subject. He emphasized his special feeling of closeness to Phi Kappa Psi, and then he charged into his peroration loud and strong with the words: "And finally, Brother Elks. . . ."

To establish rapport with the special group to whom you are writing, sincerity as well as accuracy is essential—as in all communications writing. Contrived "connections" are no better here than in communications to individuals. They are, in fact, worse because they are spread out for more people to see through.

Memo to an Individual—Copies to Whom?

The interoffice memorandum addressed to an individual with "copies-to-others" illustrates reaching several people with a single message. Inept or self-seeking use of this device has sparked many wisecracks.

But, judiciously used, its potentials for good are great. Ability to inform without obligating the reader to respond or react is this technique's chief strength. When being informed will benefit the extra readers, this device serves well. When self-seeking is its true purpose, it can backfire.

Its widespread misuse as an office-politics ploy makes copies-to-others suspect as a self-seeking device. So honesty of purpose is a vital element in its every use. It is never effective when used to tell the extra-copy-receiver something you would be embarrassed to say to his face. It shouldn't convey a threat to receiving associates that by approving its recommendations the boss will be ruling on the associates' concerns. But, the same information, in a form in which it gives associates advance warning so that they can speak their pieces before action is taken, is helpful to them. In this case, copies-to-others can alleviate possible frictions and actually build goodwill.

The suggested memorandum from the newly employed accountant to the general manager of a small manufacturing company (pages 66–67) can illustrate. The memorandum suggested, you will recall, ran:

> TO   General Manager
> FROM   Accountant
> I suggest establishment of a special receiving department responsible for:
> 1. Inspection of all merchandise on its way into our plant
> 2. Checking of incoming invoices against purchase orders
> 3. Recording of all incoming material on proper receiving forms
> 4. Prompt delivery of incoming shipments to using departments
> Such a facility—set up under the supervision of the production, administrative, or accounting department manager's supervision—could, I believe, save money, time, and errors.

Copies of this memorandum went to the production manager and the administration manager. This clearly gave them a chance to oppose or support the proposals while still in the recommendation stage. They *could* act before the general manager made up his mind and even before he asked their opinion—as he undoubtedly would. The memo's last sentence, in addition, made clear that the recommendation did not include naming the accountant as supervisor.

There is good reason for copies-to-others when the memorandum is about actions taken, decisions made, or statistical data related to the sender's operations. Factual information is rarely self-seeking unless the writer consciously makes it so. Usually everybody benefits from having a little more—rather than a little less—information than he absolutely needs. It is a short distance to the wastebasket for the copy that goes to the uninterested reader. When the memo's main idea is placed first, the receiver can quickly decide whether to read it or ditch it.

The worst misuse of copies-to-others is not the self-seeking at which critics jibe. It is the tendency of the uncommunicative to substitute copies-to-others for more surefire methods. Most executives say: "Deliver me from the associate who cries: 'Certainly you knew about that! Maybe I didn't tell you personally, but here it is, clear as day, right on page 5 of my memo of August 5. I'm sure I sent you a copy. Yes, I did. Your name heads the list of copies-to-others.' "

In short, copies-to-others is a useful communication device of very limited impact. It is good to use because it is easy to use. But the strength of its impact is proportionate to the ease of its use.

Summary

Writing to a group, you still must aim at the individuals in it. But beware of writing to the "average" member of the group. He doesn't exist.

Speak the special language of a group only when you really are an insider.

It is best to consider each group member as a human being. Write to surmount the barriers to intake common to most people.

There is good reason for sending copies to many concerned people when a memorandum is about actions taken, decisions made, or statistical data related to the sender's operations.

But copies-to-others are poor alibis for failure to communicate. You haven't communicated when you have put information on someone's desk.

20

Writing for Speaking

WRITING FOR SPEAKING falls into two general categories:

1. Writing that is to be more or less memorized and then spoken as though it were extemporaneous (e.g., most public speeches by businessmen and politicians, sermons, lectures, etc.)

2. Writing that is to be read out loud to a live audience, with hopes that it will be published later (e.g., most papers read before technical, scientific, educational, and other professional societies or groups or at conferences, seminars, forums, and the like)

The major difference: A speaker's delivery sets the pace at which listeners must listen. The words register in their minds or fail to register, depending on whether the speaker's delivery pace matches a listener's hearing pace. To know that, on the average, people listen three or four times as fast as the average person speaks is of little practical use.

The complexity of thought content and degree of listener concentration influence each individual situation greatly. No two listeners take in ideas or information at exactly the same rate. There are fast listeners and slow listeners, just as there are fast readers and slow readers. So the spoken communication can never be paced exactly right for everyone in an audience. The speaker's problem is to express his ideas slowly enough to reach most of a given audience, and yet not so slowly as to bore half of it.

The skilled "presenter" is conscious of what is happening to his listeners. He realizes that some quick-minded people are slow emotionally—and vice versa. He senses when some listeners need time for emotional readjustment. He may even slow up his presentation—"overtalk" on some points which *mentally* need no amplification—to give time for emotions to catch up.

When writing material that is to be spoken, always remember: The rate at which the ideas are spoken sets the pace at which listeners must listen.

Writing for Speaking

Writing in the first of these categories can be designed specifically for its single purpose. Though the words are written in advance, the communication is an oral one. It communicates through the ear; it enters a listener's mind, not a reader's. So it follows different rules, for a good speech rarely makes good reading—and vice versa. Two completely separate documents are necessary if both oral and written versions are to reach separate goals with equal impact.

Writing for listeners rather than readers, you should pick carefully the specific points you want to make—then equip yourself to make them within the time allotted for your presentation. Develop your manuscript along the lines of a thirty-minute speech. Include only the amount of information or ideas you can express in ten or eleven pages of loosely phrased, double-spaced typewriting.

Then read aloud your final draft to friends, associates, or a tape recorder, as soon as you have finished it. (This will pay big dividends. It will help your oral presentation to be a great success.) In addition, unless you are an experienced speaker, show up at the meeting room ½ hour before your session is scheduled to start. Meet other speakers on the program and familiarize yourself with the mikes, the projection facilities, and the room layout. (By the time you get on your feet, you will feel at home—among friends in familiar surroundings.)

As you prepare your draft for reading aloud, you will be conscious continually of how it must differ from the manuscript you might write for publication. Men experienced in both writing and speaking say the speeches they write differ from their articles chiefly in the following ways:

• The main idea is stated at the beginning as it is in an article, but less succinctly. If it is stated in a crisp, marching first sentence, the following few sentences will back off from it and return to it in easy steps during the next paragraph. At the end of two brief paragraphs, in other words, the speech may get back to where it started, giving slow listeners a chance to get aboard. For example:

> I'm going to start right off by saying that I don't think scheduled overhauls of aircraft components are really necessary.
>
> Now I realize that's a pretty radical statement. There are, for instance, government regulations which specify certain overhaul schedules that the airlines must meet. Most of the development work done on improving aircraft maintenance has involved attempts to make these schedules more accurate and more certain to result in increased safety. So I don't expect you folks to agree with that statement of mine unless I can give you proof of its truth, proof which is satisfactory to *you*.
>
> And that's just what I'm going to try to do in the next thirty minutes. I'm going to give you the facts resulting from four specific studies (relating to four different important aircraft units) which we've made at Lexicon Airlines in the last twelve months. I'm going to let you see why it now seems to me that scheduled overhauls of aircraft components aren't really necessary anymore.

• A reasonable number of say-nothing words—which would slow up a reader badly—actually make listening easier, more relaxed. (Less than half the words used in the above example told the same story to readers of the magazine published by the organization to whom the speech was made.) Much oftener than in writing, phrases like "on the other hand," "in the light of," "nevertheless," "for example," and "of course" serve a useful purpose. A speech can be overloaded with them, too. But sometimes they are needed to keep the flow of ideas or information from coming faster than most of an audience can listen.

• Repetition of the same ideas in different words often is desirable in a speech; rarely is it desirable in good communications writing.

Material written to be spoken, in short, should be less closely packed than material written to be read. Of eight specific actions suggested in *Clear Writing for Easy Reading* [1] to produce sentences that march, only the five in boldface type are really important to the speech writer:

1. Get rid of say-nothing words.
2. Eliminate "introductory" words.
3. **Stick to direct statement and active verbs.**
4. **Keep the ideas per sentence low.**
5. **Beware of qualifying clauses.**
6. Aim for short sentences.
7. **Personalize your thinking.**
8. **Be specific.**

The pace at which a speaker delivers ideas to his listeners is more important than the speed at which he speaks.

Is a Choice Necessary?

You may feel that you are too busy to do two separate writing jobs when invited to present a paper before an organization. Urged to do so—and given limited time for presentation—you may settle for cutting down the manuscript you already have written. At the meeting, you may leave out enough parts of the written presentation to permit reading the remainder in the allotted time.

Of course that doesn't constitute writing a paper effective in reaching *listeners*. It doesn't make your oral presentation any better—just more bearable.

So, if you are like most of us, you will often find yourself making a choice. Shall you write a paper which—read at the meeting—will have maximum impact on your live audience? Or shall you aim primarily for the usually very much larger audience to be reached by publication?

If you choose the live audience as your main objective, you

[1] Norman G. Shidle, *Clear Writing for Easy Reading*, McGraw-Hill Book Company, New York, 1964.

will develop your manuscript along the lines outlined earlier in this chapter. You will make sure to do the best possible job. You will realize that chances of subsequent printing of this excellent listener-oriented paper will be small. If it is printed at all, its *relatively* limited thought-and-information content will probably be rewritten to one-third or one-half of the already curtailed length.

For Publication after Presentation

If publication is your aim, learning the publication procedures of the particular organization is worthwhile. Most professional societies establish judgment routines for selecting for publication the best of the papers given at meetings. You can usually find out how selection is made and also get some idea of the criteria for determining the "best"—at least informally. Each such organization has its own desired format for a manuscript, which facilitates publication mechanics but which is usually unrelated to the evaluation and selection processes.

Suggestions on writing a paper which do relate to its evaluation are made to authors by a large professional society. They are generally applicable:

> Good organization of thought with subsequent revisions are two ingredients common to good papers. Good organization reflects your having thought through the facts and conclusions you wish to pass along to your readers. Careful revision improves the readers' chance of fully understanding what you're saying.
>
> A written outline is the most common tool used for "thought-organization." It is easy to assemble and reassemble your ideas in this form. Also, the outline can serve as a source of headings for the sections of your paper. Generally a simple outline is all that's necessary. If you find you have multiple subheadings, this may be a sign that your reader will get lost along the way.
>
> Revisions are best generated by your colleagues. After you have written a manuscript that satisfies you, try it out on a knowledgeable associate. If portions are not clear to him, you can be sure they will trouble many others. However, don't ask your colleague to rewrite for you. Have him tell you about sentences that don't read correctly. Have him alert you to unnecessary statements, unsupported conclusions, or faulty logic. (Professional men tend to

inject true but irrelevant information.) Have him make a note of places where more depth of fact would be of interest—or of anything that would make a better paper from his reader's point of view.

Put Main Ideas First

Put first in your paper the main ideas you want to leave with your readers—as you would in any other communications writing. Often this will mean your summarization of the significance of your conclusions. Or you may have recommendations to make. Either your conclusions or your recommendations should come at the beginning of your paper.

This practice orients your reader to the subject of your paper. Also, it gives him the order in which you plan to approach the subdivisions of your subject. For you're not ready to write a finished draft until you have your conclusions and/or recommendations clearly down in summary form. They are the core of your paper, the reason for your writing it. So you convey a maximum of information to your reader by stating those first. Then go on to amplify, qualify, explain, or prove them. Thus you ensure both unity and coherence.

This attack is peculiarly effective in papers—many of which are referred to rather than read. Having the main idea first is especially necessary in contributions to the professional literature of a subject. Summarized conclusions or recommendations at the start serve the reference reader by:

1. Making it easier for him to finger data he wants as he flips through library bound volumes. (A glance at the opening paragraph is enough to signal interest or no interest.)

2. Making it easier for him to scan the entire published paper and extract what he wants without detailed reading.

3. Ensuring more accurate indexing and abstracting—thus making the essential information more accurately and readily available to researcher-readers.

Don't Start with the Creation of the World

The antithesis of starting with the main idea is all too common among writers of professional-society papers. Amateur writers, they often fail to see their paper as related to a body of knowledge.

Speaking or writing to fellow professionals, they open with the beginning of the world and arrive at the specific subject of today's paper on page 14. There is no better way to ensure unfavorable reader opinion or to lose the very readers most writers of professional papers want to reach—their fellow experts.

Examples of this blinders approach to writing a paper are available at almost any scientific or other professional society meeting.

A paper entitled "Powered-axle Concept for a Mobile Army," for instance, began literally with the creation of man:

> Since the creation of man and his inability to get along with his fellow man, he has had the need for a well-equipped Army to defend his rights and privileges.

You might enjoy trying to guess the subject of another engineering-society paper which began:

> Since the beginning, man has been dissatisfied with the "lay of the land" and has endeavored to alter the original shape of the earth in many ways. This is well illustrated by the art of earth-moving. . . .

It's unlikely that you have guessed the main idea of this paper —which the author never did get around to expressing in well-pointed sentences. It was:

> To utilize newer, larger diesels efficiently, earth-moving equipment manufacturers must have simple, lightweight power trains that will provide customers with profitable haulage equipment.

Many authors for the automotive engineering society which produced both the supertangential examples quoted go only as far back as the invention of the wheel. But those who get the most attentive listeners and most satisfied readers orient their readers for easy reading. They start with their conclusions or recommendations; then they confine their papers to explaining, amplifying, or proving them.

"Editorial" Comments

Editorializing is out of place in most professional papers. In such papers you should label clearly as opinion any such expressions. Statements should be as objective as you can make them. Professional-society publication committees put black marks next to statements like this:

> The international jet aircraft costs $5,500,000. This is a substantial sum of money, despite the casualness with which billion-dollar sums are bandied about these days.

Also they give low rating to items of personal history, such as:

> The first military prestressing problem that came to my desk was in 1950 in connection with a request by the Navy that we increase the displacement of its diesel powerplant.

Commercialism, of course, is seriously frowned on. Too frequent use of company or trade names, promotional expression of product performance data, and discussion of product advantages while ignoring possible disadvantages are all suspect in a professional-society paper. Direct sales promotion of a product or an idea will ensure a paper's being discarded from publication lists.

Specific versus General

Specific information, specific examples, and specific recommendations go far toward getting a paper favorably considered for publication. Generalities—no help to any communications writing—are the kiss of death to a professional-society paper. Low impact results when a paper is full of statements like:

> Practically every failure of new or retreaded jet tires has proved to be the result of a manufacturing error.

A professional-society reader opens his mind more readily when he is given specific data to make the statement self-supporting:

> One of two kinds of manufacturing error was found responsible for failure of thirty-five out of forty new, and thirty-eight out of forty retread, jet tires tested. The manufacturing errors to which the failures were traced were (1). . . .

Abstracts Should Be News

The abstract, which many professional societies want to accompany a paper, has a single purpose: to let a prospective reader find out whether he wants to read the paper. So the abstract should whet his appetite. It should tell him what new data, conclusions, or point of view he will find in the paper. It should indicate the significance of the paper's material, and it should do all this in about one hundred words. A good abstract should help a potential reader seeking problem solutions months or years hence. That is why he needs the new ideas your paper contains, rather than a summary of the subject it treats. A good abstract—like the following example—should tell what your paper says, not just name the subjects it covers.

> A recently developed metallic coating shows promise as a gasoline-engine cylinder liner.
>
> It offers a wear-resistant material which combines the hardness of carbides with the economy of electroplating practices. This coating consists of electroplated dispersion of microscopic-size hard particles.

This abstract is specific enough to let a reader decide to read the article, if he is interested in gasoline-engine cylinder liners, or to give him a fair idea of the product if he reads no further. He could only guess at what he might get from the article had the abstract read:

> This paper describes a recently developed metallic coating. It discusses the coating's wear-resistance qualities, gives the composition of the material, and covers various elements of its economic use.

With the second abstract, the decision to read or not read will be harder to make, too, and the paper would have to be read to give the abstract reader take-home information. The generality-filled abstract gives only the "news" that a new metallic coating exists.

Format and Timing

Most professional societies lay great stress on details of manuscript format and the date on which the manuscript is due. Each organization has its own "requirements." These are designed to facilitate processing of the many manuscripts which usually arrive at nearly the same time. There is no uniformity in details of format or of timing requirements because each organization has different processing facilities and capabilities.

Meeting the organization's detailed format requirements has little if anything to do with whether your manuscript will be published. The timing requirements are something else again. Early delivery of a manuscript makes possible prompt consideration for publication and speeds up the date of publication. Too late delivery, in many organizations, automatically eliminates a paper from consideration for publication.

To ensure accuracy and to attain the most attractive publication possible are your chief reasons for following an individual society's preferred format.

Citing another work, for example, is a usual way to authenticate data, credit another worker in the field, and guide the reader to collateral information. Each professional society has its own preferred form for making such references. One society's "instructions to authors" read:

> REFERENCES—Number references consecutively in order of appearance. In the text, type the reference number in brackets thus [4]. The first one should be [1].* The footnote for this asterisk should read: *Numbers in brackets designate references at end of paper.

Many societies send several pages of similar instructions to authors invited to write papers.

If pressure of time requires that you skimp on editing and rewriting the paper itself or that you neglect to follow format details, forget the format details. It is the quality of the content and the writing which will determine whether or not your paper is worth publishing.

Just be sure to send in "clean copy" at the end. Start off with a title page, giving the paper's title, your name, your title, and your company and its location. Have your final draft retyped on one side of letter-size paper (8½ by 11 inches) and double spaced. To ensure accuracy, make certain that each illustration or figure is referred to in the text and that you have a list of all figure numbers—with a caption for each—attached at the end. And make sure that your illustrations are clear and reproducible. (If in doubt, check with somebody who knows.)

Summary

Manuscripts that are written to be effective when spoken are seldom good written communications. Listeners get only one chance at ideas—which come to them at a pace determined by the speaker. A reader sets his own pace. He can go back over a sentence as often as he likes.

When you write a manuscript that is to be spoken:

• Pick carefully specific points you want to make. Then equip yourself to make them within the time allotted for your presentation.

• Read your final draft aloud to friends, associates, or a tape recorder.

• Get to your meeting ½ hour ahead of time. Meet other speakers and familiarize yourself with the mikes, projection facilities, and the room layout.

• State your main idea at the beginning, as you would in a written communication. But back off from it and return to it in easy steps during the next paragraph.

• Use a reasonable number of say-nothing words. They would irritate a reader, but they relax a listener. He doesn't have to listen so hard to keep abreast of you.

Material written to be spoken, in short, should be less closely packed than material written to be read.

When you write a manuscript for publication after presentation:

• Learn the publication procedures of the organization before which you are presenting your paper.

• Put first in your paper the main ideas you want to leave with your readers. State them specifically, crisply, briefly.

• Don't start with the history of the world. Include only what is needed to make clear your special contribution.

• Don't editorialize. Don't promote your own products or personality.

• Be specific. Shun generalities.

21

Writing
Articles for Business
or Technical Magazines

IS THERE SOMETHING you know more about than most others in your business, industry, or profession? Is it something likely to help others do their jobs better or to make their jobs more personally rewarding?

If the answer is "yes" to these questions, you can properly aspire to make an occasional magazine article part of your communications writing.

Such an article will spread your knowledge to more people than any other communication you write. It is almost certain to enhance your standing in your company and your field. Before it gets to readers, it will have been evaluated (and perhaps revised) by a professional editor—a benefit foreign to other communications-writing forms. If your article is accepted and published, you know you have achieved a passing mark as a communications writer. If it is refused, you may be able to get the editor to suggest how to do better next time. (Most business and technical magazine editors are would-be teachers at heart.)

Most everyday writers think in terms of an article each year or so.[1] They want every so often to give others information or ideas evolved from their own experiences. They see articles as occasional extensions of everyday communications-writing opportunities. They have neither the time nor the need to qualify as professional or even semiprofessional authors. Their only question is: "How does article writing differ—if at all—from good communications writing in general?"

Answer: Not at all basically. But certain elements of good communications writing require special emphasis.

The occasional article writer will do well to concentrate on:

• Getting the main idea of the article into one or two specific, positive statements—and using those statements (or a rewording of them) as the opening paragraph

• Using specific ideas, facts, and "for instances" abundantly

The writing itself, of course, should consist of sentences that march, full of words that live (see Chapter 8). But specific focus at the beginning of the article is of paramount importance.

"If I could teach our occasional contributors only one thing," a veteran editor says, "I'd teach them to integrate the article's main idea in a single sentence—then start the article with that sentence.

"Once they've done that," he goes on, "its hard for them to go wrong. That 'lead' sentence guides and limits everything else in the article. In fact, half the work of writing the article is done once that peg or lead sentence has been written."

This editor speaks with the voice of experience. In any one article, you can hope to convey only one idea—or at most a few—clearly. Insist on putting in too many, and you ensure that none will get off the page and into the reader's mind. So force yourself to select the most important idea or ideas.

Then write that idea down. Write it in one specific statement

[1] If you think of writing articles as an avocation, you will want to learn about the different kinds of articles and, about how to find and develop article ideas. You will need to study how to make an outline, how to deal with editors, and how to develop and use illustrations, tables, and charts. You will want to read at least chaps. 1–9 of Tyler G. Hicks, *Successful Technical Writing*, McGraw-Hill Book Company, New York, 1959. (Despite the book's title, these chapters apply equally well to writing any article for business or professional publications.

which can be the "peg" on which your whole article hangs. Thus you fix your own thinking clearly, so that "thinking worries" will not intrude too much after you start to write.

But make this peg a specific, not a general, statement. Suppose you plan an article about the use of titanium in airplane structures. Your peg might be:

> More titanium will be used in airplane structures next year than in any recent year.

not:

> Data on prospects for use of titanium next year. . . .

A few years ago, the author of an article on the economics of the guaranteed wage wrote a good peg. It was:

> The American people object to equal payments to workers whether they work or are idle.

But he didn't know it was his peg until after the article was finished. He put it last instead of first.

The article led up to this main idea—instead of flowing out from it.

Result: Only the few readers who plowed through four magazine pages ever found out exactly what he had on his mind. They were misled and misoriented by his lead (opening) sentence, which suggested a totally different (and incidentally much less interesting) idea:

> The guaranteed annual wage, guaranteed employment, guaranteed wages, or whatever term, promises to become a major economic issue in the next few years.

A subsequent reader-research study indicated that the real peg —which had been buried—would have provoked considerably more readership than the one used as a lead. Many readers had a "so-what?" attitude to the statement about becoming a "major economic issue in the next few years."

Mental steps by an airline chief engineer to develop a potent article peg provide a practical illustration of how to do it. This technical executive had directed to completion an evaluation of the usefulness of a data-collecting device called a "multiparameter recording unit." "If devices like this are practical," he told a magazine editor, "we're going to be able to reduce considerably the percentage of jet transport flights delayed because of mechanical reasons. And these evaluations of ours indicate that the device *is* practical—if you know how to use the results it gives."

The editor asked the chief engineer to write an article "telling other airline engineers how they can make practical use of your findings." Knowing that this engineer-executive had written only one or two articles in his life, the editor added words of warning. To guide this contributor to selection of the right peg and lead, he said:

"I'm hoping you won't do what one of your confreres did in an engineering-society paper I heard on this subject recently. Don't start off with a discourse on the importance of reliability—now and in the future. Don't follow with ten or fifteen paragraphs outlining the increasing complexity of modern aircraft and its operation. (We've all known for a good many years that the 'basic jet engine was a major step in increasing the state-of-the-art of airlines' aircraft and their physical systems.') No, don't do that, please. Just give the results of your own evaluation of whatever it is you evaluated!"

Guided by the editor's admonition, this contributor came up with a lead paragraph—as a peg for his article. It contained the main ideas he wanted to leave with his readers:

> Overhauling airplane components at scheduled frequencies is hardly ever necessary. Only for specific cases to prevent specific modes of failure is scheduled overhaul required. Recent Quality Air Lines studies show, in fact, that rigid adherence to arbitrary—often unreasonably low—TBOs (Time Between Overhauls) can actually do more harm than good.
>
> Four special maintenance programs currently in use at Quality Air Lines support these conclusions—and illustrate a more rational and economical program. These programs are organized explorations of the age-versus-reliability characteristics of components. They cover electronics, accessories, hydraulics, and air conditioning.

The article went on to describe the four programs in terms which showed their support of the main conclusions. The multiparameter recording device was discussed in terms of its contributions of data which made possible the new-type maintenance programs—on the basis of which the useful-to-readers conclusions had been drawn. (The published article was headlined: "Scheduled Unit Overhauls Not Needed, QAL Programs Reveal.")

Deciding on the peg—the focus of all the projected article's ideas and data—is the single most important step in writing a creative "communicating" article. Thought out and written clearly, the peg becomes both guide and limitation for the rest of the article—a sort of summary outline. Reference to the peg should decide the fate of every fact and idea that knocks for admission to the article. After the peg is established, the rest of the writing —for maximum clarity—should flow naturally, almost inevitably. It should amplify, prove, explain, or further define the idea expressed in the peg.

How much content comes to rest in a reader's mind is directly proportionate to your success in achieving a good peg. That achievement, in turn, rests on your ability to synthesize a series of relatively unrelated facts or concepts.

One business magazine editor defines such synthesis as: "Ability to envision and/or create relationships between scattered, isolated data and/or ideas."

When hiring new writers, he illustrates by listing the following requirements for business and technical magazines:

- Industry needs more engineers.
- Industry needs more engineering technicians.
- Fewer engineers are being graduated than in the past.
- Engineering curricula have moved toward the "sciences."
- Technician curricula have moved up in mathematics and sciences.
- Engineers (young ones especially) complain when put on routine jobs.
- Engineers (older ones especially) think every young engineer should go through a period of doing routines—a sort of apprenticeship approach.

• Engineers (some younger, but more older) resent injection of technicians.

• Etc., etc., etc.—with much statistical data and other supporting information.

Then he points out: "It's easy to determine and get agreement on the general subject of an article to be drawn from such information. It's 'engineers and engineering technicians—today and tomorrow.'" But the all-important step, the really difficult step, remains to be taken. We must determine what *is* the article we shall write—by writing a lead paragraph. The writer must do his own synthesizing.

Specifics and Examples

The quality of your article will be above that of the average occasional contribution if, besides getting clear focus in your opening paragraph, you do the following:

1. Be specific; shun generalities.
2. Use plenty of "for instances."

A reader always likes specific facts or incidents better than generalities. An article filled with generalities will lose readers early. If it is filled with specifics, it will hold many to the end. To a reader, a generalities-full passage of fifty words may seem "longer" than a 100-word passage dotted with thought-stimulating specifics. For instance:

Generalities

Actually, instrumentation has long been used in specific phases of industrial processes.

Many devices had become commonplace in the American home, while others were used in industry and in communications.

Some of these go far back into technological history, but they were on the road toward this so-called automation.   (50 words.)

Specifics

Actually, instrumentation has long been used in specific phases of industrial processes.

Such simple devices as the thermostat using the feed-back principle had already become a commonplace in the American home. Certain chemical processes used automatic controls of heat, pressure, flow, liquid, and gas. In the mechanical sphere there were safety controls, automatic switching, automatic inspection of work, and devices for turning on and off electric or hydraulic equipment. In communications, there was machine switching.

Some of these go far back in technological history, but they were on the road toward this so-called automation.[2]   (94 words)

Most readers will prefer the ninety-four word passage, though it's nearly twice as long. (But adding specific data is the *only* excuse for the extra length—and specific data can be overdone, too.)

To write the specific-data passage required more work. The writer probably had to consult library files or flip through indexes to find references—or ask a qualified engineer if the examples were correct. This is almost always true. Try it for yourself.

Try to summarize in a sentence or so what the speaker said at the last meeting you attended.

The last speaker I heard told, as I recall, about how a great deal of steel could have been saved during World War II if some of the shells for the Allies had been produced by some new manufacturing process. But I had to check back to a magazine report of the talk to be able to tell you that he said: "One million tons of steel could have been saved during World War II if just the 105 mm shells produced for the Allies had been cold-formed."

Because being specific means more work for the writer, being specific makes his articles stand out. Few occasional article writers will take the necessary pains.

"For instances" are even more work—and make your article even more outstanding. Every time you state a generality, follow it immediately with a "for instance"—for instance:

> Only a fine line distinguishes suggestions from complaints—and to many people the difference is not at all clear.
>
> If employee Abbott says: "It isn't safe for a man to work on a machine like this," his remark would no doubt be regarded as a complaint. When employee Bruce, commenting on the same situa-

[2] Roger Burlingame, *Endless Frontiers: The Story of McGraw-Hill,* McGraw-Hill Book Company, New York, 1959, p. 368.

tion says: "A protective guard, such as the one being used by the XYZ company would make this a safe operation," his words would be looked upon as a suggestion.[3]

Useful words are lost to the language if they are persistently misused. This results in impoverishment of speech.

The other day, for instance, I was reading an article on television in which the writing mentioned the large staff required for a certain program—ending with the phrase: "the enormity of the operation."

Now "enormity" does not mean size alone, but a large wickedness, or an outrageous act of offense.

"Enormous" means size alone, but if we keep using "enormity" for this meaning, then we have lost a useful word to describe some particularly heinous offense.[4]

Attitudes Influence Success

Self-centeredness is the chief inside-the-writer barrier to be surmounted in article writing. Whether writing of lasers or labor unions, manufacturing or motivational research, ask yourself first: "What good will it do *XYZ Magazine* subscribers to read what I plan to write?"

The answer will open the doors of your mind to development of material which will stimulate readers to reach for your ideas. Make this approach, and you will find your writing in line with magazine editors' thinking.

Summary

Articles will spread your knowledge to more people than any other communications you may write.

To write good articles:

• Be sure to get the article's main idea into one or two specific positive statements, and reword those statements to make your opening paragraph.

[3] Charles E. Redfield, *Communication in Management,* The University of Chicago Press, Chicago, 1953.

[4] N. B. Sigmund, *Effective Report Writing,* Harper & Row, Publishers, Incorporated, New York, 1960.

• Be prolific in your use of specific ideas and data, and cite many "for instances."

• In focusing your main idea, try to envision and create relationships between the scattered, isolated data and the ideas with which you probably started.

• Deciding on the main idea, answer this question: "What good will it do *XYZ Magazine* subscribers to read what I plan to write?" (This will alleviate your natural self-centeredness and help you to decide in terms of your readers' interests.)

22 | Practical Listening Aids Creative Writing

CONSCIOUS LISTENING is a practical aid to better communications writing. There is no better way to improve your ability to convey ideas to others than to work hard at efficient listening.

A behavior-researcher once asked a group of semantics-studying executives: "Which would you rather do: listen to the other fellow or speak your own mind? Which is harder or more unpleasant, less satisfactory?"

He got the expected answer: "Of course, the other fellow doesn't make sense very often. You have to listen to so many stupid things these days." Commenting, the researcher summarized: "Of course, the other fellow doesn't make sense very often. But when you broadcast your own wisdom, what a wonderful message it sounds like—to you!"

This common self-centeredness makes most listening unfruitful. We listen with our ears—and often because we have to. While others speak, we think mostly about what we are going to say in response. We react, rather than absorb; we affirm or deny, rather than examine.

Yet sooner or later, occasionally or often, we will write to most people to whom our ears are exposed. They may be business associates or people we work with on civic or community projects.

They may be men or women from whom we buy or to whom we sell ideas, information, or products. In any case, they are people on whom our lives impinge and with whom we exchange concepts. They are the people to whom we listen most.

Whatever they say and however they say it, they reveal likes and dislikes, enthusiasms and prejudices. They expose the way their minds work and how they approach problems. They reveal the psychological barriers our written communications must surmount as well as the paths most open to them.

Listening for these hidden harmonies and discords makes us familiar with the character of their idea-grabbing equipment. We become better able to harmonize viewpoints and actions. We can improve later communications to mutual advantage.

Thus approached, listening can be made moderately fruitful, regardless of the quality of what is listened to. "The more one accepts the philosophy that everyone has something worth listening to, the more one gets out of listening," says Alfred G. Larke.[1]

By conscious listening, we can also acquire much knowledge of how to convey ideas. Listening to a torrent of unfamiliar words, for example, may impress on us the need for using words familiar to our reader. Listening to prejudiced expression of a viewpoint may emphasize the need for an objective approach in our own written communications. Finding concentration difficult, we may recall that *our* audience will do a minimum of reaching.

This practical listening builds a store of knowledge about the people our writing will seek to reach. When we sit down to write, we will draw on this store of specific knowledge. If it doesn't exist, we probably won't take time out to accumulate it—unless the communication is of great importance. This listening-generated knowledge will be solid gold when following the advice given in Chapter 10 on writing to individuals: Get all the specific data you can about your one-man or one-woman audience. At least let your mind focus on what you already know about the person to whom you intend to write. Consider, even though fleetingly, his general mental traits and his habitual mental reactions.

[1] Alfred G. Larke, "Be a Good Listener Yourself," *Dun's Review and Modern Industry*, April, 1955, p. 46.

Conscious good listening will almost certainly result in favorable reception for later, unrelated written communications. Everybody likes a good listener and tends to be prejudiced in favor of what he later may write. Who doesn't think well of the listener who lets us get troubles off our chest? Who isn't complimented by the listener who doesn't yield to distractions and who maintains obvious interest?

Good listeners make more friends and promote more cooperative effort than indifferent listeners. Besides, they have a better chance to present their own ideas effectively than most of us do. In addition, of course, they get more information. In short when you write to a man after listening to him, he is likely to listen to you.

So mastering the art of listening can be well worthwhile. Few of us are adept at this. If you doubt it, check yourself sometime during a conference while someone else is talking. Are you actually listening to what is being said? Are you letting ideas enter your mind? Are you permitting them to get acquainted with your own? Are you giving them any chance to make a permanent home along with concepts already in your mind? Are you at least asking them to stop for a moment for a casual chat before sending them on with a "Glad to have met you"?

Or are you running to shut your mind's door to permit concentration on what you so badly want to say as soon as you can break in? Most of us do the latter, most of the time—especially if we are interested in the subject. Only through effort can we free our minds to welcome guest ideas when we are readying our own for voyaging.

Good listeners really listen. They grant new or opposing thoughts the courtesy of a warm welcome, even while rejecting most visitors as permanent guests. Good listeners look interested —not as though they were wool-gathering. Good listeners stimulate added ideas by pertinent questions. They prepare the ground for favorable reception of their own brainchildren by having patent sympathy for those of others.

Good listeners overcome the common fault of self-centeredness —and thus improve the quality of their communications.

23

Reading Is Writing in Reverse

YOU CAN USE what you have learned about the art of success-ful communication to facilitate your reading for information if you start looking for the peg—the main idea—of every piece of writ-ing that comes to you. Identify it. Then examine it. See whether reading further promises to yield information or stimulation com-mensurate with the time the reading will take.

If you decide that it may, then use that main idea as a peg around which to orient the exposition, argument, or description which makes up the total communication.

This kind of scanning is akin to the thinking-before-writing that is the core of the art of successful communication. It's the same process you've learned to use in creative, effective communica-tions writing.

If most writers practiced that art well, you could acquire their ideas and information by:

• Starting to read at the beginning
• Deciding with assurance after reading a sentence or two that you will or will not profit from reading further
• Reading right on through (if you decided "yes")

But too few writers put the main idea first. They don't concen-trate on giving you their message in the way that requires least ef-fort on your part. Yet, as a reader, you have to know what the article, memorandum, letter, or report is really about before you can know how much time to spend on it.

Too many writers bury that main idea somewhere in the middle of the text—where you must ferret it out. You have to have it before reading in order to:

1. Decide whether or not to read
2. Have a point around which to orient your thinking as you read

Once you have found that peg—and decided to read further—your intake will be speeded up greatly. A case in point follows.

Some New York University reading-speed researchers split average student groups into two equal sections. Both sections of each group were given the same article to read. One section was instructed to start at the word "go" to read from the first word to the last. The other half was told: "First scan the article quickly. Then go back to the beginning and read it through word for word." (Criteria for checking content absorption were applied to both sections.) Each individual raised his hand as he finished reading.

Result: A majority of those who first scanned and then read finished ahead of the fastest of those who simply started to read. By the time the scanners started to read through, they had acquired an idea of what the article had to say. They had fashioned their own pegs. Then it was easy to relate the various ideas and bits of information as they ran through word for word.

There is little doubt that concepts enter more quickly into a mind prepared to receive them. More importantly, the concepts have greater significance after they get in. The peg-finder has something to relate them to as he reads.

So to get the most the fastest, make a habit of looking for the peg—a specific statement of the main idea—as you pick up any communication. If you are lucky, it will be in the first paragraph. If it isn't, jump to the end, especially if you are reading a report, an article, or a technical paper. (Many unskilled communications writers live in a dream world. They believe that people read information-giving material as they would read a mystery story—unable to tear themselves away until the denouement.)

If you find no peg at either the beginning or the end, scan the piece. Run down the first sentence of each paragraph. When you come to one you think might be the true theme, tuck it away in your mind. Then go on to complete the scanning process. (You may hit on two or three ideas that seem at first glance to be the peg.)

In any case it's wise to identify the main idea of any piece before reading it through. Identification reduces the total time needed to absorb a given amount of ideas or information. Also, it ensures your retaining a clearer concept of what you have read. (The good communications writer does the identifying for you, when he brings his thoughts into focus before starting to write.)

This approach to reading for information fits neatly with what the reading-speed researchers have been proclaiming in recent years. It meshes also with applied techniques developed for use by executives and professional men. "Once you've mastered the mechanics of faster reading, the trick is to look for the main idea" is the main idea one executive got from his company's speed-reading course. A publishing executive, after studying speed-reading techniques, concludes that "most of our reading mistakes are forms of patient plodding." Prominent among these mistakes are (1) reading all material at the same rate and (2) wool-gathering and daydreaming while continuing to follow the lines automatically.

To summarize: Using the arts of successful communication while reading for information will cut your reading time and effort. Whether you read slowly or quickly, these arts will speed up your information intake. You will get more faster than if you just start reading.

Reading Helps Writing

Next to writing frequently, reading regularly as described is the best possible way to increase your writing skills.

Constant looking for, and finding, pegs in poorly focused writings improves your facility to integrate your own thoughts. Thinking in terms of integrated statements of main ideas becomes a habit. Looking for pegs becomes a game. Finding one brings the same thrill a crossword puzzler gets when he's tracked down the right word for an obscure definition.

24

Satisfactions and Success from Communications Writing

GOOD COMMUNICATIONS WRITING pays its author in both satisfactions and success. Its rewards far outweigh its achievement costs.

But rewards accrue only after effort has become a habit. Good communications writing is five-tenths mental discipline, four-tenths willingness to rework first drafts, and one-tenth aptitude.

Secondary are the direct returns from readers. Most important are the rewards manifested in improved ability to use your mind effectively. These result from practice of the mental disciplines required for good communications writing.

Establishing both objective and purpose before writing, for example, gives practice in using procedures needed to solve any problem. Considering your reader's needs and desires is a habit readily convertible to any human relations. Exorcising self-centeredness is a good routine to establish.

Bringing to focus the main idea of each communication makes one adept in taking decision making's first and most vital step. Habitually reworking first drafts routinizes a positive patience often useful in the business of living.

No way to creative mental habits is so open to so many people as good communications writing. Its intangible rewards are inevitable by-products of acquiring the ability to communicate well in writing.

To gain these waiting rewards, however, one has to discipline, but not limit, his thinking. He has to make a habit of thinking before he acts—not only before he writes. Regularly, he must do plain hard work (editing and rewriting) to lift his every communication to the standard his sound thinking has set.

There is no other way. Good communications writing is work. But it is rewarding work—if you persevere in doing it well.

Doing It Well

Doing it well is summarized in the thirty suggestions that follow. The first ten concern thinking before writing; the next ten concern how to write. The final ten are hints to help in a variety of special-purpose writing situations.

Before You Write:

1. Resolve to be sincere, careful, and interested in the other fellow's problems.

2. Bring your ideas or information into focus—by means of a written sentence.

3. Fit your communication to the realities of the particular situation.

4. Plan your communication, combining the analysis, integration, and synthesis good executives use in making decisions.

5. Remember: Skill in disputing is the opposite of skill in communicating.

6. Think constructively. Then your words will accentuate the positive.

7. Make certain that neither self-justification nor self-will predominates in your approach. (If either does, your words will reflect it.)

8. Clear your thought (if need be) of pride, envy, laziness, and anger—and also of fear, impatience, supiciousness, and anxiety.

9. In planning your communication, expect impatient, touchy

readers whose minds are easily diverted or who think tangentially.

10. Plan to write *through,* as well as *to,* a reader, when that might help him achieve his aims. (He might pass your writing on to others without rewording it.)

When You Write:

1. Put the main idea at the beginning—in the first sentence if possible.

2. Present material in the order that the main-idea opening sentences lead the reader to expect.

3. Express yourself in terms of the reader's interests, so that passing your communication to others may serve his own purposes.

4. Build into each communication some attraction to stimulate a reader to reach for what it contains. Include some thought-starters, stick to the point, and aim at a reader's needs as well as his wants.

5. Make a habit of using short words and sentences averaging twenty words or less—sentences that march.

6. Write sentences that can mean only one thing.

7. Lean toward active verbs.

8. Put the main idea first—even in sentences.

9. Make your communication look good: neat, typewritten, and with generous amounts of white space.

10. Shun special terminology (professional slang) if it narrows an audience to those familiar with it, when more familiar language would permit others to benefit.

Special-purpose Writing Hints:

1. *Asking for information,* you are always under obligation to your reader. Do whatever work is needed to make responding easy.

2. *Writing for approvals,* shape your communication to meet your reader's need. (If you don't know what it is, find out.)

3. *Writing reports,* emphasize the conclusions, the recommendations, the implications and the significance of what you are reporting.

4. *Writing interoffice memoranda,* remember that your memo-

randa convey the image associates are getting of your business thinking.

5. *Writing to congratulate or condole,* the qualities most needed are sincerity, appropriateness, brevity, tact, and holding to a single idea.

6. *Writing minutes,* don't—in the traditional style. Rather, write reports of meetings. Tell the action taken, the consensus reached, and the plans projected. Report-type minutes can be made a dynamic part of any group's operating pattern.

7. *Inviting a speaker,* be neither apologetic nor overly prideful. Give him background, as well as factual, information. Make the invitation attractive.

8. *Looking for a job,* use writing effectively in all four steps: deciding what to look for, preparing your qualifications, finding prospective employers, and convincing them.

9. *Writing a piece to be spoken,* remember that listening and reading are totally different forms of information intake. Write more loosely for listening.

10. *Writing an article,* be sure to get the main idea into your opening paragraphs, and use "for instances" plentifully.

How Are You Doing?

You can check the degree of your communications-writing success by its direct results. You are doing an increasingly good job in your memoranda, reports, papers, and letters if:

• You find yourself increasingly being asked to suggest a decision, lead a group, or take new responsibilities. (People have been experiencing the clarity, wisdom, and impact that spell leadership.)

• Your associates seem to be making more sense when they communicate with you. (People are mirrors.)

• Fewer people ask you to explain something about which you have already written them.

• More people say "yes" promptly to ideas you suggest and proposals you make. (Hesitancy due to not understanding sidetracks more approvals than disagreement. Most folks think it is safer to say "no" than "yes" when they aren't entirely sure.)

• More people turn to you for advice, expose their problems

to you, and see you as a source of guidance. (You have overcome self-centeredness, the major barrier to good communications writing.)

• You will find yourself less often explaining or debating the same points over and over again. (Especially will this be true in the case of committee or group effort—if *your* minutes, reports, or agenda are involved.)

• Fewer people will ask you the question: "Exactly what did you have in mind about so-and-so?"

Reactions Spell Success

Reactions like these are worth much more than any pile of compliments on your writing. They spell success for your endeavors.

Such success is itself a chief satisfaction to the man who sees opportunity besides obligation in everyday communications writing.

Index

263

r- 69